# PRAISE FOR
# WHAT IS THE SOUL?

"I applaud Rev. Langton for his critical thinking. *What Is the Soul?* dissects this creature amiably well, and the way it leads the reader to Jesus Christ is simply wonderful. Very interesting, and thought-provoking!"

—**Amar Rambisoon, ThD, PhD,**
Senior Pastor, Deeper Life Assembly, Ocoee, FL

"This book deserves the stamp of a PhD thesis. It is more than that. It is a discourse of a scholar where armies of scholars abound. I marvel at the content and admire the author's courage to raise and answer the questions that very few venture to ask, afraid to lift the veil and find something they might not want to discover.

"*What Is the Soul?* is inviting in uncommon ways. Several times, on a single page, I found myself questioning my own beliefs, even after the author planted the location of the various source texts. God has granted Rev. Langton the gift to enlighten and awaken so many of us who are walking in a trance. I am sure his invitation to question the TRUTH will make us all better."

—**Raj Rawat,**
author of *Find Your Everest*

"A brilliant attempt to define the soul of man according to the Scriptures. This question of the soul has baffled many, even today; but Rev. Langton's thought-provoking book has given much clarity to the subject and enrichment to the body of Christ."

—**Rev. Ransford Clarke**,
Senior Pastor, Faith Tabernacle Worship Center,
Orlando, FL

"The use of Scripture as the primary source of fact and data was done extremely well. The more I read, and the more you repeated your point in different contexts was very helpful in helping me understand the position you were taking. I woke up and couldn't go back to sleep as I thought through your presentation and the implication of Adam's sin and the biology of it all—fascinating!

"And finally, the manner and thoroughness in the way you point people to Jesus, again with your use of Scripture, and the pastoral way you lead people to Christ was incredible. I was blessed to read the words you wrote and believe I caught your passion for their lost souls."

—**Mike Larkin, Ph.D.**,
Founder, IGNITE Academy International,
Christiansburg, VA

"What Rev. Langton has written is truly a blessing. Because of its honesty, practicality, viewpoints, and most of all hope, I believe it was a work that was all God-directed. This book has truly impacted me a great deal. I was waiting with expectation for what was coming next, and that's what caught me. I know that it will impact many people, believers, and non-believers alike. With unfailing love, may God's blessings be upon *What Is the Soul?* and everyone who reads it!"

—**Rev. Sam Kalloo**,
Senior Pastor, Gift of Grace Worship Center, Kissimmee, FL

"Of all the books that I have read, *What Is the Soul?* is the first that has made me more curious to seek and to want to know more about this creature called 'man' and his spirit, soul, and body relationship with a Holy God who lives in heaven. *What Is the Soul?* has taken the doctrine of the soul in the Bible and opened a clearer understanding of this relationship that body, soul, and spirit have with each other, and has established clearly that this relationship is present in each human being. Very safely and very wisely the author splits hairs in his quest to accurately interpret the true meaning of the Word of God, as it relates to the soul of man. May God bless the time and effort that has been invested in writing this manuscript."

—**Rev. Dan Dhoray**,
Foursquare Evangelist, Ocoee, FL

"*What Is the Soul?* is a goldmine of information and spiritual insight. This book explores profound spiritual and biblical truths in a conversational style which appeals to both the scholar and the layperson. A welcome addition to any personal or theological library or classroom."

—**Mrs. Rosa Bailey**

"This book surpasses everything I have ever read on the explanation of the soul. It is an inspired word that will reach your mind, heart, and soul and it will convince you to make a decision that will guarantee your soul's salvation. May this book be a blessing to everyone that reads it."

—**Dr. Margarita D'Andrade, DLitt**,
author of *Women: Don't Take the Blame*

"I liked the analogy about the presidential pardon; I especially liked the announcement that Jesus was not connected genetically to Mary, and with that, the fact that His blood was not from anyone on earth."

—**Rev. Jerry Bartholomew**,
author of *The Identity of Jesus*

"This book is more than exceptional, and every believer should hold a copy. With biblical reference and accuracy, the book properly answers the question in its entirety of *What Is the Soul?* In this book, I found the entire answer for the curious mind of anyone—whether he is a believer or not, no matter what age, demographic, or country of cultural origin. It takes discipline and the obedience of the Holy Spirit to successfully write a book on a topic that can be debatable and broad. This book speaks the truth."

—Karen Charlot, MBA

"*What Is the Soul?* is an inclusive and thorough explanation of the 'Soul.' The author left no stone unturned in this very thought-provoking read! The material is fresh and not thrown haphazardly: every line is intentional and packed with dimension. I highly recommend this book for anyone wanting a new take on the subject matter."

—Nooshin Ghazi-Moghaddam

"*What Is the Soul*'s message about Jesus and the Gospel of Christ is clear: Giving up everything … and wholly and totally depending on and trusting in the Lord Jesus is the only way! There is no way anyone can find fault or be dismissive of that truth.

"I pray in the mighty name of Jesus Christ, Yeshua Hamashiach, that the Father of glory will give its readers the spirit of wisdom and revelation and that the eyes of their understanding shall become enlightened, and they will come to know the hope of His calling (Ephesians 1:17-18). May God continue to use this book in a mighty way to bring to salvation souls in the thousands and hundreds of thousands! To God be the glory."

—Rose Achong

"In this well-crafted book, Desmond Langton unpacks the truth of the Gospel by asking and answering the crucial question: *What is the Soul?* Get ready to delve into an insightful journey of discovery as Rev. Langton guides us through the true story and journey of the soul."

—Phillip A. & Karen Lee Fatt,
Riverview, FL

"This work clearly shows the author's passion and love for God and His Word! After reading this book, I now have a renewed enthusiasm to help the willing and even the unwilling recognize that Jesus is the only one who can save them. There will be such rejoicing in heaven over that one lost soul if he chooses Jesus! Thank you, Rev. Langton, for doing what your Spirit led you to do, and may it touch many lives and remind them there is only one way back to God."

—**Carine Dorce**

"My husband is a very passionate man who became quite disillusioned with the church and its teaching yet is always seeking to honor and revere God in his daily life. Whatever you shared with him, he understood it! I thank God for the gift in you and your labor in developing and sharing your ministry. We are both looking forward to more of what God has deposited in your heart to share with 'whomsoever.' May your ministry achieve its fullest potential as God gives opportunity and favor! Know that you have my prayers and support toward that goal."

—**Coreen Pedroso**

# WHAT IS THE SOUL?

# WHAT IS THE SOUL?

Eternal Answers to Spiritual Questions

REV. DESMOND LANGTON
FOREWORD BY DR. BARRY DAVIES

Copyright © 2017 CSM Publishers, Orlando, Florida.

All Rights Reserved.
First Edition 2017
Second Edition 2022

Editor: Rev. Diana Richardson, Moravian Falls, NC 28654
Proofreader: Nina Shoroplova, ninashoroplova.ca/wp/book editor
Layout design: Amit Dey, amitdey2528@gmail.com
Cover design: Pagatana Designs, pagatana.com
Publishing consultant: Geoff Affleck, AuthorPreneur Publishing Inc., geoffaffleck.com

ISBN: 978-0-9984945-2-4 (paperback)
ISBN: 978-0-9984945-4-8 (hardcover)
ISBN: 978-0-9984945-3-1 (ebook)

Library of Congress Control Number: 2017900558

Except for brief quotations in printed reviews, no part of this book may be reproduced, in whole or in part without written permission from the holder of the copyright.

Because of the dynamic nature of the Internet, one or more of the web addresses or links within this book may have changed since it was published and may no longer be valid.

The views of this work are solely the views of the author and do not necessarily reflect the views of the publisher, and the publisher respectfully disclaims any responsibility for them.

For information about special discounts for bulk purchases, please contact the author: desmondlangton@gmail.com | www.desmondlangton.com

Usually, an author reserves a dedication for people who have either influenced him or in some way contributed to his life's experiences. Were I to attempt to list all who did, it is certain that my list would be incomplete! So, to ensure that I slight no one through omission, I choose instead to dedicate this book to one person only.

You.
If you're a person
who wonders what will happen
to your soul after you die,
or what will happen
to the souls of your loved ones after they die,
this book is for you.
Chances are we may not yet know each other, or maybe we do.
Either way, I dedicate this book to you.
May you be blessed as you read.
And, having read, may you seek to develop your very
own personal and eternal relationship
with Our Lord and Savior, Jesus Christ!
To him be glory both now and forever!

**Amen.**

# TABLE OF CONTENTS

Praise for What Is the Soul? . . . . . . . . . . . . . . . . . . . . . . . . . . . . . i

Foreword . . . . . . . . . . . . . . . . . . . . . . . . . . . . . . . . . . . . . . . . . . xv

Preface . . . . . . . . . . . . . . . . . . . . . . . . . . . . . . . . . . . . . . . . . . . xix

Acknowledgements . . . . . . . . . . . . . . . . . . . . . . . . . . . . . . . . . xxi

Introduction . . . . . . . . . . . . . . . . . . . . . . . . . . . . . . . . . . . . . . . . 1

Chapter 1: What Is the Soul? . . . . . . . . . . . . . . . . . . . . . . . . . . 15

Chapter 2: Seven Types of Souls . . . . . . . . . . . . . . . . . . . . . . . 27

Chapter 3: Does Everyone Have a Soul? . . . . . . . . . . . . . . . . . 51

Chapter 4: What About Your Soul? . . . . . . . . . . . . . . . . . . . . . 73

Chapter 5: Who Am I? . . . . . . . . . . . . . . . . . . . . . . . . . . . . . . . 89

Chapter 6: Who Made Me? . . . . . . . . . . . . . . . . . . . . . . . . . . 111

Chapter 7: Self-Examination . . . . . . . . . . . . . . . . . . . . . . . . . 127

Chapter 8: Spiritual Disconnect . . . . . . . . . . . . . . . . . . . . . . . 139

Chapter 9: Surrogacy vs Gestational Surrogacy . . . . . . . . . . . 151

Chapter 10: The Lost Glory . . . . . . . . . . . . . . . . . . . . . . . . . . 171

Chapter 11: The Restored Glory . . . . . . . . . . . . . . . . . . . . . . 187

Chapter 12: The Rejected Gift, the Four Sons of God, and
the Re-membered Man . . . . . . . . . . . . . . . . . . . . . 203

Chapter 13: What Others Believe About the Soul. . . . . . . . . . . . . 223

Chapter 14: The Conclusion of It All. . . . . . . . . . . . . . . . . . . . 243

About the Author . . . . . . . . . . . . . . . . . . . . . . . . . . . . . . . 249

Notes. . . . . . . . . . . . . . . . . . . . . . . . . . . . . . . . . . . . . . 251

# FOREWORD

In his first published book, *What Is the Soul?* Desmond Langton clearly states at the beginning the ultimate purpose and object for his writing—to draw people closer to God and so lead them to live a Christ-like life. Langton's personal style gives the feeling that he wrote this book for each person reading it; he uses words that assure each person that s/he will be able to search the sentences, words, and meanings of the Bible texts.

For this book, a vast amount of research has taken place from the Bible itself and an extensive range of commentaries and other resources. The author has very thoughtfully and painstakingly provided the reader with the *Strong's Exhaustive Concordance* number system that he can use to check the reference in the Bible itself. For persons wanting to do further research, the information is well documented. The author is clearly a deeply committed Christian who thoroughly knows his Bible, which he extensively quotes to justify his well-developed convictions boldly and clearly. The book takes the form of a very personal account of his journey to his arriving at his conclusions, and he teaches his readers with the facts and opinions he has discovered and which he shares.

Langton uses a Biblical-literalist and inerrancy approach to present an interesting combination of scholarly teaching and evangelism. Since the subject matter is intense, to make his points clear, he uses mostly non-academic language and has chosen to write in a popular and often very colorful way so that the arguments he makes are understandable and available to all levels of readers. He uses a style which is both personal and often familiar with expressions such as "listen"; and his examples are very likely to be well-known. He does not hesitate to give even the most intimate of details to get his points across, and he also uses Scripture to back up his approach to a wide variety of topics relating to current situations such as same-sex marriage and sex changes.

In *What Is the Soul?* Langton combines the skills of the academician, evangelist, teacher, and preacher; and his fervor, sincerity, and enthusiasm for his subject are obvious on every page. This is a serious book which warrants careful and thoughtful reading.

Rev. Dr. Barry Davies MDiv, D. Min
Palm Coast, FL

*Study  
to shew thyself approved  
unto God,  
a workman  
that needs not to be ashamed,  
rightly dividing  
the word of truth.*

2 Timothy 2:15

# PREFACE

This book has been for me a labor of love. It is a book that has taken me countless hours over more than five years to compile. And even as we are about to go to press, God continues daily to quicken my spirit and reveal to me biblical truths that in my estimation have so far been overlooked. Is it any wonder therefore that the Bible is called "The Living Word"?

The writings within these pages are my opinions and are based on my personal study and research. At all times and to the best of my ability I have tried to give credit where credit is due. Any omission is purely unintentional. Accordingly, dear reader, I would appreciate receiving both your comments and your feedback for future study. My contact information is in the back of the book.

# ACKNOWLEDGEMENTS

I would like to express my thanks to the many people who reviewed this manuscript, provided support, made suggestions for improvement, wrote, or offered comments, and assisted in the overall and final editing, proofreading, cover design and interior layout.

For reviewing the book and allowing me to quote their remarks and I would like to thank, my pastor, my friend and spiritual daddy Dr. Amar Rambisoon ThD. Doc, your feedback assured me that I had passed the acid test. Dr. Mike Larkin whose suggestion to have the book professionally edited was pure gold. In no special order, I must thank the following servants of God for their reviews: Revs. Ransford Clarke, Sam Kalloo, Dan Dhoray, and Jerry Bartholomew; also, Dr. Margarita D'Andrade, Phillip A. and Karen LeeFatt; Karen Charlot, Nooshin Ghazi-Moghaddam, Rose Achong, Coreen Pedroso, and Carine Dorce.

For editing the final manuscript, I thank Nina Shoroplova, ninashoroplova.ca/wp/book editor. For layout design, Amit Dey, amitdey2528@gmail.com. For cover design, Pagatana Designs, Pagatana.com. For assistance with publishing the book on the web, Geoff Affleck, geoff@geoffaffleck.com.

None of this would have been possible without the support of my wife, Pat, my children Phillip and Michelle, my God daughter Jada, granddaughter

Kamryn, sister Brenda, brother Lawrence, cousins Rose and Coreen, and my nephew, Felipe, and all the rest of my friends and family members who also supported and encouraged me during this journey.

Last and not least: I ask forgiveness of all those who have been with me throughout this journey and whose names I may have failed to mention.

# INTRODUCTION

## Quotable Quotes

Deuteronomy 29:29

> The secret things belong unto the LORD our God: but those things which are revealed belong unto us and to our children forever, that we may do all the words of this law.

Author Unknown

> "The more you look, the more you'll see. The more you see, the simpler will become everything—even in its complexity."

## Notes to Keep in Mind

### Polyglot Bible, King James Version

Throughout the pages of this book, some of the referenced Bible texts will appear with numbers immediately beside the words as seen immediately below from Mark 8:36.[1]

> For[1063] what[5101] shall it profit[5623] a man,[444] if[1437] he shall gain[2770] the[3588] whole[3650] world,[2889] and[2532] lose[2210] his own[848] soul?[5590]

When these texts appear, know that they are taken from the online Polyglot Bible, King James Version (KJV) with Strong's Concordance Numbers. These are found online at https://www.sacred-texts.com/bib/poly/index.htm. The numbers [1063, 5101, 5623] and so on are the numbers assigned by James Strong, identifying the English equivalent of the original Hebrew and Greek.

Simple word searches in the King James Bible can be found online for at http://quod.lib.umich.edu/k/kjv/simple.html

The way to look up these references is to insert the superscripted number—for instance, the first one, [1063]—into this URL https://www.sacred-texts.com/bib/poly/hxxxx.htm, replacing the xxxx with the superscript number, for https://www.sacred-texts.com/bib/poly/h1063.htm.

Any of these numbers can be researched in *Strong's Concordance* to allow the reader to compare contextually how the same word occurs elsewhere in the Bible. Additionally, this provides a way for anyone to perform an independent check of a particular word (or set of words) and see how their usage and meanings change from one translation of the Bible to another. More importantly, this offers everyone an opportunity to get a more biblically accurate understanding of a text so that they can rightly divide God's Word as He commands us to do in 2 Timothy 2:15.

There are no emphases in the King James Version of the Bible, so where emphases occur in this book, know that they are mine. The "a," "b," "c," and "d" refer to the breaks in the thoughts or actions in the verse.

For example: Genesis 2:7 when broken down, will look like this:

(2:7a) And the LORD God formed man of the dust of the ground,

(2:7b) and breathed into his nostrils the breath of life.

(2:7c) and man became a living soul.

In the Bible when we refer to the creator God, we use an upper case "G"; when we refer to Satan who is the god of this world, we use a lower case "g."

I have chosen to capitalize "he, his, him" when the pronoun refers to Jesus or God.

## New International Version

Occasionally, I use the New International Version (NIV) of the Bible. It has no superscript numbers.

## Masculine Terms

Throughout this book, to simplify literary flow, I will be using the male or the masculine terms rather than any combination thereof. And, whenever I use it, you need to see it as being all-inclusive of and applicable to all and any male, female, boy, girl, baby, or an LGBTQ person.

## Possible Misinterpretation in the Old Testament

Also, using the KJV Online Polyglot Bible (www.sacred-texts.com/bib/poly/index.htm), I will be quoting Bible verses liberally. Beside each verse reference, there is a number that is called the Strong's Concordance number. That number represents a Hebrew word (if in the Old Testament) or a Greek word (if in the New Testament). From each number, you can do further study for a clearer understanding.

In this book, my position is that Strong was not one hundred percent accurate with every word he translated. If I am right, then it must follow that we have been misinterpreting some areas of God's Word! So, whenever I refer to a number in *Strong's Exhaustive Concordance*, I invite you to look up the number for yourself in Strong's Lexicon or other lexicons that use Strong's numbers and verify everything for yourself.

For example, Genesis 1:27 says,

> So God[430] created[1254] [853] man[120] in his own image,[6754] in the image[6754] of God[430] created[1254] he him; male[2145] and female[5347] created[1254] he them.

Now, why did God create "he him"? Why did God not create "he her"? The answer is simple. God created "he him" because "him" was created in the image of God's Only Begotten Son, that is "The Man Christ Jesus" who was, is, and ever shall be God's only Mediator between God and Man (1 Timothy 2:5).

According to Strong, the word translated "man" in Genesis 1:27 is 'âdâm—aw-dawm' - אדם —אָדָם [Strong's H120], from 119. And according to his interpretation, it means "ruddy," that is, a human being (an individual or the species, mankind).

Could Strong's interpretation be wrong?

The Bible is clear that, when God creates, He speaks (Genesis 1:1; Psalm 33:6). And when God speaks, the Bible says that the words that He speaks, "they are spirit, and they are life" (John 6:63). Therefore, I am saying that, based upon the Law of First Mention, since Genesis 1:27 states that God created man, it must follow that the man that God created had to have been an invisible spirit being that God spoke into existence, in which there was life.

Now, if my interpretation is accurate, it must follow that Strong's interpretation that the MAN that God created was a human being in the day that he was created must necessarily be one hundred percent incorrect and inaccurate.

Note, however, that I am not saying that MAN is not a human being nor that he did not become a human being. I am simply stating that contextually in Genesis 1:27, the MAN that God created was a spirit or a spirit-man if you will. God had not yet taken the dust of Genesis 2:7a and fashioned or formed a body for the spirit-man. Only after God formed a body for the created spirit-man, did that man become a human, that is a spirit-man who lived in a body that was made of dust.

Genesis 5: 1-2 confirm that "in the day" that God created man, God named that spirit-man, ADAM. This fact escaped our interpretation of Scripture. I say this, because in Genesis 2:7, when God took the dust and formed (a body for) the man, that man, who had then become a spirit in a dirt body, also was called Adam.

Genesis 5:1-2 say:

> This²⁰⁸⁸ is the book⁵⁶¹² of the generations⁸⁴³⁵ of Adam.¹²¹ In the day³¹¹⁷ that God⁴³⁰ created¹²⁵⁴ man,¹²⁰ in the likeness¹⁸²³ of God⁴³⁰ made⁶²¹³ he him;
>
> Male²¹⁴⁵ and female⁵³⁴⁷ created¹²⁵⁴ he them; and blessed¹²⁸⁸ them, and called⁷¹²¹ ⁸⁵³ their name⁸⁰³⁴ Adam,¹²¹ in the day³¹¹⁷ when they were created.¹²⁵⁴

Recap: (1) The man that God created (Genesis 1:27) was one hundred percent spirit, he was the product of a seed, which was the word of God, which was both male and female, and he was called ADAM (Genesis 5:2); (2) The man for whom God took the dust and for whom God formed a body (Genesis 2:7a) was also called Adam. The one was one hundred percent pure spirit; the other was one hundred percent spirit in a dirt body. The presence of the spirit in the dirt body made the body of dirt come alive or become animate.

According to James 2:26,

> For¹⁰⁶³ as⁵⁶¹⁸ the³⁵⁸⁸ body⁴⁹⁸³ without⁵⁵⁶⁵ the spirit⁴¹⁵¹ is²⁰⁷⁶ dead,³⁴⁹⁸

How is this possible? Romans 1:20 tells us why. It says,

> For¹⁰⁶³ the³⁵⁸⁸ invisible things⁵¹⁷ of him⁸⁴⁶ from⁵⁷⁵ the creation²⁹³⁷ of the world²⁸⁸⁹ are clearly seen,²⁵²⁹ being understood³⁵³⁹ by the³⁵⁸⁸ things that are⁴¹⁶¹ made, even⁵⁰³⁷ ³⁷³⁹ his⁸⁴⁸ eternal¹²⁶ power¹⁴¹¹ and²⁵³² Godhead;²³⁰⁵ so that they⁸⁴⁶ are¹⁵¹¹ without excuse:³⁷⁹

When we interpret Romans 1:20, we find the text

> the³⁵⁸⁸ invisible things⁵¹⁷ of him⁸⁴⁶ from⁵⁷⁵ the creation²⁹³⁷ of the world²⁸⁸⁹

becomes the creative words that God spoke (John 6:63) at creation (Genesis 1:1; 1:21; 1:27; Ezekiel 28:15; Colossians 1:15). And the things that were made become the manifestations of the invisible things that became visible (John 1:3; Genesis 2:2-3).

Here's the deal from Genesis 2:2-3:

> And on the seventh[7637] day[3117] God[430] ended[3615] his work[4399] which[834] he had made;[6213] and he rested[7673] on the seventh[7637] day[3117] from all[4480 3605] his work[4399] which[834] he had made.[6213]
>
> And God[430] blessed[1288 853] the seventh[7637] day,[3117] and sanctified[6942] it: because[3588] that in it he had rested[7673] from all[4480 3605] his work[4399] which[834] God[430] created[1254] and made.[6213]

Don't forget that.

Two Phases: (1) God created and (2) God then made.

First, there was the "creating" or "spoken word" or "invisible" phase, and then there was the "making" phase, that is the manifestation from the invisible into the "visible" of God's spoken Word.

Now we know why God instructed the Apostle Paul to include in Romans 1:20, the fact that

> his[848] eternal[126] power[1411] and[2532] Godhead;[2305] so that they[846] are[1511] without excuse:[379]

What is God's eternal power and Godhead?

Would you like to know my thoughts on that question? I believe that God's eternal power and Godhead was God's only begotten Son, and He was represented as the man Christ Jesus (1 Timothy 2:5). I say that because it was, He who became manifest in the flesh (John 1:12). It was He who lay down His deity because He thought it not robbery to be equal with God (Philippians 2:6-11). And it was He who became a human being so He could die on the cross to redeem all humanity from God's Adamic curse.

Think about this: If you were the Creator, and you were about to create an image of yourself, wouldn't you have had to have been in existence before you created anything? Of course, you would. And since you would, when we read John 1:1, which states: "In the beginning was the word," we need to read it as if it said, "Before the beginning, there was the Word." We need to do that because the word "before" places the Creator in an accurate position about the creation He created.

A spirit is invisible!

Now, do you know? I looked up the meaning of the word *spirit*, and there was not one definition in any of the online dictionaries that stated clearly and specifically that a spirit is invisible or that it is an invisible being. And yet when he was speaking with the Colossians 1:15 about the risen Christ, Paul said of God's only begotten Son that He is, was, ever shall be

> the image$^{1504}$ of the$^{3588}$ invisible$^{517}$ God,$^{2316}$ the firstborn$^{4416}$ of every$^{3956}$ creature:$^{2937}$

I don't know about you, but I need no further confirmation. God is a Spirit, and as Spirit, God is invisible. So, when we read the Book of John and it tells us that the Word that was God (John 1:1) was made flesh (v. 12), what else should we conclude other than the fact that He (God's Son) who was invisible had become visible? As Sherlock Holmes would say, "Elementary, my dear Watson!" Now, if you need further proof that the eternal power and Godhead of Romans 1:20 was referring to God's only begotten Son (1 Timothy 2:5; John 1:14), here's what the Bible says in 2 Corinthians 5:19,

> God$^{2316}$ was$^{2258}$ in$^{1722}$ Christ,$^{5547}$ reconciling$^{2644}$ the world$^{2889}$ unto himself,$^{1438}$

This verse refers specifically to the Word of John 1:1 that was made flesh in John 1:14.

Colossians 2:9 tells us:

> For[3754] in[1722] him[846] dwelleth[2730] all[3956] the[3588] fullness[4138] of the[3588] Godhead[2320] bodily.[4985]

In the preceding verse, "Him" refers to God, but more specifically it refers to the Son of God in His office as the Man Christ Jesus (1 Timothy 2:5). And this man Christ Jesus was the Logos (John 1:1) minus His deity. In Philippians 2:6-8, it is written that it was He who became human because He

> thought it not robbery to be equal with God, but made himself of no reputation, and took upon him the form of a servant, and was made in the likeness of men.

And then, of course, there is Hebrews 11:3, which ties it all together.

> Through faith[4102] we understand[3539] that the[3588] worlds[165] were framed[2675] by the word[4487] of God,[2316] so that things which are seen[991] were not[3361] made[1096] of[1537] things which do appear.[5316]

So much for a sample of the Old Testament (OT); now let's look at one in the New Testament (NT).

### Sample Misinterpretation in the New Testament

In John 3:3 it is late at night. Jesus is speaking with Nicodemus, a ruler of the Jews. Nicodemus asks a question, and the Bible says,

> Jesus[2424] answered[611] and[2532] said[2036] unto him,[846] Verily,[281] verily,[281] I say[3004] unto thee,[4671] Except[3362] a man[5100] be born[1080] again,[509] he cannot[1410 3756] see[1492] the[3588] kingdom[932] of God.[2316]

Here is Strong's entry for the word *man*:

> τίς—tis—tis—An enclitic indefinite pronoun; some or any person or object: —a (kind of), any (man, thing, thing at all), certain (thing), divers, he (every) man, one (X thing), ought, +

partly, some (man, -body, -thing, -what) (+ that no-) thing, what (-soever), X wherewith, whom [-soever], whose ([-soever]).

Even as we have been misinterpreting the word *man* in the Old Testament, so too in the New, we have continued the practice of interpreting "man" as being a "human being."

But remember, God created a spirit-man. So, when we eavesdrop on Jesus as He was conversing with Nicodemus, we need to understand that Jesus was not referring to the physical Nicodemus, but rather He was referring to the procreated, fallen, or sinful, spirit-man who was resident in the body of Nicodemus ("Nick").

Please understand: Up until the moment when Nick's mother conceived, Nick's daddy's seed was in liquid form as it traveled from the cervix through the uterus to the fallopian tubes. Then, over the next nine months, as God formed a body in his mom's womb (1 Corinthians 15:38) that would become Baby Nick, the seed and egg morphed into a spirit or an invisible form so that when Nick was born both his daddy's seed and mommy's egg were completely invisible. God had taken daddy's seed and mommy's egg and given them increase (1 Corinthians 3:6). That increase was represented by the body of the newly born infant, named Baby Nick. In John 12:24 and in Mark 4:28-29, Jesus describes the process that every seed must undergo, before it can produce life. And, in Genesis 1:11, HE informs us that once life is produced in any form, we may rest assured that the "seed is within itself."

We all know that anyone can count the number of seeds in an apple, but can anyone count the number of apples or apple trees that are in one apple seed? Similarly, we know that all human life is produced from the union of one male seed and one female egg; but can anyone tell how many seeds any male will sow or how many babies a male will eventually father? Can anyone tell how many babies any female will eventually birth? Obviously not. And the reason is because God is the architect who unites the male seed with the female egg and forms the resulting zygote, the one flesh that becomes the parents' offspring.

Of that miraculous event, the Bible says, "What therefore God hath joined together, let not man put asunder" (Mark 10:9). Somebody needs to reveal this truth to Planned Parenthood. Somebody needs to tell them that life is precious, and God is its architect.

Now I must tell you that this process whereby God takes the seed of the male and the egg of the female and forms a body is the same process that occurred for almost every human being. Exceptions would be Adam, Eve, and God's Son, Jesus Christ. But, in all cases, the result was the same. Whether it was Adam, Eve, or Jesus, all three were spirits or spirit-seeds for whom God made a body (Genesis 2:7 and 22; Hebrews 10:5).

In Adam's case, God spoke a word called "man," and that word was spirit and life (John 6:63). When God placed Adam's spirit-man in the dust, it became manifest in the flesh in the person of Adam. Adam was no longer just a man; he had become a hu-man. He was now a created spirit who was living in a body made of dust.

In Eve's case, the Bible says that God took a rib from Adam (Genesis 2:22) and with it, he made for Adam a companion or a helper. Adam would call that helper "woman." Later, Adam would name his helper Eve. She became the female equivalent of Adam who was now one hundred percent male. And, like Adam, Eve was merely a pro-created spirit-seed called wo-man, who was one hundred percent female and was the result of a spirit-seed called man that was both male and female. Like Adam, Eve's pro-created spirit-seed also lived in a dirt body. Neither Adam nor Eve was bisexual!

In Jesus' case, His spirit-seed was uncreated! Before the foundation of the world, He was called "the man Christ Jesus" (1 Timothy 2:5). This man Christ Jesus was the Word of God (John 1:1) who was God's only begotten Son, who was taken out of God's bosom (John 1:14) and had become flesh (John 1:18). Revelation 13:8 says He was "the Lamb, slain from the foundation of the world." And it was this spirit-man Christ Jesus that God sent into the world (John 3:16) to become a human being (John 1:18) so He could die on the cross and save all mankind. Now, in His human state, we need to remember and never forget that the Spirit-man that resided in Jesus' human body was a Spirit that was one hundred percent God, minus His deity! (John 1:3c; Philippians 2:6-8).

Bottom Line: God created, God formed, and then God delegated to the man named Adam and the woman (whom Adam later called Eve) while they were both in the Garden of Eden, the responsibility to be fruitful and multiply. God specified how they were to accomplish this. From creation to the present time, nothing has changed. The process is still the same.

Reproduction and perpetuation of the species are contingent upon the male and the female getting "to know" each other in a biblical sense (Proverbs 5:18-19).

God's intention, then as now, never was for the male and male or the female and female to reproduce (Romans 1:24-32; Leviticus 20:13; Deuteronomy 22:5).

## What's the Message?

The message is that the Bible has always had and will continue to have every answer concerning everything about life and the universe in general. So why did it take men so long to prove that the earth was round?

What can I say?

As men and women, we learn nothing from the books we don't read.

I invite you, therefore, to take a fresh look at some new interpretations of some very old subjects.

An open mind is all you need.

Allow your mind to be like a parachute—you must open it for it to work. And know for a surety that I believe, as I have often heard many people say, that one of the greatest mistakes we can make is to believe something we only think we know for sure.

Eternity is a long time to be wrong!

## Q & A

### Genesis 1:27

The Bible says in Genesis 1:27,

> So, God created man in his own image, in the image of God created he him; male and female created he them.

### Genesis 1:28

Immediately after "God created man" (Genesis 1:27), here are ten things that God did. Genesis 1:28 says,

1. "And God *blessed them*, and
2. "God *said unto them*,
3. "*Be fruitful*, and
4. "*multiply*
5. "and *replenish* the earth
6. "and *subdue* it
7. "and *have dominion*
8. "*over the fish* of the sea,
9. "and *over the fowl* of the air,
10. "and *over every living thing* that moves upon the earth."

**Question:** Who is the "him" who created all things?
**Answer:** (a) God the Father _____ (b) God the Son _____

**Question:** Who is the "him" who made all things?
**Answer:** (a) God the Father _____ (b) God the Son _____

**Question:** Who or what does God look like?
**Answer:** John 4:24 says, "God is a Spirit."

**Question**: Since God is a Spirit, what must a creature, created in the image of God look like? Would it look like a spirit, or would it look like a human being?

*Answer:* Spirit _____. Human being _____.

**Question**: Since man was created in the image of God, did God use a model from which He created this man in His image?

*Answer:* 1 Timothy 2:5, "The man Christ Jesus."

**Question**: Was the man Christ Jesus (a) fully God (b) fully man (c) both fully God and fully man or (d) neither fully God, nor fully man?

*Answer:* (a) _____ (b) _____ (c) _____ (d) _____

**Question:** Did God pronounce His blessings of fruitfulness and multiplication on a spirit or on a human being?

See Genesis 1:28, then answer: Spirit _____ Human being _____.

**Question:** If God created one man, why did He bless "them"? Why did He not bless "him"?

See Genesis 1:27, then answer: God created him _____ and created he them _____.

**Question:** Who are the "them" that God blessed?

See Genesis 1:27, then answer: Genesis 1:27 _____ and _____.

## Genesis 5:1-2

Following the creating and the blessing of man, the Bible tells us that God then named the man. Genesis 5:1-2 says,

1 This is the book of the generations of Adam.

In the day that God created man, in the likeness of God made he him.

2 Male and female created he them; and blessed them,

and called their name Adam, in the day when they were created.

**Question**: When did God give the created man his name?

*Answer:* (Genesis 5:2a) In the day he was _____.

**Question**: When God gave the created man his name, was the man a spirit or was he a human-being?

*Answer:* Genesis 5:2: Man was (a) a spirit. _____. (b) Man was a human being. _____.

## Colossians 1:16

For by him were all things created, that are in heaven, and that are in earth, visible and invisible, whether they be thrones, or dominions, or principalities, or powers: all things were created by him, and for him.

## John 1:1-3

[1] In the beginning was the Word, and the Word was with God, and the Word was God. [2] The same was in the beginning with God. [3] All things were made by him; and without him was not anything made that was made.

CHAPTER 1

# WHAT IS THE SOUL?

## Bible Verses About the Soul

### John 1:12-13

> And the LORD God ...breathed into his nostrils the breath of life; and man became a living soul.

### Ezekiel 18:4

> Behold ... the soul that sinneth, it shall die.

### Ezekiel 28:16

> Thou hast sinned: therefore, I will cast thee as profane out of the mountain of God: and I will destroy thee, O covering cherub.

### Hebrews 9:22

> And almost all things are by the law purged with blood; and without shedding of blood is no remission.

### Leviticus 17:11

For the life of the flesh is in the blood: and I have given it to you upon the altar to make an atonement for your souls: for it is the blood that maketh an atonement for the soul.

### Hebrews 9:22

And I will say to my soul, Soul, thou hast much goods laid up ... take thine ease, eat, drink, and be merry. But God said unto him, Thou fool, this night thy soul shall be required of thee: then whose shall those things be, which thou hast provided?

### Acts 4:12

Neither is there salvation in any other: for there is no other name under heaven given among men, whereby we must be saved.

### Acts 16:30-31

Sirs, what must I do to be saved? And they said, believe on the Lord Jesus Christ, and thou shalt be saved, and thy house.

## Why Should You Read This Book?

Let me ask you a question:

At the very instant you take your last breath, and your body becomes lifeless, do you know that you know for sure that even before your body is buried or cremated, you will be in heaven with Jesus Christ and with God our Father for all eternity? (Note: when I say "you," I am referring to your inner spirit-man or inner life force if you will.)

And what I am asking is, if you should die tonight, are you one hundred percent confident that though your inner spirit-man will be absent from the body, it will be present with the Lord? (See 2 Corinthians 5:8.)

This book may not be for you.

If your answer to both questions is an emphatic "YES!" then this book may NOT be for you. You see the Bible calls such as you "blessed," because you "have not seen and yet have believed" (John 20:29, KJV). And what is it that you would have believed? Very simply, you would have believed in or would have placed your faith in the virgin birth and life, death, burial, resurrection, and ascension into heaven of Jesus Christ—God's ONLY begotten Son. In other words, you would have placed your faith in the finished work of the Cross.

And then again, this book may be for you.

Are you saved? Do you understand what it means to be "saved"? Other than the fact that "the Bible says so," do you have a ready answer for the faith you have, and can you lead another person to Christ? Can you make salvation make sense? If you can't, then this book is definitely for you.

Here's what this book will do for you.

I promise you this book will give you the information you'll need to make an informed decision concerning your eternal destination.

Additionally, the information in this book will equip you with the tools necessary for you to witness to and share your testimony with anyone who does not believe what you believe. Remember, unbelievers do not believe the Bible! So, you cannot go to them citing the Bible.

When Jesus spoke to fishermen, He spoke in fish terms; when He spoke to farmers, He spoke in planting and harvesting terms; when those versed in the law challenged Him, He responded in legal terms.

Similarly, if you're a believer, you need to understand that when you share your faith with others who aren't, you must speak to them in a language they understand. The information in this book will equip you to do just that.

I must let you know that the information contained herein is not new—only my interpretation of some of it is. The information contained herein has been around for millennia. This author is approaching it from the point of view that quite a lot of the information with which we have become familiar with may not be one hundred percent accurate. Note: Misinterpretation is an error. Misinterpretation will cause us to make erroneous conclusions.

Before you condemn the present, remember the past.

Emma Miller Bolenius wrote an American schoolbook published in 1919. When commenting on Columbus Day, she stated,

> When Columbus lived, people thought that the earth was flat. They believed the Atlantic Ocean to be filled with monsters large enough to devour their ships, and with fearful waterfalls over which their frail vessels would plunge to destruction. Columbus had to fight these foolish beliefs in order to get men to sail with him. He felt sure the earth was round.

Years before, Nicolaus Copernicus, a Polish astronomer, put forth the theory that the sun is at rest near the center of the universe, and that the earth, spinning on its axis once daily, revolves annually around the sun.[2] Though Greek philosophers and others used mathematics and logic to arrive at the conclusion that the earth was indeed a sphere, it was hundreds of years later when Magellan proved that it was indeed round, by sailing around it. Now, had the powers that be taken the time to read the Bible, they would have learned well in advance of any assumptions or theories that the earth was indeed round. Speaking for the Lord, the prophet Isaiah says in chapter 40, verse 22,

> It is He that sits upon the circle of the earth, and the inhabitants thereof are as grasshoppers; He stretches out the heavens as a curtain and spreads them out as a tent to dwell in.

## These Few Things I Know

**First:** Beginning with Cain and Abel and up to the present time, within the body of every newborn, there is resident in him or her a pro-created inner spirit-man or fertilized seed comprised of two gametes—the one a male sperm, the other a female egg. This condition is true no matter how cute, or how socially, politically, or financially connected one may be. Today that seed is called a zygote. It is a term that no one knew before 1887; yet at Creation, God called that seed "MAN" (Genesis 1:27).

More importantly, I submit that the "man" God created was an invisible Spirit (Romans 1:20). The biblical record is clear:

1. God created or spoke a spirit-man into existence (Genesis 1:27).
2. That man was a spirit because God speaks words that are spirit (John 6:63).
3. God blessed the created man (Genesis 1:28).
4. God named that created man Adam (Genesis 5:2).
    a. Having done 1, 2, and 3,
5. God then took dust and formed for the invisible created man, a body (Genesis 2:7a).

Were we to begin with Seth (Genesis 5:3) and backtrack to Cain and Abel (Genesis 4:1-2), we would note that when Cain, Abel, and Seth were born, they bore the image of Adam and not the image of God. The Bible record confirms that this is so because of Adam's sin (Genesis 3:6c). In other words, Adam's first three sons were made in the image of a fallen or sinful human being (Genesis 5:3). And, from then to the present day, the Bible records that every newborn baby is born in sin and has come short of the glory of God (Romans 3:23).

What is this "glory" and how did we come short of it? The answer will follow in a later chapter, but for now, I am quite content to agree with the Psalmist who stated that he "was shapen in iniquity, and in sin did [his] mother conceive (him)" (Psalms 51:5). Since the Bible records that "all have sinned" (Romans 3:23), it means that at birth, even though I was one hundred percent physically alive, I was also one hundred percent totally and completely spiritually dead (Ephesians 2:1-3).

**Second:** Know this to be true! If you are reading this book, then it is certain that you were born physically alive yet spiritually dead. To be spiritually dead means that your inner spirit-man was born spiritually separated from God. For you to get spiritually reconnected to God, God has provided one way, and only one way, and that is for your inner spirit-man to accept Jesus Christ as your Lord and Savior. The window of opportunity within which your inner spirit-man reconnects itself to God is between the day your mother gave birth to you and the day everyone says goodbye to you. The only way to restore the spiritual connection is to follow Romans 10:9.

> Confess with your mouth the Lord Jesus and believe in thine heart that God hath raised him from the dead.

That's it! It does not get any simpler. Just open your mouth and say: "Jesus! Save me!"

As you age, you'll note that you'll be attending more funerals. The more funerals you attend, the more you would or should become aware that you too are mortal, and you too shall die. Death to your physical body is not a matter of *if*; it is just a matter of *when*; not so with your inner spirit-man. He lives on forever. And he'll do that either in God's presence or out of it. My recommendation, therefore, is that you seize every moment—from the moment you took your first breath to the moment you take your last—and use each as an opportunity for you to make right your relationship with God. Make no mistake: There is indeed Life and Death in the Power of Your Tongue.

Know of a surety that there's a day coming when three words will follow you into eternity. If you are male, they are "and he died." If you are female, then they are "and she died." Either way, everyone dies. Your mission should you choose to accept it is to use the time you have to strategically position yourself, so that when you die, your loved ones who survive you will know for a surety that though your inner spirit-man is absent from your body, it is most definitely present with the Lord.

So today, my prayer for you is this: If you should hear God's voice, do not harden your heart, for today is your day of Salvation. The exact moment of your physical death may yet be unknown, but be assured, it's coming. No one gets out alive!

Make sure that when it's your time to leave, you'll leave knowing that you had taken the ONLY step possible that was provided by God to ensure that you shall live again in the glory and happiness of heaven.

Romans 10:9-10 give us the formula. They say it very simply.

9 That if thou shalt confess with thy mouth the Lord Jesus, and shalt believe in thine heart that God hath raised him from the dead, thou shalt be saved.

10 For with the heart man believeth unto righteousness; and with the mouth confession is made unto salvation.

John 1:12-13 says it also:

But as many as received him, to them gave he power to become the sons of God, even to them that believe on his name, Which were born, not of blood, nor of the will of the flesh, nor of the will of man, but of God.

## The Soul Defined

When defining the soul, one answer that is very popular today, whether in the pulpit, in the mission field, or in Christian-TV land, is that your soul is your mind, your will, and your emotions. Against that interpretation, I present to you the words of Jesus Christ Himself. We find them in the Book of Mark, chapter 8, verses 35 through 37.

> 35 For$^{1063}$ whosoever$^{3739\ 302}$ will$^{2309}$ save$^{4982}$ his$^{848}$ life$^{5590}$ shall lose$^{622}$ it;$^{846}$ but$^{1161}$ whosoever$^{3739\ 302}$ shall lose$^{622}$ his$^{848}$ life$^{5590}$ for my sake$^{1752\ 1700}$ and$^{2532}$ the$^{3588}$ gospel's,$^{2098}$ the same$^{3778}$ shall save$^{4982}$ it.$^{846}$
>
> 36 For$^{1063}$ what$^{5101}$ shall it profit$^{5623}$ a man,$^{444}$ if$^{1437}$ he shall gain$^{2770}$ the$^{3588}$ whole$^{3650}$ world,$^{2889}$ and$^{2532}$ lose$^{2210}$ his own$^{848}$ soul?$^{5590}$

37 Or²²²⁸ what⁵¹⁰¹ shall a man⁴⁴⁴ give¹³²⁵ in exchange⁴⁶⁵ for his⁸⁴⁸ soul?⁵⁵⁹⁰

## My Definition of the Soul

I define the soul as a heaven-based created creature that lives in a place called Eden, which is the garden of God in heaven (Psalms 148:5; Ezekiel 28:13, 15). The word *Eden* means "presence." So, you could say that, in heaven, all created souls live in the very presence of God and worship God unceasingly.

## More Definitions of the Soul

1. The soul is the Spirit, or the breath of God that God breathed into the nostrils of ADAM (Genesis 2:7b).
2. That breath was a spirit of power, of love, and of a sound mind (2 Timothy 1:7).
3. The soul is the Spirit or the Dove that descended on Jesus after John baptized Him (Matthew 3:16).
4. The soul is the Spirit of the risen Christ that everyone receives when they accept Jesus Christ as Savior, and they are given the poser to become a son of God (John 1:12).
5. The soul is the Spirit of the Holy Ghost whom the disciples received when Jesus Christ breathed on them (John 20:22).
6. The soul is the Spirit of Power that others received on the Day of Pentecost when a mighty rushing wind filled the house, and they began speaking in other tongues (Acts 2:1-4).
7. The soul is that same Spirit that Believers receive after they accept Jesus Christ as Savior (John 1:12; John 20:22).
8. The soul is the Spirit of God that Paul says is the treasure that lives in the earthen vessel that is the body of every Believer (2 Corinthians 4:7).

9. The soul is a Spirit of God who lives in a person's body and reveals to that person the things of God. (1 Corinthians 2:11; see also Genesis 2:7b).

10. The soul is the Spirit of Christ who is the Light of the world, which needs to shine in the life of every believer so that men will see their good works and come to "glorify your Father which is in heaven" (Matthew 5:16).

11. The soul is the Spirit of God who can change a person's life for the better and changes it from the inside out: "Let this mind be in you, which was also in Christ Jesus" (Philippians 2:5).

12. From 2 Timothy 1:10, the soul is the eternal Spirit of the risen Christ

    who hath abolished[2673] [3303] death,[2288] and[1161] hath brought life and immortality to light[5461] [2222] [2532] [861] through[1223] the[3588] gospel.[2098]

13. The soul is the Spirit of God who guarantees eternal life in heaven with God to everyone who receives it, as it is written in John 17:3.

    And this is life eternal, that they might know thee the only true God, and Jesus Christ, whom thou hast sent.

14. The soul is the Spirit of God that a believer receives while he is yet in his mortal and corruptible body. 1 Corinthians 15:54 states,

    So[1161] when[3752] this[5124] corruptible[5349] shall have put on[1746] incorruption,[861] and[2532] this[5124] mortal[2349] shall have put on[1746] immortality,[110] then[5119] shall be brought to pass[1096] the[3588] saying[3056] that is written,[1125] Death[2288] is swallowed up[2666] in[1519] victory.[3534]

15. The soul is the Spirit of the Risen Christ who quickened the procreated spirits of the Ephesians and others (Ephesians 2:1a) and that Spirit is the "Christ in you, the hope of glory" (Colossians 1:27).

### How Valuable Is Your Soul?

Now, I want you to think about this very carefully. Do you get the idea that Jesus Christ has placed the soul as being more important and more valuable than all of the wealth in the entire world?

If you do, then can you please tell me how one can be so casual as to equate the soul merely with one's "mind, will, and emotions"?

Correct me if I am wrong, but is it not a fact that when you are casual about anything, the potential exists for you to become a casualty? Let's get serious; if God was willing to sacrifice His only begotten Son to save your soul, should you not want to know what your soul is?

Question: If it is true that the soul is your (i) mind (ii) will, and (iii) emotions, then, how do you account for your (1) memory, (2) imagination, (3) conscience, and (4) heart? You do know that you have them, don't you?

### Ezekiel 28:16

God banished Lucifer, the first sinner, from heaven.

> By the multitude of thy merchandise, they have filled the midst of thee with violence, and thou hast sinned: therefore, I will cast thee as profane out of the mountain of God: and I will destroy thee, O covering cherub, from the midst of the stones of fire.

### Isaiah 12: 12-15

Lucifer was filled with pride and cast out of heaven. Note the five repetitions of "I will."

> [12] How art thou fallen from heaven, O Lucifer, son of the morning! how art thou cut down to the ground, which didst weaken the nations! [13] For thou hast said in thine heart, I will ascend into heaven, I will exalt my throne above the stars of God: I will sit also upon the mount of the congregation, in the sides of the

north: [14] I will ascend above the heights of the clouds; I will be like the most High. [15] Yet thou shalt be brought down to hell, to the sides of the pit.

**Luke 22:42**

Jesus humbled himself by surrendering His will to God's even to His death on the cross.

Father, if thou be willing, remove this cup from me: nevertheless, not my will, but thine, be done.

**Luke 11:2**

Believers are called to surrender their will to God's and do as Jesus did.

When ye pray, say, Our Father which art in heaven, Hallowed be thy name. Thy kingdom come. Thy will be done, as in heaven, so in earth.

## What are the Characteristics of the Soul?

Souls may be perceived as being either visible or invisible.

Souls may have names, or they may not:

- Lucifer (Isaiah 14:12),
- Michael (Daniel 10:13, 21; 12:1; Jude 1:9; Revelation 12:7),
- Gabriel (Daniel 8:16; 9:21; Luke 1:19; 1:26).

Souls may be identified by group names, some of which include host, angel(s), and sons of God.

- Host (Genesis 2:1),
- Hosts of the Lord (Exodus 12:41; Josh. 5:14),
- Host of God (1 Chronicles 12:22),

- Host of heaven (Deuteronomy 4:19; 17:3; 2 Chronicles 18:18; 2 Chronicles 33:3, 5; Nehemiah 9:6; Isaiah 34:4; Jeremiah 8:2; 19:13; 33:22; Daniel 8:10; Ephesians 1:5; Acts 7:42),
- Host of the heavens (Psalms 33:6; Isaiah 45:12).

Angels and Archangels are too numerous to name.

Sons of God (Job 1:6; 2:1; 38:7).

Note: Excluded from this group are the sons of God in Genesis 6:2, 6:4. These are fallen angels who sinned. We'll talk about them later.

Now, if my interpretation conflicts with what you presently hold to be true, please hold on and bear with me. I am going somewhere, and I will make the connection when I address the soul that dies.

Earlier I mentioned that Lucifer was the first creature (also the "covering cherub" or "anointed cherub") or angel to have sinned.

With Lucifer's sin came Lucifer's fall. He and one third of the angels were cast out of heaven, and clearly, Lucifer was not human, yet he was the first creature to have sinned. We read in Ezekiel 28:16:

> 16 By the multitude[7230] of thy merchandise[7404] they have filled[4390] the midst[8432] of thee with violence,[2555] and thou hast sinned:[2398] therefore I will cast thee as profane[2490] out of the mountain[4480] [2022] of God:[430] and I will destroy[6] thee, O covering[5526] cherub,[3742] from the midst[4480] [8432] of the stones[68] of fire.[784]

Ezekiel 18, verses 4 and 20 both tell us that

> the soul[5315] that sinneth,[2398] it[1931] shall die.[4191]

CHAPTER 2

# SEVEN TYPES OF SOULS

## Seven Soul Types

I believe I have identified seven different types of souls in the Bible.

1. A soul
2. A dead soul
3. A living soul
4. A lost soul
5. A redeemed soul
6. A reprobate soul
7. A glorified soul

Here is my interpretation of each type.

| Term | My Interpretation | Scripture Support |
|---|---|---|
| **Soul** | He is a heaven-based created spirit-being who dwells in the very presence of God | Ezek. 18:20 |
| **Dead Soul** | He is a created spirit being that sinned and was cast out of heaven or removed from the presence of God | Think Lucifer and the fallen angels. Ezek. 28:16 Isaiah 14:12-20 |
| **Living Soul** | He is a sinless spirit-man, created in the image of God + dust + the breath of God | Think Adam and Eve before they sinned. Gen. 1:27; 2:7 |
| **Lost Soul** | He is a Living Soul that sinned. He is human. God used to live in his body, and in turn, he resided in God's presence. Sin caused God to exit his body, and also evict the lost soul from his presence. Adam replaced God with the evil spirits of the God of this world. Satan became his ruler. | Think Adam and Eve after they sinned. They became spiritually dead. And God evicted them from of Eden. Gen. 4:1; 5:3; 3:6; 2:7; Rom. 6:16; John 8:34 |
| **Redeemed Soul** | He is a Lost Soul who accepted Jesus Christ. He was reconnected to God spiritually. God re-entered his body, But the evil spirits of the god of this world did not leave. | 1 John 3:2; 1 Thessalonians 4:17; Eph. 6:12; John 1:12; Rom. 10:9-10; 2 Cor. 5:17 |

| | | |
|---|---|---|
| **Reprobate Soul** | He is a Redeemed Soul that backslid. He is one refuses to repent and will spend eternity out of God's presence. | 2 Cor. 13:5-7; Titus 1:16 |
| **Glorified Soul** | This is a glorified human who was once mortal but is now immortal; once had a corrupted body but swapped it for an incorruptible one. He lives in heaven, in God's presence where there's no sin. | 1 Cor. 15:53-54; John 1:12 |
| **Man** | He is a spirit. God created him. And he is a male (seed) and female (egg) combination. | Gen. 1:27; 5:2; John 6:63; Luke 8:11 |
| **Human being** | He is a procreated spirit called "Man" who lives in a body. At birth, this spirit-man is in a body that is either 100 percent male or 100 percent female. | Gen 1:27; 2:7; James 2:26 |

## What Is a Dead Soul?

A dead soul is a soul that sinned. The Bible says, "The soul that sinneth, it shall die" (Ezekiel 18:4, 20; Isaiah 14:12-14). Scripture confirms that Lucifer was the first sinner (Isaiah 14:12-14).

Since it is impossible for any creature other than a soul to sin, I conclude therefore that Lucifer was the first soul mentioned in the Bible and also the first soul that died, "for the devil sinneth from the beginning" (1 John 3:8). See also Ezekiel 18:4, 20 and Isaiah 14:12-14.

The Bible says, "The wages of sin is death" (Romans 6:23). Obviously, the death referred to in that verse is spiritual and spiritual death results in spiritual separation from God.

Both Lucifer and the angels that sided with him suffered the consequence of separation from God because of sin (1 Peter 2:4). When Adam and Eve sinned, the same fate—separation from God—befell them (Genesis 3:24). Even though Romans 6:23 appears in the New Testament, the reality is that correct application must link it first to Lucifer's sin, because the wages of Lucifer's sin was spiritual death or spiritual separation from God (Luke 10:18).

Can a believer who sins become spiritually from God again? I believe the Bible says no, because Jesus said, "I give them eternal life, and they shall never perish; neither shall anyone snatch them out of My hand" (John 10:28). I see no way that believers can be separated twice from God. The Bible says in Romans 5:17,

> If by one man's offence death reigned by one; much more they which receive abundance of grace and of the gift of righteousness shall reign in life by one, Jesus Christ.

In Lucifer's case, he was in God's presence. He was God's chief worshipper. When he sinned, he was cast out of God's presence. As a result, Lucifer lost his soul, and so did one third of the angels who sided with him in rebellion against God (See Ezekiel 28:1-16). When Lucifer's soul died, my understanding is that it fell to the earth (See Ezekiel 28:16-19). On earth, it became a disembodied spirit.

By divine decree, however, in the earthly realm, a spirit needs a body to exist or to become physically alive. Many believe that in the Garden of Eden Lucifer entered or took possession of the body of the serpent where he became the Tempter.

Of that process, whereby a disembodied spirit inhabits the body of an animal or a person, in John 10:1, Jesus says,

> He that enters not by the door into the sheepfold but climbs up some other way; the same is a thief and a robber.

In the earthly realm, God designed, from the beginning, that every living creature, including humans, would reproduce after its own kind through the process of sexual intercourse and every living plant would reproduce after its own kind through the process of germination. This process occurs when its seed falls to the ground and then reproduces more of the same.

More importantly, God designed for every seed, regardless of the type of seed, that it was He, God, who would give it a body (1 Corinthians 15:38).

## What Is a Living Soul?

A living soul is a creature called "man," who was created in God's image (Genesis 1:27; Romans 1:20; Colossians 1:15; Psalms 33:6), who was both male and female (Genesis 1:27) and who was named ADAM (Genesis 5:2). That spirit creature was blessed by God (Genesis 1:28) and then placed in a body made out of dirt that God had prepared for him (1 Corinthians 15:38; Genesis 2:7a; Romans 1:20).

I must let you know that when it is used correctly the term "living soul" can be applied only to Adam and Eve before they sinned. It may also be applied to Jesus because He never sinned. But it is my contention that once Adam and Eve sinned, they became lost souls.

### What happened when Adam sinned?

Once Adam and Eve sinned, no longer could they say, "Greater is He that is in me, that he that is in the world" (1 John 4:4), because they had lent their members to sin, and as a result had become the servant of sin (Romans 6:16). A heaven-based soul lives in the presence of God, whereas, with an earth-based living soul, the presence of God lives in his and her bodies.

The Bible says that the sin of one man named ADAM (Genesis 5:2; Genesis 3:6b), who was a spirit-being in a dirt body, caused God to remove His presence from the body of the first two human beings. Symbolically this was accomplished by God putting the man and the woman out of Eden or out of the very spot where His presence was.

As it is written in Genesis 3:22-24,

> 22 And the LORD[3068] God[430] said,[559] Behold,[2005] the man[120] is become[1961] as one[259] of[4480] us, to know[3045] good[2896] and evil:[7451] and now,[6258] lest[6435] he put forth[7971] his hand,[3027] and take[3947] also[1571] of the tree[4480][6086] of life,[2416] and eat,[398] and live[2425] forever:[5769]
>
> 23 Therefore the LORD[3068] God[430] sent him forth[7971] from the garden[4480][1588] of Eden,[5731] to till[5647][853] the ground[127] from whence[4480][8033][834] he was taken.[3947]
>
> 24 So he drove out[1644][853] the man;[120] and he placed[7931] at the east[4480][6924] of the garden[1588] of Eden[5731][853] Cherubims,[3742] and a flaming[3858] sword[2719] which turned every way,[2015] to keep[8104][853] the way[1870] of the tree[6086] of life.[2416]

Because of Adam's sin, or more specifically because of the sin of the created spirit-man that resided in the body of the first male named Adam, every descendant of Adam was a lost soul in the day he was born. A lost soul is a soul that does not know God, nor was it made in the image of a holy God, because the glory of God had departed (Romans 3:23; 1 Samuel 4:21; Colossians 1:27).

Genesis 5:3 says,

> 3 And Adam[121] lived[2421] a hundred[3967] and thirty[7970] years,[8141] and begot[3205] a son in his own likeness,[1823] after his image;[6754] and called[7121][853] his name[8034] Seth:[8352]

Please note: Adam was created, in the image of God (Genesis 1:27) and was then made into God's likeness (Genesis 2:7a; 5:2). Seth, however, was made in the likeness of a fallen or sinful Adam (Genesis 5:3).

When God placed the created spirit-man in the dirt, at that point the man that God had created became human, meaning he was now a combination of dirt plus spirit. Later, when God breathed His Spirit into the nostrils of the first human being, that first human being was then made into the likeness of God (Genesis 2:7b; 5:2).

It took three components for the first human to become a living soul. It took spirit-man (Genesis 1:27), the body (Genesis 2:7a), and the breath of God (Genesis 2:7b). In other words, those first two humans were the only ones of God's creatures who were given the privilege and honor, of having a personal relationship with our heavenly Father.

Once God had finished His work in creating and making the Adamic man, God placed the living soul that He had created and made in a Garden called Eden (Genesis 2:15, 1:26, 1:28). Genesis 1:28 says that before making the created man into His likeness, God had blessed the man, who was both male and female, to

> 28 Be fruitful,[6509] and multiply,[7235] and replenish[4390] [853] the earth,[776] and subdue[3533] it: and have dominion[7287] over the fish[1710] of the sea,[3220] and over the fowl[5775] of the air,[8064] and over every[3605] living thing[2416] that moveth[7430] upon[5921] the earth.[776]

Once God formed Adam's body, the created Adam became the human Adam. He became a spirit that lived in a dirt body (Genesis 2:7a).

When God breathed the breath of life into Adam's nostrils (Genesis 2:7b), the Bible says that Adam became a living soul. I submit that Adam became a living soul because he had no sin and resident in his body was his created male-female spirit-man (Genesis 1:27) and the breath of God (Genesis 2:7a), which was also Spirit. It took the Spirit of God and Adam's spirit-man for human Adam to become a living soul. With God's Spirit in his body

Adam now had a personal relationship with God who lives in heaven. Adam became a person who carried the Spirit of God in his body. Here's the proof:

The first man whom God created was a male-female spirit called ADAM (Genesis 5:1-2). The first human was spirit + dust (Genesis 1:27 + Genesis 2:7a. He was also called Adam. And the first living soul who was spirit-man + dust + Spirit of God (Genesis 1:27 + Genesis 2:7a + Genesis 2:7b) was also called Adam. I believe in all three cases that spirit-man Adam was also male and female (Genesis 1:27, 28; 5:1-2).

Unlike the heaven-based soul that lives in the presence of God, the living soul had the presence of God living in him.

In the Bible, the presence of God that lives within the body of every believer is described as a "treasure in an earthen vessel" (2 Corinthians 4:7). In the Old Testament, the first living soul was called ADAM. He was both male and female, and I contend that when we view them in New Testament context, we must also view them as one who had the same treasure in the earthen vessel that was his body (2 Corinthians 4:7).

Additionally, we must see Adam's body as a temple of God's Holy Spirit because God's Spirit lived in Adam's body (1 Corinthians 6:19; 2 Corinthians 6:16).

At present my position is that there are no living souls on planet earth, neither have there been any since our first parents, Adam and Eve, sinned and were driven out by God from the Garden of Eden (Genesis 3:22-24).

Biblical history records that there were only two humans who were living souls:

1. The first human, who was called Adam, was both male and female (Genesis 2:7, 15, 18, 20-21; 5:1-2);
2. The first male, who was also called Adam, became fully male or masculine after the woman was taken out of him (Genesis 2:21-22); and

3. The first female human, who was the woman whom Adam called both woman (Genesis 2:23) and Eve (Genesis 3:20), became fully feminine only after she was taken out of the body of that first human that had become the first living soul (Genesis 2:22-23; Genesis 2:7b).

## What's with this Word "Nephesh"?

In the original language, the word translated "soul" is *nephesh*. Strong's Concordance defines *nephesh* as a man, a breathing creature, or a person that is mortal.[3]

However, Strong makes no connection to the fact that in Ezekiel 18:4, *nephesh* was referring to Lucifer.

At no time does Strong indicate that a *nephesh* refers both to an earthly creature as well as a heavenly creature. At no time does Strong make any connection or reference to the fact that a soul is a creature created by God and was created to worship God 24/7/365 and for all eternity, which is what all the angels in heaven have been doing since the beginning of time and are doing still, even to this day (Revelation 4:8).

Let's be very clear about one thing: The very first time the word "sinned" is mentioned in the Bible (Ezekiel 18:4, 18:20), it refers NOT to a human being BUT to an angel named Lucifer. And since the Bible has established that when Lucifer sinned and was cast out of heaven (Ezekiel 28:16), one third of the angels who sided with him were also cast out of heaven (2 Peter 2:4), then the only logical conclusion we can make is that all (the good) angels are souls. It could not be otherwise.

Moreover, we must note that in some places in the Bible the word *nephesh* (Strong's 5315) is interpreted to mean animals or lower life forms.[4] And, as far as I know, animals are totally incapable of committing sin. Five times in the Book of Genesis the word *nephesh* is used to refer to animals or lower life forms. So clearly, when we categorize all souls as *nephesh*, we err.

Here are these five references: Genesis 1:21, 1:24, 1:30, 2:7, 2:19.

> 21 And God⁴³⁰ created¹²⁵⁴ ⁸⁵³ great¹⁴¹⁹ whales,⁸⁵⁷⁷ and every³⁶⁰⁵ living²⁴¹⁶ creature⁵³¹⁵ that moveth,⁷⁴³⁰ which⁸³⁴ the waters⁴³²⁵ brought forth abundantly,⁸³¹⁷ after their kind,⁴³²⁷ and every³⁶⁰⁵ winged³⁶⁷¹ fowl⁵⁷⁷⁵ after his kind:⁴³²⁷ and God⁴³⁰ saw⁷²⁰⁰ that³⁵⁸⁸ it was good.²⁸⁹⁶
>
> 24 And God⁴³⁰ said,⁵⁵⁹ Let the earth⁷⁷⁶ bring forth³³¹⁸ the living²⁴¹⁶ creature⁵³¹⁵ after his kind,⁴³²⁷ cattle,⁹²⁹ and creeping thing,⁷⁴³¹ and beast²⁴¹⁶ of the earth⁷⁷⁶ after his kind:⁴³²⁷ and it was¹⁹⁶¹ so.³⁶⁵¹
>
> 30 And to every³⁶⁰⁵ beast²⁴¹⁶ of the earth,⁷⁷⁶ and to every³⁶⁰⁵ fowl⁵⁷⁷⁵ of the air,⁸⁰⁶⁴ and to every thing³⁶⁰⁵ that creepeth⁷⁴³⁰ upon⁵⁹²¹ the earth,⁷⁷⁶ wherein⁸³⁴ there is life,⁵³¹⁵ ²⁴¹⁶ I have given ⁸⁵³ every³⁶⁰⁵ green³⁴¹⁸ herb⁶²¹² for meat:⁴⁰² and it was¹⁹⁶¹ so.³⁶⁵¹
>
> 7 And the LORD³⁰⁶⁸ God⁴³⁰ formed³³³⁵ ⁸⁵³ man¹²⁰ of the dust⁶⁰⁸³ of⁴⁴⁸⁰ the ground,¹²⁷ and breathed⁵³⁰¹ into his nostrils⁶³⁹ the breath⁵³⁹⁷ of life;²⁴¹⁶ and man¹²⁰ became¹⁹⁶¹ a living²⁴¹⁶ soul.⁵³¹⁵
>
> 19 And out of⁴⁴⁸⁰ the ground¹²⁷ the LORD³⁰⁶⁸ God⁴³⁰ formed³³³⁵ every³⁶⁰⁵ beast²⁴¹⁶ of the field,⁷⁷⁰⁴ and every³⁶⁰⁵ fowl⁵⁷⁷⁵ of the air;⁸⁰⁶⁴ and brought⁹³⁵ them unto⁴¹³ Adam¹²¹ to see⁷²⁰⁰ what⁴¹⁰⁰ he would call⁷¹²¹ them: and whatsoever³⁶⁰⁵ ⁸³⁴ Adam¹²¹ called⁷¹²¹ every living²⁴¹⁶ creature,⁵³¹⁵ that¹⁹³¹ was the name⁸⁰³⁴ thereof.

I believe we would be more accurate if we say that every soul or every living creature is a *nephesh,* but every *nephesh* (living creature) is not a soul.

Search the concordance, and you'll see that every time the word *soul* is used in relation to a personal relationship with God, it refers always to a human being or angel, never to an animal or lower life form. Here are some more Bible verses to drive the point home: Ezekiel 18:4; Psalm 16:10, 23:3, 25:1, 34:22:

4 Behold,[2005] all[3605] souls[5315] are mine; as the soul[5315] of the father,[1] so also the soul[5315] of the son[1121] is mine: the soul[5315] that sinneth,[2398] it[1931] shall die.[4191]

10 For[3588] thou wilt not[3808] leave[5800] my soul[5315] in hell;[7585] neither[3808] wilt thou suffer[5414] thine Holy One[2623] to see[7200] corruption.[7845]

Note: Jesus' soul was the Holy Spirit.

3 He restoreth[7725] my soul:[5315] he leadeth[5148] me in the paths[4570] of righteousness[6664] for his name's sake.[4616 8034]

This means that the heavenly connection between God and man was being restored.

1 A Psalm of David.[1732] Unto[413] thee, O LORD,[3068] do I lift up[5375] my soul.[5315]

22 The LORD[3068] redeemeth[6299] the soul[5315] of his servants:[5650] and none[3808 3605] of them that trust[2620] in him shall be desolate.[816]

Personally, I feel that Strong's translation or interpretation is severely deficient because it does not specify that the *nephesh* that became the living soul was a human being who was a "breathing creature that had a personal relationship with God and in whose body God lived."

Be that as it may, when we put Ezekiel 28:16 and 18:20 together we see that:

1. Lucifer was an angel who was the covering cherub (Ezekiel 28:16).
2. Lucifer sinned; he said in his heart, "I will ascend into heaven" (Isaiah 14:13a).
3. Spiritually speaking, Lucifer died; and we'll see later that he was "cast out of heaven" (Isaiah 14:21a).
4. Therefore, I conclude that Lucifer was a soul because the Bible has established clearly that only souls are capable of committing sin (Ezekiel 18:4, 20).

What's your opinion? I'd like to know.

## What Is a Lost Soul?

A lost soul is a living soul that sinned. The first living soul to have sinned was the woman that God made from a rib of the first human named Adam. She sinned because she was deceived. The Bible says, "Adam was not deceived, but the woman being deceived was in the transgression" (1 Timothy 2:14).

The second living soul to have sinned was the man called Adam. It is extremely important to note that this man called Adam was a combination of a created spirit-being called ADAM and a body of dirt that made him human. The finished product was also called Adam.

### Bible Verses
#### Genesis 1:27

> So, God created man in his own image, in the image of God created he him; male and female created he them.

#### Genesis 2:7

> And the LORD God formed man of the dust of the ground and breathed into his nostrils the breath of life; and man, became a living soul.

#### Genesis 3:6

> And when the woman saw that the tree was good for food, and that it was pleasant to the eyes, and a tree to be desired to make one wise, she took of the fruit thereof, and did eat, and gave also unto her husband with her; and he did eat.

### Genesis 3:23-24

> [23] Therefore, the LORD God sent him forth from the garden of Eden, to till the ground from whence he was taken. [24] So he drove out the man; and he placed at the east of the garden of Eden Cherubims and a flaming sword which turned every way, to keep the way of the tree of life.

### What Happened When the Woman Sinned?

When the woman—that is the second human being that God made—sinned, did you ever notice that God did not show up and ask her what was it she did? Why didn't He? I will tell you: God didn't show up because the woman was "taken out of" the first man. She was just a branch if you will; she was not the tree.

Imagine for a moment that you have a cake, and you cut a slice of it. I'd like you to take that slice of cake and place it on a table and then place the rest of the cake in the refrigerator. After that I'd like you to imagine that a roach is crawling on the slice of cake or a maybe a mouse is nibbling on it.

Now answer this question: Did the act of either the roach or the mouse affect the rest of the cake?

Obviously, the answer is no. Why? Because the rest of the cake was in the refrigerator.

Now, do you remember the Bible saying the God took the dust and formed the man (Genesis 2:7a)? I'd like you to see that dust as a lump of clay that God took and made a body for the man that he had created (Genesis 1:27) and called ADAM (Genesis 5:2).

Now, in Genesis 2:21 the Bible says,

> 21 And the LORD[3068] God[430] caused a deep sleep[8639] to fall[5307] upon[5921] Adam,[121] and he slept:[3462] and he took[3947] one[259] of his ribs,[4480] [6763] and closed up[5462] the flesh[1320] instead[8478] thereof.

Imagine for a moment that the rib is the equivalent of the slice of cake and that the roach crawling on the slice of cake is the equivalent of the woman disobeying God and eating of the tree of the knowledge of good and evil.

Question: When the slice of clay ate of the tree, was the lump that was Adam affected?

Answer: The only answer is an emphatic NO. The only answer is that the woman sinned alone. The only answer is that the woman suffered spiritual death alone because the male had not as yet eaten of the tree.

When the woman ate, did the Bible say that God showed up and asked: "Hey Eve, what is this that you have done?" It doesn't say that, does it? Do you know why? It is because when the slice of clay sinned, only the slice was affected.

The rest of the proverbial lump of clay that was in the refrigerator was still intact and sinless. This means that when the woman sinned, she sinned alone. Case closed.

Since the penalty for sin is death, it also meant that when she sinned, she died; and not only that, but she also died alone! But we both know that she did not die a physical death. Therefore, since she did not die physically, the only other alternative is that she died spiritually.

But how could she become spiritually dead had it not been for the fact that she had to have been spiritually alive? And if she was, what was it that made her spiritually alive? I submit to you that it was the Genesis 2:7b Spirit of God that lived in her.

When she sinned, God's Spirit left her. It is simple logic. One cannot become spiritually dead unless one first was spiritually alive. One cannot lose what one never had.

And how did she become spiritually alive? She became spiritually alive because she was the slice of cake taken out of the first man, Adam; and because she was, she had everything that the first man Adam had. When God breathed into the nostrils of a lump of clay, the entire lump became holy. Romans 11:16 says,

> 16 For[1161] if[1487] the[3588] first fruit[536] be holy,[40] the[3588] lump[5445] is also[2532] holy: and[2532] if[1487] the[3588] root[4491] be holy,[40] so[2532] are the[3588] branches.[2798]

In Eve's case, she was just a branch. Adam was the root. In Adam's case, he was the branch, Jesus was the vine.

When Eve sinned, she died spiritually. Adam was still safe. But when Adam sinned, it was only then that the entire human race—who was as yet resident and unborn in Adam's loins—all died spiritually because God removed His Spirit from the body of the first human.

Of that experience, the Bible says in Hebrews 4:12 that:

> 12 For[1063] the[3588] word[3056] of God[2316] is quick,[2198] and[2532] powerful,[1756] and[2532] sharper[5114] than[5228] any[3956] two-edged[1366] sword,[3162] piercing[1338] even[2532] to[891] the dividing asunder[3311] of[5037] soul[5590] and[2532] spirit.[4151]

The dividing of the soul and spirit had to have happened when our first parents sinned. Before Adam sinned, the lump of clay that was the house for the first man was a holy lump. It was a lump in which God had taken up residence. God had come to earth, in spirit form and tabernacled with the first human being.

The body or the house that God had built for that first human was designed by God to be a house for two spirits and only two spirits: the spirit called man and the spirit called God that was the breath of God (Job 33:6).

Alone in his body without having received the Breath of God, the spirit-man became a natural man, and his body became a house for his spirit-man. However, with the Breath of God in his body, his body became a temple for the Holy Spirit, and the (first) man became the son of God (Luke 3:38).

## What Happened When the Man Sinned?

The account of what happened when the man sinned is well documented in the Book of Genesis, chapter 3. God showed up on the scene, asked a few questions, and then applied the punishment.

The Bible says that the woman was deceived, but the man (that is the male called Adam) sinned willfully (Genesis 3:6; 1 Timothy 2:14).

Why would Adam have eaten of the tree? What was his motivation?

In my opinion, the Bible gives us the answer, but we've never put two and two together.

Please note: This is merely my opinion, so don't build a doctrine on this. Stick with the basics: The Virgin Birth; the death, burial, resurrection, and ascension of Christ; salvation by grace; and so on.

In the Book of John, Jesus says, "Greater love hath no man than this that a man lay down his life for his friends" (John 15:13).

And while it is true that Christ did lay down His life for His friends, we must not forget that Christ also laid down His life for His enemies. Check the Bible, and you'll see that on Crucifixion Day, Jesus had not a single friend in the entire world! John 3:16 tells us that He laid down His life for the entire world and whosoever believes in Him shall not perish.

In Adam's case, however, Adam did not have any enemies. In the Garden of Eden, other than the woman, there was no one else in the world. Genesis 2:23 reads thus:

> 23 And Adam[121] said,[559] This[2063] is now[6471] bone[6106] of my bones,[4480] [6106] and flesh[1320] of my flesh:[4480] [1320] she[2063] shall be called[7121] Woman,[802] because[3588] she[2063] was taken[3947] out of Man.[4480] [376]

So, can we agree that the first woman was a friend of the first man? And if we can, can we also agree that it is possible and highly probable that when Adam ate of the fruit, that he was laying down his life for his friend? Remember, the woman was deceived. The man wasn't.

What type of person do you know who will lay down his life for his friend? If you have a wife, will you lay down your life for her? Would you do it for your son or daughter?

I will tell you that the person that would do that is the person who has *agape* (from Greek and pronounced *a-ga-pay*) or a God kind of love. It is called unconditional love.

The crew who took down the plane in 9-11 had the *agape* kind of love. The guy who donated his eyes so his blind girlfriend could see had the *agape* kind of love. If you're reading this, you probably have it as well.

It's just that you may not yet have had the opportunity to put it to the test.

In the Bible, Adam is portrayed as a type of Christ; that is, as a person who laid down his life for his friend. When Eve sinned, humanity was NOT affected. However, when Adam did (Genesis 3:6c), all humanity became sin infected because resident in seed form, in the loins of that first male, was the entire human race. When Adam ate of the tree, essentially, he revoked his allegiance to Jehovah God and became the servant of Satan (Romans 6:16; Ezekiel 18:4, 20).

It is important to note that though the Bible records that the female or the woman was the first to sin, or the first to transgress God's law or the first to violate God's command (Genesis 2:6), God did not impose the penalty (Genesis 2:23-24) until after the man, or the male, or the first human (Genesis 2:7) had violated God's command as well.

Check the Bible, and you'll see: When the woman ate of the fruit of the tree, God did not show up and say to her, "Where art thou?" (Genesis 3:9). Why not? Was God showing favoritism? Didn't God say in Genesis 2:17b, for³⁵⁸⁸ in the day³¹¹⁷ that thou eatest³⁹⁸ thereof⁴⁴⁸⁰ thou shalt surely die.⁴¹⁹¹

Why didn't God expel her from the garden? Why didn't God say, "Because the female has become one of us, she must be put out?"

The Bible says in Genesis chapter 3,

> 22 And the LORD³⁰⁶⁸ God⁴³⁰ said,⁵⁵⁹ Behold,²⁰⁰⁵ the man¹²⁰ is become¹⁹⁶¹ as one²⁵⁹ of⁴⁴⁸⁰ us, to know³⁰⁴⁵ good²⁸⁹⁶ and evil:⁷⁴⁵¹ and now,⁶²⁵⁸ lest⁶⁴³⁵ he put forth⁷⁹⁷¹ his hand,³⁰²⁷ and take³⁹⁴⁷ also¹⁵⁷¹ of the tree⁴⁴⁸⁰ ⁶⁰⁸⁶ of life,²⁴¹⁶ and eat,³⁹⁸ and live²⁴²⁵ forever:⁵⁷⁶⁹
>
> 23 Therefore the LORD³⁰⁶⁸ God⁴³⁰ sent him forth⁷⁹⁷¹ from the garden⁴⁴⁸⁰ ¹⁵⁸⁸ of Eden,⁵⁷³¹ to till⁵⁶⁴⁷ ⁸⁵³ the ground¹²⁷ from whence⁴⁴⁸⁰ ⁸⁰³³ ⁸³⁴ he was taken.³⁹⁴⁷
>
> 24 So he drove out¹⁶⁴⁴ ⁸⁵³ the man;¹²⁰ and he placed⁷⁹³¹ at the east⁴⁴⁸⁰ ⁶⁹²⁴ of the garden¹⁵⁸⁸ of Eden⁵⁷³¹ ⁸⁵³ Cherubims,³⁷⁴² and a flaming³⁸⁵⁸ sword²⁷¹⁹ which turned every way,²⁰¹⁵ to keep⁸¹⁰⁴ ⁸⁵³ the way¹⁸⁷⁰ of the tree⁶⁰⁸⁶ of life.²⁴¹⁶

Because God applied the penalty for sin to the first human who was named Adam rather than to the first female whom Adam called Eve, we can now understand clearly what the Bible means when it says that "in Adam, all die" (1 Corinthians 15:22a; Genesis 5:1-2).

Similarly, when it says that every single human being is born spiritually dead, because it is separated from God "in trespasses and sins" (Ephesians 2:1), we can understand that too.

The Bible says that by the sin of one man—that would be that first human who was named Adam (Genesis 1:27, 5:1-2; Romans 5:12, 5:15, 5:17, 5:19)—the entire human race, who at that time was resident in seed form in that first man Adam (Genesis 1:27, 5:1-2) became corrupt in that all who have been reproduced through sexual intercourse between a male and a female and from within the DNA of the reproductive seed of that first human have sinned and come short of the glory of God (Romans 3:23).

So, the Bible is accurate when it says that there is "none righteous, no, not one" (Romans 3:10; Job 15:14). It is important to note that the Eden from which the Man and the Woman were expelled was in the earth. We find the location of that Garden of Eden in Genesis 2, verses 8-14.

Also, it is important to note that the woman was not called Eve until after she sinned. We learn that in Genesis 3:20 where she was now Adam's wife and was called "the mother of all living."

> And Adam[121] called[7121] his wife's[802] name[8034] Eve;[2332] because[3588] she[1931] was[1961] the mother[517] of all[3605] living.[2416]

## What Is a Redeemed Soul?

A redeemed soul is a human being who is born spiritually dead or spiritually separated from God and who accepts the free gift of salvation (Ephesians 2:8) through accepting Jesus Christ as Lord and Savior. Anyone who wants to make Jesus Christ Lord of his life must first repent of his sin and believe that God raised Jesus from the dead (Romans 10:9). For those who do, the Spirit of the Risen Christ enters into their bodies and at that time they will have positioned themselves to become (redeemed) sons of God, even as Adam became the son of God when the Lord breathed into his nostrils (Luke 3:38).

Romans 10:8-11 describes the process:

> 8 But[235] what[5101] saith[3004] it? The[3588] word[4487] is[2076] nigh[1451] thee,[4675] even in[1722] thy[4675] mouth,[4750] and[2532] in[1722] thy[4675] heart:[2588] that is,[5123] the[3588] word[4487] of faith,[4102] which[3739] we preach;[2784]

> 9 That³⁷⁵⁴ if¹⁴³⁷ thou shalt confess³⁶⁷⁰ with¹⁷²² thy⁴⁶⁷⁵ mouth⁴⁷⁵⁰ the Lord²⁹⁶² Jesus,²⁴²⁴ and²⁵³² shalt believe⁴¹⁰⁰ in¹⁷²² thine⁴⁶⁷⁵ heart²⁵⁸⁸ that³⁷⁵⁴ God²³¹⁶ hath raised¹⁴⁵³ him⁸⁴⁶ from¹⁵³⁷ the dead,³⁴⁹⁸ thou shalt be saved.⁴⁹⁸²
>
> 10 For¹⁰⁶³ with the heart²⁵⁸⁸ man believeth⁴¹⁰⁰ unto¹⁵¹⁹ righteousness;¹³⁴³ and¹¹⁶¹ with the mouth⁴⁷⁵⁰ confession is made³⁶⁷⁰ unto¹⁵¹⁹ salvation.⁴⁹⁹¹
>
> 11 For¹⁰⁶³ the³⁵⁸⁸ Scripture¹¹²⁴ saith,³⁰⁰⁴ Whosoever³⁹⁵⁶ believeth⁴¹⁰⁰ on¹⁹⁰⁹ him⁸⁴⁶ shall not³⁷⁵⁶ be ashamed.²⁶¹⁷

Two passages in John (1:12 and 14:6) explain this:

> 12 But¹¹⁶¹ as many as³⁷⁴⁵ received²⁹⁸³ him,⁸⁴⁶ to them⁸⁴⁶ gave¹³²⁵ he power¹⁸⁴⁹ to become¹⁰⁹⁶ the sons⁵⁰⁴³ of God,²³¹⁶ even to them that believe⁴¹⁰⁰ on¹⁵¹⁹ his⁸⁴⁶ name:³⁶⁸⁶
>
> 6 Jesus²⁴²⁴ saith³⁰⁰⁴ unto him,⁸⁴⁶ I¹⁴⁷³ am¹⁵¹⁰ the³⁵⁸⁸ way,³⁵⁹⁸ the³⁵⁸⁸ truth,²²⁵ and²⁵³² the³⁵⁸⁸ life:²²²² no man³⁷⁶² cometh²⁰⁶⁴ unto⁴³¹⁴ the³⁵⁸⁸ Father,³⁹⁶² but¹⁵⁰⁸ by¹²²³ me.¹⁷⁰⁰

## What Is a Redeemed Soul?

Now, let's see what Scripture says about the Redeemed Soul.

1. The Spirit comes in by individual invitation only according to Romans 10:9-10

   > 9 That³⁷⁵⁴ if¹⁴³⁷ thou shalt confess³⁶⁷⁰ with¹⁷²² thy⁴⁶⁷⁵ mouth⁴⁷⁵⁰ the Lord²⁹⁶² Jesus,²⁴²⁴ and²⁵³² shalt believe⁴¹⁰⁰ in¹⁷²² thine⁴⁶⁷⁵ heart²⁵⁸⁸ that³⁷⁵⁴ God²³¹⁶ hath raised¹⁴⁵³ him⁸⁴⁶ from¹⁵³⁷ the dead,³⁴⁹⁸ thou shalt be saved.⁴⁹⁸²
   >
   > 10 For¹⁰⁶³ with the heart²⁵⁸⁸ man believeth⁴¹⁰⁰ unto¹⁵¹⁹ righteousness;¹³⁴³ and¹¹⁶¹ with the mouth⁴⁷⁵⁰ confession is made³⁶⁷⁰ unto¹⁵¹⁹ salvation.⁴⁹⁹¹

2. The Spirit makes himself available to all according to Revelation 3:20:

> 20 Behold,[2400] I stand[2476] at[1909] the[3588] door,[2374] and[2532] knock:[2925] if[1437] any man[5100] hear[191] my[3450] voice,[5456] and[2532] open[455] the[3588] door,[2374] I will come in[1525] to[4314] him,[846] and[2532] will sup[1172] with[3326] him,[846] and[2532] he[846] with[3326] me.[1700]

3. The Spirit has stated that once He comes in, He will not leave, not at any time, "For he hath said, I will never leave thee, nor forsake thee" (Hebrews 13:5).

4. John 1:12-13 says only those who receive the Spirit qualify to become sons of God:

> 12 But[1161] as many as[3745] received[2983] him,[846] to them[846] gave[1325] he power[1849] to become[1096] the sons[5043] of God,[2316] even to them that believe[4100] on[1519] his[846] name:[3686]
>
> 13 Which[3739] were born,[1080] not[3756] of[1537] blood,[129] nor[3761] of[1537] the will[2307] of the flesh,[4561] nor[3761] of[1537] the will[2307] of man,[435] but[235] of[1537] God.[2316]

5. Luke 3:23 and 3:38 confirm this, saying, "And Jesus … was the son of Adam, which was the son of God."

Note: My position is this: if Adam had not received the Spirit of God, Adam could not have been called the son of God.

The Spirit of God is a tripartite Spirit that is comprised of the Spirits of the Father, Son, and Holy Spirit. 2 Timothy 1:7 says,

> 7 For[1063] God[2316] hath not[3756] given[1325] us[2254] the spirit[4151] of fear;[1167] but[235] of power,[1411] and[2532] of love,[26] and[2532] of a sound mind.[4995]

### One: You Get the Power from the Holy Spirit

Acts 1:8 says,

> But ye shall receive power, after that the Holy Ghost is come upon you: and ye shall be witnesses unto me both in Jerusalem, and in all Judaea, and in Samaria, and unto the uttermost part of the earth.

John 20:22 says, "And when He had said this, He breathed on them, and said to them, 'Receive the Holy Spirit.'"

Acts 8:17 says, "Then laid they their hands on them, and they received the Holy Ghost."

See also Acts 19:2 and John 14:16.

### Two: You Get the Love from God

Verse 16 in 1 John 4 says,

> And we have known and believed the love that God hath to us. God is love, and he that dwelleth in love dwelleth in God and God in him.

Romans 8:9 says,

> But ye are not in the flesh, but in the Spirit, if so be that the Spirit of God dwells in you.

Two verses later, Romans 8 says,

> But if the Spirit of him that raised up Jesus from the dead dwell in you, he that raised up Christ from the dead shall also quicken your mortal bodies by his Spirit that dwelleth in you.

### Three: You Get the Sound Mind from Jesus Christ

In Philippians 2:5, we read, "Let this mind be in you, which was also in Christ Jesus."

Romans 7, verses 23 and 25 say,

> But I see another law in my members, warring against the law of my mind, and bringing me into captivity to the law of sin which is in my members.... I thank God through Jesus Christ our Lord. So then with the mind I myself serve the law of God, but with the flesh the law of sin.

And finally, 1 Peter 4:1 says,

> Forasmuch then as Christ hath suffered for us in the flesh, arm yourselves likewise with the same mind: for he that hath suffered in the flesh hath ceased from sin.

### What About Reincarnation

When God takes the seed of a human and makes a body for it, the resulting human is said to be incarnate or clothed in flesh.

When a creature takes it upon himself and enters a body that God did not specifically prepare for him, I call that process reincarnation.

Incarnation is of God. Reincarnation is not. That's the way I see it. How about you?

So, you ask, is it possible for disembodied spirits or demons to enter a person's body? The answer is an emphatic YES!

Remember now, at the Last Supper, Judas was in the very presence of Jesus Christ when, according to the Bible, "Satan entered into him" (John 13:27); "Him" would be Judas. In other places in the Bible, it is recorded that demons or wicked spirits inhabited or took up residence in the bodies of humans (Matthew 12:45; Luke 8:2; 11:26).

Remember also, when Jesus walked this earth, HE cast out many devils (Matthew 8:16, 8:32; 12:27-28; Mark 1:34, 1:39, 9:25; Luke 4:35, 11:14, 18-20, 13:31). He also gave to His disciples the power to cast out devils (Matthew 10:8; Mark 3:15). And He has empowered everyone who believes on HIM with the same power (Matthew 7:22; John 1:12).

As to the penalty for sin, for the souls, or the angels whom God cast out of heaven, their penalty was eternal separation from God. They have absolutely no hope of redemption (2 Peter 2:4).

## What Is a Reprobate Soul?

A reprobate soul is a soul that was born dead in trespasses and sin (Ephesians 2:1a), was quickened (Ephesians 2:1b; Romans 10:9), and then backslid and refused to repent. The penalty for the earth-based reprobate soul is the same as the penalty for the heaven-based dead soul in that both souls are condemned to spend eternity in hell, as is stated in Matthew 18:8 and restated in 25:41:

> 8 Wherefore[1161] if[1487] thy[4675] hand[5495] or[2228] thy[4675] foot[4228] offend[4624] thee,[4571] cut them off,[1581] [846] and[2532] cast[906] them from[575] thee:[4675] it is[2076] better[2570] for thee[4671] to enter[1525] into[1519] life[2222] halt[5560] or[2228] maimed,[2948] rather than[2228] having[2192] two[1417] hands[5495] or[2228] two[1417] feet[4228] to be cast[906] into[1519] everlasting[166] fire.[4442]
>
> 41 Then[5119] shall he say[2046] also[2532] unto them[3588] on[1537] the left hand,[2176] Depart[4198] from[575] me,[1700] ye cursed,[2672] into[1519] everlasting[166] fire,[4442] prepared[2090] for the[3588] devil[1228] and[2532] his[846] angels:[32]

## What Is a Glorified Soul?

A glorified soul is a glorified human who was once mortal but is now immortal; once had a corrupted body but swapped it for an incorruptible one. He lives in heaven, in God's presence where there's no sin (1 Corinthians 15:53-54; John 1:12).

CHAPTER 3

# DOES EVERYONE HAVE A SOUL?

## Bible Verses

### Genesis 2:7b

7 And the LORD³⁰⁶⁸ God⁴³⁰ formed³³³⁵ ⁸⁵³ man¹²⁰ of the dust⁶⁰⁸³ of⁴⁴⁸⁰ the ground,¹²⁷ and breathed⁵³⁰¹ into his nostrils⁶³⁹ the breath⁵³⁹⁷ of life;²⁴¹⁶ and man¹²⁰ became¹⁹⁶¹ a living²⁴¹⁶ soul.⁵³¹⁵

### Genesis 2:19

19 And out of⁴⁴⁸⁰ the ground¹²⁷ the LORD³⁰⁶⁸ God⁴³⁰ formed³³³⁵ every³⁶⁰⁵ beast²⁴¹⁶ of the field,⁷⁷⁰⁴ and every³⁶⁰⁵ fowl⁵⁷⁷⁵ of the air;⁸⁰⁶⁴ and brought⁹³⁵ them unto⁴¹³ Adam¹²¹ to see⁷²⁰⁰ what⁴¹⁰⁰ he would call⁷¹²¹ them: and whatsoever³⁶⁰⁵ ⁸³⁴ Adam¹²¹ called⁷¹²¹ every living²⁴¹⁶ creature,⁵³¹⁵ that¹⁹³¹ was the name⁸⁰³⁴ thereof.

### 1 Corinthians 2:11b

1 For¹⁰⁶³ what⁵¹⁰¹ man⁴⁴⁴ knoweth¹⁴⁹² the things³⁵⁸⁸ of a man,⁴⁴⁴ save¹⁵⁰⁸ the³⁵⁸⁸ spirit⁴¹⁵¹ of man⁴⁴⁴ which³⁵⁸⁸ is in¹⁷²² him?⁸⁴⁶ even²⁵³² so³⁷⁷⁹ the things³⁵⁸⁸ of God²³¹⁶ knoweth¹⁴⁹² no man,³⁷⁶² but¹⁵⁰⁸ the³⁵⁸⁸ Spirit⁴¹⁵¹ of God.²³¹⁶

## 1 Corinthians 2:14

> 14 But[1161] the natural[5591] man[444] receiveth[1209] not[3756] the things[3588] of the[3588] Spirit[4151] of God:[2316] for[1063] they are[2076] foolishness[3472] unto him:[846] neither[2532] [3756] can[1410] he know[1097] them, because[3754] they are spiritually[4153] discerned.[350]

## Did Adam Have a Soul?

I say yes, Adam had a soul! Most definitely yes! And further, I say, that if he didn't, then God would be a respecter of persons. And the Bible is clear that God is not! (Acts 10:34).

Romans 3:23 states that "all have sinned and come short of the glory of God." What does that mean? I believe it means that from the day we were born we were all spiritually dead or disconnected from God. We were spiritually dead because, at birth, there is not one of us who had the Holy Spirit or the Spirit of the Risen Christ living inside our bodies.

I realize that accepting this fact may be a bitter pill for us to swallow. How could a Holy and Just God allow your newborn to be born in sin? God could because the seed that daddy sowed was a sinful seed and whatsoever daddy sowed, that was what he reaped. A corrupt tree cannot produce good fruit.

Now as bad as that may be and sound, you've got to know that before the foundation of the world, God had already provided His antidote for sin in the person of His Son. The fact that you were born means that you now can be born again, and it doesn't cost you a thing. Your Salvation is free! And, because your baby was born, you now can train him (or her) in the way he should go, and at the appropriate time, he too will seize the opportunity for his inner spirit-man to be born again.

Here are a few questions that you've probably never asked, but which, most definitely, need answers.

- Did Adam have a soul?

- What about Eve? Did she have a soul?
- If they did, from where or from whom did they get it?
- And what exactly is or was this glory of God?

As I said earlier, I believe that the glory of God was the Spirit of God that comes and lives in a person when that person accepts Jesus Christ as Lord and Savior. And I said that the breath that God breathed into the nostrils of Adam was the Spirit of God that became Adam's soul.

There are eight verses in the Bible that account for the first two human beings coming into existence. We find them in the Book of Genesis verses 1:26, 27, 28; 2:7, 21, 22; 5:1-2.

As you read them, understand that these verses were taken from the Polyglot Online Bible, King James Version. The numbers you see are the Strong's Concordance numbers. These are important because they can be used to set the tone for you to interpret the Bible accurately.

## Bible Verses about Adam and Eve, the First Human Beings
### Genesis 1:26-28

> 26 And God[430] said,[559] Let us make[6213] man[120] in our image,[6754] after our likeness:[1823] and let them have dominion[7287] over the fish[1710] of the sea,[3220] and over the fowl[5775] of the air,[8064] and over the cattle,[929] and over all[3605] the earth,[776] and over every[3605] creeping thing[7431] that creepeth[7430] upon[5921] the earth.[776]
>
> 27 So God[430] created[1254] [853] man[120] in his own image,[6754] in the image[6754] of God[430] created[1254] he him; male[2145] and female[5347] created[1254] he them.
>
> 28 And God[430] blessed[1288] them, and God[430] said[559] unto them, Be fruitful,[6509] and multiply,[7235] and replenish[4390] [853] the earth,[776] and subdue[3533] it: and have dominion[7287] over the fish[1710] of the sea,[3220] and over the fowl[5775] of the air,[8064] and over every[3605] living thing[2416] that moveth[7430] upon[5921] the earth.[776]

## Genesis 2:7

7 And the LORD[3068] God[430] formed[3335] [853] man[120] of the dust[6083] of[4480] the ground,[127] and breathed[5301] into his nostrils[639] the breath[5397] of life;[2416] and man[120] became[1961] a living[2416] soul.[5315]

## Genesis 2:21-22

21 And the LORD[3068] God[430] caused a deep sleep[8639] to fall[5307] upon[5921] Adam,[121] and he slept:[3462] and he took[3947] one[259] of his ribs,[4480] [6763] and closed up[5462] the flesh[1320] instead[8478] thereof;

22 And [853] the rib,[6763] which[834] the LORD[3068] God[430] had taken[3947] from[4480] man,[120] made[1129] he a woman,[802] and brought[935] her unto[413] the man.[120]

## Genesis 5:1-2

1 This[2088] is the book[5612] of the generations[8435] of Adam.[121] In the day[3117] that God[430] created[1254] man,[120] in the likeness[1823] of God[430] made[6213] he him;

2 Male[2145] and female[5347] created[1254] he them; and blessed[1288] them, and called[7121] [853] their name[8034] Adam,[121] in the day[3117] when they were created.[1254]

## God's Divine Process

In the preceding verses, you should have made note that

- God proposed to make man (Genesis 1:26).
- The first step in the process was that God created man (Genesis 1:27).
- When God creates, He speaks (Psalms 33:6).
- And the words that He speaks are spirit and life (John 6:63).
- It follows, therefore, that the man that God created was a spirit.
- But there's more. The Bible says that the word of God is a seed (Luke 8:11).

I conclude therefore that the first "man" that God created was a spirit that was a seed and that was both male and female.

## First Create, Then Bless

The very first thing that God did with the spirit-man He created (Genesis 1:27) was blessed him to be fruitful and multiply (1:28). After blessing him, God then took dust and made a body for the man. The man had now become a human being, and it was then that God placed that first human in the garden and commissioned him to name all the animals.

## How Did Adam Get So Smart?

Have you ever asked yourself: "What was it about Adam that enabled him to name all the animals?" On the sixth day of creation, who was the only person who could have known the name of all the animals? Would that not have been God? How did Adam get to know what was in God's mind? Only one way I know: "God breathed His Spirit into the nostrils of that first man and man became a living soul" (Genesis 2:7).

## The Natural Man Knows Not

Before God breathed into the nostrils of Adam, Adam was a natural man. He was just a spirit-man in a body. As a natural man, Adam could not have named any of the animals. Of the natural man, the Bible says the following in 1 Corinthians 2:14:

> 14 But[1161] the natural[5591] man[444] receiveth[1209] not[3756] the things[3588] of the[3588] Spirit[4151] of God:[2316] for[1063] they are[2076] foolishness[3472] unto him:[846] neither[2532] [3756] can[1410] he know[1097] them, because[3754] they are spiritually[4153] discerned.[350]

## The Spiritual Son of God Knows All

When God breathed into the nostrils of Adam, Adam then became the son of God. He was in the garden, which is to say he was in the presence of God; and more importantly, the presence of God was in him.

With the presence of God in him, Adam was then equipped to speak or to verbalize what God was thinking. Of that phenomenon, the Bible says in 1 Corinthians. 2:11,

> 11 For[1063] what[5101] man[444] knoweth[1492] the things[3588] of a man,[444] save[1508] the[3588] spirit[4151] of man[444] which[3588] is in[1722] him?[846] even[2532] so[3779] the things[3588] of God[2316] knoweth[1492] no man,[3762] but[1508] the[3588] Spirit[4151] of God.[2316]

My position is that Adam could never have named those animals had it not been for the fact that the Spirit of God was in him.

## God's Plan

Let's face it: At creation, wouldn't you agree that it was only God who could have known what He intended to call each animal and each bird, fish, or plant? Why did God leave the naming of them to the man?

I believe He did because God fully intended to give to the man complete dominion and authority over everything that crept and walked.

Have you ever noticed that of everything that God created and made, "MAN" was the only creature to whom He gave a name and into whom He breathed His breath of life?

I am saying that the Spirit of God that was in Adam, or that Breath of life that was in him, was Adam's soul.

Being earthbound, yet possessing within his body the Spirit of God who lives in heaven, is what enabled Adam to communicate with His Heavenly Father. That same Spirit was what qualified Adam to be called both (1) the son of God and (2) a living soul.

### Heavenly Soul vs. Living Soul

Now, check this out. In heaven, Lucifer was in the presence of God. Then he sinned. The Bible says that the soul that sins, surely dies (Ezekiel 18:4);

and the Bible confirms that Lucifer did die (Ezekiel 28:16). From those two verses, I conclude that Lucifer was the first soul to have sinned. What is important to note is that Lucifer was heaven-based, and he was only "in the presence" of God. God was not living in Lucifer's body.

On earth, however, God took His presence and breathed it into Adam's body; first into Adam and later into Eve. God's breath transformed them from being just human beings to living souls. Had they remained sinless, they would have remained living souls. But, when they sinned, they became lost souls, and with them, every unborn soul that was resident in Adam's loins became a lost soul as well.

For those of us who have accepted Jesus Christ as Savior, at best we have redeemed souls. We are works in progress. With our confession, our inner spirit-man became positionally sanctified. Then the Spirit of God came into our earthly house, and He now lives in us and empowers us to work out our salvation with fear and trembling. We may not see evidence in us of that spiritual transaction immediately, but we've got to exercise our faith and believe the same to be so.

## Work Out Your Salvation

When we receive Christ, from then till we die, what we've got to do is yield our every thought, word, and deed to the leading of God's Holy Spirit and allow Him to guide us into all truth (John 16:13), so that we do not conform to the ways of this world (Romans 12:2).

With the Holy Spirit helping, we must seek to transform ourselves into the image of God's Son, and we do that by the renewing of our minds, that we may prove what is that good, and acceptable, and perfect, will of God (Romans 12:2).

How do we do that? As I said, we've got to surrender our will, and through the agency of the Holy Spirit allow Him to teach us, all there is to know about God and Jesus, and just continue to pray for God's will to be done in our lives while our will takes a back seat.

Here's what the Bible says in John 14:26,

> 26 But[1161] the[3588] Comforter,[3875] which is the[3588] Holy[40] Ghost,[4151] whom[3739] the[3588] Father[3962] will send[3992] in[1722] my[3450] name,[3686] he[1565] shall teach[1321] you[5209] all things,[3956] and[2532] bring all things to your remembrance,[5279 3956 5209] whatsoever[3739] I have said[2036] unto you.[5213]

And 1 Corinthians 2:10 and 2:12 say,

> 10 But[1161] God[2316] hath revealed[601] them unto us[2254] by[1223] his[848] Spirit:[4151] for[1063] the[3588] Spirit[4151] searcheth[2045] all things,[3956] yea,[2532] the[3588] deep things[899] of God.[2316]

> 12 Now[1161] we[2249] have received,[2983] not[3756] the[3588] spirit[4151] of the[3588] world,[2889] but[235] the[3588] Spirit[4151] which[3588] is of[1537] God;[2316] that[2443] we might know[1492] the things[3588] that are freely given[5483] to us[2254] of[5259] God.[2316]

## How Did Man Become a Living Soul?

The simple answer and the only answer is that man became a living soul when God breathed the breath of life into the nostrils of the first human being (Genesis 2:7b). Read the words of the prophet Job, and you'll see that Job understood that his body was made from clay and that resident in that body was not one but two spirits of God. One of God's spirits was called the created spirit-man, and the other spirit was called the *neshâmâh* (the very breath of God).

## Two Spirits from Job's Account of Man in Polyglot Online Bible

In any translation other than one with the Strong's Concordance numbers, the presence of the two spirits that live in the body of man are not readily apparent. These verses are in Job 33.

> 4 The Spirit[7307] of God[410] hath made[6213] me, and the breath[5397] of the Almighty[7706] hath given me life.[2421]

"Spirit" is translated from Hebrew *rûach* (i.e., meaning man was created, as we read in Genesis 1:27). "The breath" is translated from Hebrew *neshâmâh* (i.e., meaning man became a living soul with the very breath of God, as stated in Genesis 2:7b).

Job 33:6 says,

> 6 Behold,[2005] I[589] am according to thy wish[6310] in God's[410] stead: I[589] also[1571] am formed[7169] out of the clay.[4480] [2563]

This means the man was made into a human being, as stated in Genesis 2:7a.

## About the Breath of God

It took the breath of God (Genesis 2:7b) to transform Adam from just an ordinary human being to a living soul. It was that breath that gave Adam the ability to name all the animals (Genesis 2:19-20). It was the breath of God that transformed the Apostles and all who were in the upper room (Acts 1:8) from people who were scared, to people who valued not their life and would preach the Gospel, no matter what. It is that breath of God that transforms a person's body from just an earthly house to a temple of/for God's Holy Spirit.

In 1 Corinthians 3:16 is the question, "Know ye not that ye are the temple of God, and that the Spirit of God dwelleth in you?" And in 1 Corinthians 6:19, it asks,

> What? Know ye not that your body is the temple of the Holy Ghost, which is in you, which ye have of God, and ye are not your own?

John 2:21 says Jesus spoke of "the temple of his body."

It is that breath of God that became the redeemed soul that Paul speaks of in 1 Thessalonians 5:23 when he says,

> I pray God your whole spirit and soul and body be preserved blameless unto the coming of our Lord Jesus Christ.

## Did Jesus Have a Soul?

I believe Jesus had a soul, for these reasons:

1. When God made a body for Adam, He designed it to be a house (2 Corinthians 5:1) for the spirit called *man* that He had created.

2. When God completed Adam's house, He breathed His Spirit into the body of the first human (Genesis 2:7a), then Adam's body that was at first an earthly house became a temple for God's Holy Spirit. God's Spirit was now living in Adam's body.

3. As I see it, a house is where we live. A temple is where we worship. And because believers' bodies become God's Temples, we are commanded in the New Testament to present our bodies as living sacrifices, holy and acceptable unto God, which is our reasonable service (Romans 12:1).

4. Accordingly, it is my position that God cannot now transform the believers' bodies into temples of His Holy Spirit and not have done the same for Adam.

5. When the Psalmist says, "Except the LORD build the house, they labor in vain that build it" (Psalms 127:1), I agree that God could have been speaking about a church or a place of worship. But on the deeper level, I believe that God was (and still is) referring to the human body that He formed out of dust that became an earthly house for our inner spirit-man. Of that house, which is the human body, Paul tells us that it will dissolve, meaning it will die, but he reassures us that "we have a building of God (waiting for us)," meaning a house not made with hands, but one that is eternal in the heavens (2 Corinthians 5:1).

6. Also, I believe that God is saying to us today if we give priority to our physical, social, financial, sexual, educational, and other well-being and pay little or no attention to our spiritual well-being, then, indeed we do so at our eternal peril.

In Matthew 10:28, Jesus cautions us to "fear not them which kill the body but are not able to kill the soul: but rather fear him which is able to destroy both soul and body in hell."

## Now, Let's Look at Jesus.

In the Book of John, Chapter 1, verse 1, John identifies the Son of God as the Word of God. In the original language, He is called "the Logos." In verse 1c, John tells us that the Word is God. The Bible says that God is Spirit (John 4:24). Therefore, we conclude that the Word is Spirit. Then the Bible says that "the Word was made flesh" (John 1:14). By interpretation, it means that the Eternal Spirit who is God, laid down his deity, then donned a suit made of dust and became human. How did He do that? The Bible says that the Holy Ghost helped.

## What did the Holy Ghost do?

Luke 1:35 says this:

> 35 And$^{2532}$ the$^{3588}$ angel$^{32}$ answered$^{611}$ and said$^{2036}$ unto her,$^{846}$ The Holy$^{40}$ Ghost$^{4151}$ shall come$^{1904}$ upon$^{1909}$ thee,$^{4571}$ and$^{2532}$ the power$^{1411}$ of the Highest$^{5310}$ shall overshadow$^{1982}$ thee:$^{4671}$ therefore$^{1352}$ also$^{2532}$ that holy thing$^{40}$ which shall be born$^{1080}$ of$^{1537}$ thee$^{4675}$ shall be called$^{2564}$ the Son$^{5207}$ of God.$^{2316}$

What exactly does that mean? To keep the context, we need to fast-forward thirty years. Jesus is walking toward the river Jordan to be baptized. John cries out: "Behold! The Lamb of God who takes away the sin of the world!" (John 1:29).

Who is this Lamb? Revelation 13:8 tells us that this Lamb was "slain from the foundation of the world." So how should we interpret this miraculous birth of the baby Jesus?

The only one way I know is to accept God's Word, as it is written, before you understand. Then go to God and ask Him for wisdom to understand

His Word (James 1:5). When you go to God and ask in faith, you may rest assured that He will tell you these things:

- The Lamb that was slain from the foundation of the world was the Word of God (Revelation 13:8).
- The seed is the Word of God (Luke 8:11).
- If a seed abides on a shelf, it abides alone, but if it falls to the ground and dies, then it will bring forth fruit (John 12:24).
- The seed that fell was His Son (John 1:1; Luke 8:11) who was slain from the foundation of the world (Revelation 13:8) that God kept on a shelf in heaven until a specific moment called "the fullness of time" came.
- Isaiah prophesied of His coming (Isaiah 7:14; 9:6).
- When "the fullness of time" came, then God "sent forth his Son" who was "made of a woman" and "made under the law" (Galatians 4:4).
- How did God do it? He instructed the Holy Ghost to take the seed that was the man Christ Jesus (1 Timothy 2:5) and also was the Lamb of God that was slain from the foundation of the world (Revelation 13:8) and miraculously implant it into the Virgin Mary's womb (Luke 1:35).

## What About Mary?

Do you know that God made Mary's body and that when she died, her body went back to the dust?

Do you know that the same is true for every human being: when we die, our bodies all go back to the dust?

What should this tell you? It should tell you that no one gets out of life alive. If the human Jesus didn't, why should you? Why should I?

## What do we know about Jesus' death?

If anything, we know that Jesus' death was real. We know that He died physically because the Apostle John recorded it in John 19:33-37. The crucifixion was over. The soldiers had broken the legs of the two thieves with whom Jesus was crucified, and John 19:33 says,

> 33 But¹¹⁶¹ when they came²⁰⁶⁴ to¹⁹⁰⁹ Jesus,²⁴²⁴ and⁵⁶¹³ saw¹⁴⁹² that he⁸⁴⁶ was dead²³⁴⁸ already,²²³⁵ they broke²⁶⁰⁸ not³⁷⁵⁶ his⁸⁴⁶ legs:⁴⁶²⁸

Now, even though He was already dead, John tells us this in the next verse:

> 34 But²³⁵ one¹⁵²⁰ of the³⁵⁸⁸ soldiers⁴⁷⁵⁷ with a spear³⁰⁵⁷ pierced³⁵⁷² his⁸⁴⁶ side,⁴¹²⁵ and²⁵³² forthwith²¹¹⁷ came there out¹⁸³¹ blood¹²⁹ and²⁵³² water.⁵²⁰⁴

The shedding of blood and water was definitive proof that Jesus had died and was physically dead. Here's John's personal testimony in John 19:35:

> 35 And²⁵³² he that saw³⁷⁰⁸ it bare record,³¹⁴⁰ and²⁵³² his⁸⁴⁶ record³¹⁴¹ is²⁰⁷⁶ true:²²⁸ and he²⁵⁴⁸ knoweth¹⁴⁹² that³⁷⁵⁴ he saith³⁰⁰⁴ true,²²⁷ that²⁴⁴³ ye⁵²¹⁰ might believe.⁴¹⁰⁰

Now, why would John want us to believe that what he wrote was true? The next two verses, John give us the answer.

> 36 For¹⁰⁶³ these things⁵⁰²³ were done,¹⁰⁹⁶ that²⁴⁴³ the³⁵⁸⁸ Scripture¹¹²⁴ should be fulfilled,⁴¹³⁷ A bone³⁷⁴⁷ of him⁸⁴⁶ shall not³⁷⁵⁶ be broken.⁴⁹³⁷
>
> 37 And²⁵³² again³⁸²⁵ another²⁰⁸⁷ Scripture¹¹²⁴ saith,³⁰⁰⁴ They shall look³⁷⁰⁰ on¹⁵¹⁹ him whom³⁷³⁹ they pierced.¹⁵⁷⁴

## What Happened After Jesus Died?

Luke 23:46 tells us that just *before* Jesus died,

> 46 And²⁵³² when Jesus²⁴²⁴ had cried⁵⁴⁵⁵ with a loud³¹⁷³ voice,⁵⁴⁵⁶ he said,²⁰³⁶ Father,³⁹⁶² into¹⁵¹⁹ thy⁴⁶⁷⁵ hands⁵⁴⁹⁵ I commend³⁹⁰⁸ my³⁴⁵⁰ spirit:⁴¹⁵¹ and²⁵³² having said²⁰³⁶ thus,⁵⁰²³ he gave up the ghost.¹⁶⁰⁶

So, the very first thing that happened after Jesus died was that his spirit went back to God!

According to 2 Corinthians 5:19, that Spirit was God.

> 19 To wit,⁵⁶¹³ that³⁷⁵⁴ God²³¹⁶ was²²⁵⁸ in¹⁷²² Christ,⁵⁵⁴⁷ reconciling²⁶⁴⁴ the world²⁸⁸⁹ unto himself,¹⁴³⁸

## How Could Jesus' Spirit Have Gone Back to God?

The Apostle Peter tells us that Jesus "did no sin, neither was guile found in his mouth" (1 Peter 2:22). In other words, Jesus lived and died a perfect, sinless life. And because He was sinless, He could return freely to the presence of God from whence He came.

In John 3:13, we read,

> 13 And²⁵³² no man³⁷⁶² hath ascended up³⁰⁵ to¹⁵¹⁹ heaven,³⁷⁷² but¹⁵⁰⁸ he that came down²⁵⁹⁷ from¹⁵³⁷ heaven,³⁷⁷² even the³⁵⁸⁸ Son⁵²⁰⁷ of man⁴⁴⁴ which is⁵⁶⁰⁷ in¹⁷²² heaven.³⁷⁷²

## Don't Fear Death

One thing we should have learned from Jesus' death is that death is not something we should fear but rather it is something for which we should prepare. The death of the body is inevitable. And because it is, we need to prepare for it because it could happen at any time and sometimes quite unexpectedly. And just so you'd know, worrying about it only speeds up the process. So, stop worrying and start preparing.

If we heed Jesus' words, preparing is easy. John 6:47 records Jesus saying in His own words:

> 47 Verily,²⁸¹ verily,²⁸¹ I say³⁰⁰⁴ unto you,⁵²¹³ He that believeth⁴¹⁰⁰ on¹⁵¹⁹ me¹⁶⁹¹ hath²¹⁹² everlasting¹⁶⁶ life.²²²²

How hard is that? For us to have everlasting life all we need to do is believe on Jesus. Remember now, the Son of God, who was Spirit, became manifest in the flesh. He lived, He died, then He went back to heaven. And He is telling us that all we need to do to join Him in heaven is believe on Him. John 3:36 records that Jesus says in His Word:

> 36 He that believeth[4100] on[1519] the[3588] Son[5207] hath[2192] everlasting[166] life:[2222] and[1161] he that believeth[544] not the[3588] Son[5207] shall not[3756] see[3700] life;[2222] but[235] the[3588] wrath[3709] of God[2316] abideth[3306] on[1909] him.[846]

Now get this: The "He" to whom Jesus is referring is not your body. Jesus' is referring to the procreated spirit-man that lives inside your body.

Translation: The spirit-man that chooses to believe not on the Son shall not see (eternal) life; but the wrath of God abides on him.

## What Does the Psalmist Say?

Now, in Ecclesiastes 12:7, the psalmist writes that upon death,

> 7 Then shall the dust[6083] return[7725] to[5921] the earth[776] as it was:[7945] [1961] and the spirit[7307] shall return[7725] unto[413] God[430] who[834] gave[5414] it.

Let me repeat that: "the spirit shall return unto God who gave it."

So, if everyone was born spiritually dead (Ephesians 2:1b), and many have never confessed Jesus Christ as Lord (Romans 10:9; John 1:12), on what basis can those who didn't lay claim to spending an eternity in heaven with Jesus? How can the spiritually dead return to heaven? And if they can, why does Ephesians 2:1a say that Christ has to quicken the spirit of those who believe for them to get to heaven?

I have searched many Bible commentaries regarding Ecclesiastes 12:7, and each, across the board and without exception, interpret this verse to mean that upon death the (inner) spirit-man of every human being goes back to God who gave it. I've got to tell you that I have a hard time accepting that interpretation. If that were true, why should anyone have to accept Jesus as

Savior if both believers and non-believers end up in the same place? How does that interpretation reconcile Romans 3:23 that says,

> 23 For[1063] all[3956] have sinned,[264] and[2532] come short[5302] of the[3588] glory[1391] of God;[2316]

What does a non-believer do with John 14:6 where Jesus says,

> 6 Jesus[2424] saith[3004] unto him,[846] I[1473] am[1510] the[3588] way,[3598] the[3588] truth,[225] and[2532] the[3588] life:[2222] no man[3762] cometh[2064] unto[4314] the[3588] Father,[3962] but[1508] by[1223] me.[1700]

Don't Romans 3:23 and John 14:6 count for anything?

If it is true that the spirit of everyone goes back to God who gave it, then why was it necessary for Jesus to come and die if we could all have gotten back to God without Him dying?

Let's revisit the birth of Jesus; and then maybe, just maybe, we'll get a new understanding of why it is impossible for any human being to get into the presence of God without going through Jesus Christ.

**The Birth of Jesus**

Here's what we know about Jesus' birth:

1. God's Spirit
2. which was the spirit of the man Christ Jesus (1 Timothy 2:5),
3. who also was the Lamb of God that was slain from the foundation of the world (Revelation 13:8),
4. was placed in Mary's womb
5. by the Holy Ghost (Luke 1:35),
6. and the baby Jesus was born (Matthew 2:1).

Who was this Jesus?

He was the Spirit that was the God of John 1:1 minus His deity. Without His deity, he became the spirit of the Man Christ Jesus (1 Timothy 2:5) and that Spirit, which was one hundred percent sinless-spirit-man, was placed in a body that was made for him by God (Hebrews 10:5; 1 Corinthians 15:38) out of the dust that was manufactured by Mary's body. God did not go back to the dirt to make a body for Jesus. He used Mary's womb to make a body for Jesus.

Here's what the writer of the Book of Hebrews had to say in 10:5 about when Jesus came into the world. He said,

> 5 Wherefore[1352] when he cometh[1525] into[1519] the[3588] world,[2889] he saith,[3004] Sacrifice[2378] and[2532] offering[4376] thou wouldest[2309] not,[3756] but[1161] a body[4983] hast thou prepared[2675] me:[3427]

It couldn't be any clearer. God prepared a body for Jesus.

The Bible says, "God was in Christ, reconciling the world unto himself" (2 Corinthians 5:19). That means that God took the Spirit that was His Son and placed it in a human body, and it was that Spirit that became manifest in the flesh and made Jesus fully God and fully human (1 Timothy 3:16). He was fully human because he had laid down His deity and became a man.

This is confirmed in Isaiah 7:14 and Matthew 1:18.

> Isaiah 7:14 Therefore[3651] the Lord[136] himself[1931] shall give[5414] you a sign;[226] Behold,[2009] a virgin[5959] shall conceive,[2029] and bear[3205] a son,[1121] and shall call[7121] his name[8034] Immanuel.[6005]

> Matthew 1:18 Now[1161] the[3588] birth[1083] of Jesus[2424] Christ[5547] was[2258] on this wise:[3779] When as[1063] his[846] mother[3384] Mary[3137] was espoused[3423] to Joseph,[2501] before[4250] they[846] came together,[4905] she was found with child[2147 2192 1722 1064] of[1537] the Holy[40] Ghost.[4151]

Now, let's fast-forward to the river Jordan again. Jesus was just baptized. What happened after? Jesus was spirit, soul, and body.

The Bible in Matthew 3:16 says, "The heavens were opened unto him, and he saw the Spirit of God descending like a dove, and lighting upon him."

So, get this: at birth, Jesus had one Spirit, and that one Spirit gave him a natural or human life.

Then, after His baptism, the Spirit of God descended upon Him. This means that after baptism, there were then two heavenly spirits living in His body—the Spirit of the man Christ Jesus (1 Timothy 2:5) and the Dove's spirit, also known as the Holy Spirit.

With this new awareness, when we apply 1 Thessalonians 5:23 to these facts, can we not say and be biblically accurate that Jesus was (1) spirit, (2) soul, and (3) body?

Remember what Jesus said to John when He asked John to baptize Him. He said, "Suffer it to be so" (Matthew 3:15). In other words, had you been present, you may have heard Jesus say something like this: Brother John, I know, and I know that you know that I don't need to be baptized because there's no sin in Me. But I need to do this so they can understand that if they follow me and do as I do then they too can receive the Spirit of God and their bodies can be transformed from being just earthly houses into temples for God's Holy Spirit.

### What Did David Say?

Listen to what David said on the subject, as recorded in Psalm 16:9-10. He was prophesying about Jesus, and he said that God said that He would not leave Jesus' soul in hell nor cause it to see corruption.

> 9 Therefore[3651] my heart[3820] is glad,[8055] and my glory[3519] rejoiceth:[1523] my flesh[1320] also[637] shall rest[7931] in hope.[983]
>
> 10 For[3588] thou wilt not[3808] leave[5800] my soul[5315] in hell;[7585] neither[3808] wilt thou suffer[5414] thine Holy One[2623] to see[7200] corruption.[7845]

## What Did Paul Say?

Paul said the same thing. Acts 2:27 says,

> 27 Because³⁷⁵⁴ thou wilt not³⁷⁵⁶ leave¹⁴⁵⁹ my³⁴⁵⁰ soul⁵⁵⁹⁰ in¹⁵¹⁹ hell,⁸⁶ neither³⁷⁶¹ wilt thou suffer¹³²⁵ thine⁴⁶⁷⁵ Holy One³⁷⁴¹ to see¹⁴⁹² corruption.¹³¹²

## What Did Jesus Say?

John 12:27 tell the words of Jesus: "Now is my soul troubled; and what shall I say? Father, save me from this hour: but for this cause came I unto this hour."

## What Was Jesus' Soul?

Based on the preceding scriptures, Jesus' soul had to have been the Spirit of the Dove that descended on Him in the River Jordan.

This must be so because the first spirit that gave Jesus His natural or human life was the Spirit of the Man Christ Jesus (1 Timothy 2:5). And, that Spirit was the Word of God (John 1:1, 12) minus His deity. It also was the Lamb of God that was slain from the foundation of the world (Revelation 13:8).

Now, why did Jesus say that His soul was troubled?

I believe He said that because He knew that once God the Father would place the sins of the world on him, then the Man Christ Jesus who knew no sin would become sin (Isaiah 53:10). Jesus also knew that once He became sin, the Spirit of God would leave Him and to Jesus, that pain would be more unbearable than all the whippings he received.

## Who Lived in the Body of Jesus?

It is important to note that before Jesus became the human being who walked the streets of Jerusalem, the Spirit within his body that made Jesus a human being was indeed the spirit of the man Christ Jesus who is the one mediator between God and men (1 Timothy 2:5).

That Spirit was

1. the Word of God (minus His deity),
2. who made everything (John 1:3),
3. who created everything (Colossians 1:16), and
4. who also was the Lamb that was slain long before the foundation of the world (Revelation 13:8).

**The Pain of Jesus**

How do we know that Jesus suffered more pain when the Spirit of God left Him than He suffered at the hands of His captors? We know He did because, even though He was at the mercy of the hands of His captors who physically mutilated His body, the Bible says that He opened not His mouth (Isaiah 53:7; Acts 8:32).

And yet, when God placed the sin of the world on His shoulders, the Bible says in Mark 15:34,

> 34 And[2532] at the[3588] ninth[1766] hour[5610] Jesus[2424] cried[994] with a loud[3173] voice,[5456] saying,[3004] Eloi,[1682] Eloi,[1682] lama[2982] sabachthani?[4518] which is,[3603] being interpreted,[3177] My[3450] God,[2316] my[3450] God,[2316] why[5101] hast thou forsaken[1459] me?[3165]

**Why Did Jesus Cry in Agony?**

Could Jesus have cried because the sin of the world separated Him from Jehovah God and God the Holy Spirit? Is it possible that the sin of the world was the catalyst that caused He who was rich to become poor so that we who were poor could become rich (2 Corinthians 8:9)?

To resolve that question, I believe we can find an answer if we focus on humanity's spiritual poverty. When we read Revelation 3:17, we see that it is possible for one to be rich, to be increased in goods and have need of nothing, yet be wretched, miserable, poor, blind and naked. So obviously, riches do not eliminate one's ability to be poor.

And, while it is true that poverty manifests itself in many ways, I believe Paul was referring to humanity's spiritual poverty. Luke 4:18 begins with these words: "The Spirit of the Lord is upon me because he hath anointed me to preach the gospel to the poor." Those were the first words Jesus uttered when He began His public ministry. His priority was to preach the gospel to the poor. What is the gospel? The gospel is the Word of God. What is the Word of God? God's Word is spirit and life (John 6:63). God's Word is truth (John 17:17).

Why do we need God's Word? Matthew 4:4 tells us that "Man shall not live by bread alone, but by every word that proceeds out of the mouth of God."

The Psalmist says God's Word is a lamp unto our feet and a light unto our path (Psalm 119:105). And Hebrews tells us that He, that is God's Word, is "the source of eternal salvation" (Hebrews 5:9).

Humanity's greatest need is the salvation of their souls. Sin had separated Adam and Eve from God. From then till Christ, all humanity was spiritually poor. None were qualified enough to approach the throne of grace boldly to find mercy in time of need. But today, because of Calvary, we can.

When Jesus was on the cross, God "made Him who knew no sin to be sin on our behalf, so that we might become the righteousness of God in Him." God imputed our sin to His Son, and He became for us our paschal lamb. Symbolically, God transferred our guilt on His Son. When Jesus became our sacrificial substitute, He became spiritually poor.

But, on Resurrection Sunday when Jesus rose from the dead, access to God was restored. The veil was rent. Jesus became to all those who obey Him the source of eternal salvation. Finally, all who were poor could become rich. Jesus had shed His blood; He had paid God's price for sin; and because He had, He also consecrated for all humanity a new and living way for everyone to gain access to God; and that way was through the veil, that is to say, His flesh (Hebrews 10:20).

As I close this chapter, may I say that I believe that Adam had a soul, Eve had a soul, and Jesus had a soul. Also, I believe that both believers and unbelievers have souls, but there's a difference: The believer's soul is one that has confessed Jesus and will spend eternity in heaven with God whereas the unbeliever soul hasn't and is destined to spend eternity in hell, which is a place of eternal damnation. Read Matthew 25:41 and 1 Corinthians 6:9. The categories of unbelievers are listed there.

## Bible Verses

### John 1:12-13

12 But[1161] as many as[3745] received[2983] him,[846] to them[846] gave[1325] he power[1849] to become[1096] the sons[5043] of God,[2316] even to them that believe[4100] on[1519] his[846] name:[3686]

13 Which[3739] were born,[1080] not[3756] of[1537] blood,[129] nor[3761] of[1537] the will[2307] of the flesh,[4561] nor[3761] of[1537] the will[2307] of man,[435] but[235] of[1537] God.[2316]

### 1 John 4:16

16 And[2532] we[2249] have known[1097] and[2532] believed[4100] the[3588] love[26] that[3739] God[2316] hath[2192] to[1722] us.[2254] God[2316] is[2076] love;[26] and[2532] he that dwelleth[3306] in[1722] love[26] dwelleth[3306] in[1722] God,[2316] and[2532] God[2316] in[1722] him.[846]

### Romans 8:9 and 8:11

9 But[1161] ye[5210] are[2075] not[3756] in[1722] the flesh,[4561] but[235] in[1722] the Spirit,[4151] if so be that[1512] the Spirit[4151] of God[2316] dwell[3611] in[1722] you.[5213]

11 But[1161] if[1487] the[3588] Spirit[4151] of him that raised up[1453] Jesus[2424] from[1537] the dead[3498] dwell[3611] in[1722] you,[5213] he that raised up[1453] Christ[5547] from[1537] the dead[3498] shall also[2532] quicken[2227] your[5216] mortal[2349] bodies[4983] by[1223] his[848] Spirit[4151] that dwelleth[1774] in[1722] you.[5213]

CHAPTER 4

# WHAT ABOUT YOUR SOUL?

## Humans Are Tripartite Beings

Thus far, we have accounted for your body and your spirit but, what about your soul?

Let's return to the mirror. As you spoke to the mirror, any eavesdropper, would have heard and seen that you were having a two-way conversation between your body and its reflection in the mirror. Now the Bible says that we are tripartite beings made up of body, soul, and spirit. So, if indeed, your reflection was your spirit, then where was your soul? And, if your reflection was your soul, then where was your spirit?

To answer that question, go with me to John 20:22. Jesus breathed on his disciples and said to them, "Receive the Holy Spirit." The Online Etymology Dictionary states that the English word "receive" is a translation of the word "*receivre*," a French word that was used circa 1300 AD, meaning "to regain, to take back or to recover." So, when Jesus breathed on His disciples and told them to "receive the Holy Spirit," could He have been saying to them that the time had come for them to recover or regain the Holy Spirit that Adam lost in the Garden of Eden? I believe that He was.

The word "breathed" occurs only four times in the Bible: in Genesis 2:7; John 20:22; Joshua 10:40; and 1 Kings 15:29. In Genesis, God breathed into Adam's nostrils, and Adam became a living soul. From that moment, Adam had intimacy with God because God's Spirit was living in Adam's body.

In John 20:22, Jesus breathed on His disciples and told them to receive the Holy Spirit. When they did, the Bible says that they were justified by faith, and had peace with God through our Lord Jesus Christ (Romans 5:1). In other words, Jesus' breath had restored their spirit-man's broken relationship with God. Their souls had been redeemed.

Acts 2 1-4 tell us that on the day of Pentecost when the disciples were all in one place in one accord

> a sound from heaven as of a rushing mighty wind ... filled all the house where they were sitting, and they were all filled with the Holy Ghost.

I see this rushing wind as being a more powerful breath of God or a greater outpouring of God's Holy Spirit.

I conclude therefore that when anyone receives Jesus Christ as Lord, in the spirit-realm, Jesus breathes on that person, and by faith, that person receives the Holy Spirit. The spirit-man of that person then becomes positionally sanctified and his soul that was lost then becomes a redeemed soul. If my conclusion is correct, then it must follow that the "breath of God" in the Old Testament, also was the soul of man.

Consider this: A believer confesses Jesus Christ as Lord, while an unbeliever doesn't. With his confession, a believer receives the triune spirit of God—a spirit of power, love, and a sound mind (2 Timothy 1:7). Confessing Jesus and receiving the Holy Spirit are the only two things that separate a believer from an unbeliever.

The Bible says, "By grace are we are saved through faith; and that not of ourselves: it is the gift of God" (Ephesians 2:8). When Jesus breathed on his disciples, that was a gift of God. When God breathed into Adam's nostrils, that too was a gift of God. And on the day of Pentecost when the Holy Spirit filled everyone, everyone received gifts. Today, Salvation is that gift. And, it is FREE, but you must ask for it.

**Did You Know that Jesus Had a Soul?**

In Psalm 16 verse 10, David says, "For thou wilt not leave my soul in hell; neither wilt thou suffer thine Holy One to see corruption." This is a prophetic psalm. In it David made the soul personal to Jesus. Later, in Acts 2:31, Peter refers to this Psalm as he directed the crowd to Jesus as their Messiah. Peter says,

> 31 He seeing this before[4275] spake[2980] of[4012] the[3588] resurrection[386] of Christ,[5547] that[3754] his[846] soul[5590] was not[3756] left[2641] in[1519] hell,[86] neither[3761] his[846] flesh[4561] did see[1492] corruption.[1312]

So, even Peter personalized the Messiah's soul. What's the message? The message is that even Jesus had a soul. Our challenge is to search the scripture and find proof that confirms that Jesus' soul was the same as the soul of every believer.

Let's go to the river Jordan. Jesus entered the river and asked John to baptize him. A conversation ensued. Then Jesus told John, "suffer it to be so" (Matthew 3:15). Then John baptized Jesus. When he did, the heavens opened, and the dove descended on Jesus. Here now is the Bible's record of what happened next, from Luke 3:22:

> 22 And[2532] the[3588] Holy[40] Ghost[4151] descended[2597] in a bodily[4984] shape[1491] like[5616] a dove[4058] upon[1909] him,[846] and[2532] a voice[5456] came[1096] from[1537] heaven,[3772] which said,[3004] Thou[4771] art[1488] my[3450] beloved[27] Son;[5207] in[1722] thee[4671] I am well pleased.[2106]

Of that event, Timothy said, "without controversy great is the mystery of godliness: God was manifest in the flesh, justified in the Spirit." I conclude therefore that when the Holy Ghost descended on Jesus, the man Christ Jesus (1 Timothy 2:5) was justified in the Holy Spirit and he became body spirit and soul. Jesus' soul was the Holy Spirit.

Here's what's important: As the man Christ Jesus (1 Timothy 2:5) God's only begotten son had laid down His deity then He put on flesh and became just a regular human being. Philippians 2 verses 6 through 8 confirm this. So, when Jesus received the Holy Spirit, I am saying that He received His soul. Later when God made Him who knew no sin to become sin for us, symbolically, He lost His soul (2 Corinthians 5:21). Losing His soul is symbolic because at no time did Jesus ever sin personally. Out of obedience He allowed God to place the sins of the entire world on Him so He could die on the cross to prepare for all men the ONE way through which each person can compel God to save him or her.

**Did Adam Have the Holy Spirit?**

When an unbeliever accepts Jesus as Lord, that unbeliever becomes a believer, and by faith he receives the Spirit of the Risen Christ and the Holy Spirit.

When Jesus was preparing to do battle in the wilderness with Satan, God empowered Jesus with His Holy Spirit (Mark 1:11). God did not allow Jesus to face Satan empty handed. God equipped Him with the sword of the Spirit, which is the word of God. And every time that Jesus responded to Satan, he prefaced his words with, "It is written" (Matthew 4:4,7,10).

So, here's a question for you: If God gave Jesus His Holy Spirit; and if God gives every believer his Holy Spirit, is it conceivable that God would have placed Adam in the Garden of Eden and not given his Holy Spirit to Adam? I don't think so.

After all, according to Genesis 3:1, wasn't Satan in the garden of Eden in the form of a serpent? Seriously, if God did that to Adam, then God would be a respecter of persons and to be sure, He is not! What God did for one, He'll do for all. God does not show favoritism (Acts 10:34).

## His Servants Ye Are to Whom Ye Obey

Take the case of every newborn. Do you know that every newborn is born in sin even though his ability to sin is under-developed at birth? "The newborn can do nothing for his self so how can he be born in sin"? You ask. Let's go to the garden of Eden: Do you remember from Genesis 3:6c when Adam disobeyed God and ate of the tree? Well, Adam's act of disobedience severed his intimate relationship with God. Romans 6:16 confirms this. It states,

> Know ye not, that to whom ye yield yourselves servants to obey, his servants ye are to whom ye obey; whether of sin unto death or of obedience unto righteousness?

In the Garden, God was Adam's ONLY master. Once Adam yielded his members to that old serpent the devil, God evicted Adam from Eden, and Satan became Adam's master. Since we were all spiritual seeds who resided on the shelf of Adam's loins, when Adam sinned, the God of this world became the master of every unborn and hence every newborn baby. When Adam sinned, he yielded his self to Satan, became a servant of Satan and God withdrew His spirit from Adam.

Scripture says in Romans 5:12,

> by one man sin entered into the world and death by sin, and so death passed upon all men, for that all have sinned.

Romans 3:23 says, "and come short of the glory of God."

Now check this: When God needed a body for His Son (John 3:16), God's angel appeared to Mary and after a brief discourse Mary gave him permission to do with her as He pleased. She said to him, "Behold the handmaid of the Lord; be it unto me according to thy word" (Luke 1:38). Immediately, the Holy Spirit entered her body and she conceived in her womb.

Similarly, when Jesus was at the river Jordan, though He spoke no words, by His actions, He gave the Holy Spirit permission to enter His body (Matthew 3:17).

However, when the spirit of Satan entered Adam's body, neither Adam nor God gave Satan permission to enter. Satan was a thief and a robber who entered Adam's body through a door that was different to the door that God prescribed for spirits to enter a human's body, that is through the womb of a woman. When Adam disobeyed, he did not know what the prophet Samuel declared to King Saul in (1 Samuel 15:22) that "to obey is better than sacrifice." Because of Adam's disobedience, every human being has since been born in sin.

We have been born in sin because when Adam sinned, his blood i.e., his life's source (Leviticus 17:11) became sin-contaminated but his seed did not lose its ability to reproduce. So, when Seth was born, the Bible says that Seth bore both the image and likeness of Adam. Seth did not bear God's image (Genesis 5:3). Seth was born separated from God.

If we begin with Cain and Abel and continue up to the present day, we'll find that there is not one baby that is born of a woman that is not born in sin (Matthew 7:17-18; Luke 6:43). Why is this so?

It is so because before God breathed His spirit into the nostrils of Adam, He had already blessed the created spirit-man to be fruitful and multiply and replenish the earth (Genesis 1:28).

Adam's sin did not nullify God's command to Adam's spirit-man to be fruitful and multiply. That command stayed in effect despite Adam's sin, and because it did, the corrupt tree that Adam became could not bring forth good fruit (Luke 6:43).

On the flip side, I believe that if Adam had not sinned, then every human being would have been a sinless procreated image of God. All it took for spiritual death to affect us all was Adam's sin, because when Adam sinned, we were all spiritual seeds in his loins (Ephesians 2:1a).

Adam's physical life was in his blood (Leviticus 17:11). His spiritual life was in the breath of God (Genesis 2:7b). It was God's breath that connected Adam's earth-based spirit-man to Almighty God who is Spirit and lives in heaven. It is the breath of God that restores the Holy Spirit's presence in every believer's life.

In the earthly realm, Adam's blood kept him alive, and it is that same blood that keeps us alive today. The only way to cleanse the sin-infected blood is to get rid of it, and this is what Jesus did on the Calvary's cross. He poured out his blood. He died. He rose from the dead with a body that had no blood. And now, all He requires to save whosoever wants to be saved is their Romans 10:9 confession of faith. Jesus said,

> He that believeth on the Son hath everlasting life: and he that believeth not the Son shall not see life; but the wrath of God abides on him.

It doesn't get any simpler.

### When Did We All Die?

I am convinced that the moment conception occurs, the soul, which is male-female procreated spirit-man thus formed, is at once spiritually dead. Were that not true, how else could it be born spiritually dead in trespasses and sin as Ephesians 2:1a says?

Every life that a woman's womb produces is the result of a male seed, an egg that a female supplied and the handiwork of God who intervenes and forms a body for the conceived seed (1 Corinthians 15:38).

Whenever any male sows his seed in the manner God prescribed, that seed falls to the ground, and there it dies. John 12:24 says Jesus said,

> Except a corn of wheat fall into the ground and dies, it abides alone: but if it dies, it brings forth much fruit.

So, when the seed of any male falls to the ground, as long as that ground is the womb of a female, then that seed has the potential to produce life.

The spiritual or everlasting life of the seed begins the instant conception occurs. All that is needed to produce human or natural life is for the female to nurture that seed as God forms a body for it in the sanctuary of her womb. God used Mary's womb to prepare a body for His Son who was one hundred percent Spirit (Hebrews 10:5) and was indeed the spirit-man Christ Jesus (1 Timothy 2:5).

### Hebrews 9:27 Explained

The Bible says in Hebrews 9:27,

> 27 And[2532] as[2596] [3745] it is appointed[606] unto men[444] once[530] to die,[599] but[1161] after[3326] this[5124] the judgment:[2920]

The English translation says it is appointed unto "men" (plural). But the word *Anthropos* that is used in the original language is translated "man" not "men." So, if we are to rightly divide God's Word, instead of "men" we must stay with "man" because the Bible says in Romans 5:12,

> As by one man sin entered into the world, and death by sin; and so death passed upon all men, for that all have sinned

Also, the Bible says, **"in Adam all die"** (1 Corinthians 15:22, my bolding). It does not say in "Adams" (plural). And again, it says in Romans 5:19,

> By one man's disobedience many were made sinners

What's my point? My point is, whenever a baby is born, the soul of that baby is born in trespasses and sin and thus, is spiritually separated from God. As he grows, his mission should be to become reconnected to God. This is why the Bible commands parents to train their child in the way he should go (Proverbs 22:6). That way is the one way, one truth and one life that Jesus prescribes (John 14:6).

## Soul and Spirit Are Separate

From a biblical perspective, your soul is something that is independent of both your body and your spirit. Hebrews 4:12 states (with my bolding),

> the word of God is quick, and powerful, and sharper than any two-edged sword, piercing even to the dividing asunder of **soul and spirit**, and of the joints and marrow, and is a discerner of the thoughts and intents of the heart.

My approach to Bible interpretation is simple. I choose to believe before I understand. So, when God's Word says that it can divide the soul and the spirit, I believe that. I may not understand how, but I believe that it can and does.

### When Did the Word of God Divide Soul and Spirit?

To understand when God divided the soul and the spirit, let's revisit the Garden of Eden and see if we can find, either in type and shadow or in reality where God's Word divided the soul and the spirit.

Here's the scenario: God had just placed the man that He had formed out of dust in the Garden (Genesis 2:15). At this point in the Creation story, there is only one human being alive, and his name is Adam. God had not as yet made a female helper for Adam. And let's agree that Adam would have looked just like any regular male human being. He would not have been a hermaphrodite, as some Bible commentators have implied. Adam was not abnormal in any way. He was perfect!

Why did God put Adam in the garden? In Genesis 2:15-17, the Bible says,

> 15 And the LORD[3068] God[430] took[3947] [853] the man,[120] and put[5117] him into the garden[1588] of Eden[5731] to dress[5647] it and to keep[8104] it.
>
> 16 And the LORD[3068] God[430] commanded[6680] [5921] the man,[120] saying,[559] Of every[4480] [3605] tree[6086] of the garden[1588] thou mayest freely eat:[398] [398]

17 But of the tree⁴⁴⁸⁰ ⁶⁰⁸⁶ of the knowledge¹⁸⁴⁷ of good²⁸⁹⁶ and evil,⁷⁴⁵¹ thou shalt not³⁸⁰⁸ eat³⁹⁸ of⁴⁴⁸⁰ it: for³⁵⁸⁸ in the day³¹¹⁷ that thou eatest³⁹⁸ thereof⁴⁴⁸⁰ thou shalt surely die.⁴¹⁹¹ ⁴¹⁹¹

## To Whom Did God Give the Command to "Not Eat"?

Have you ever noticed that when God commanded Adam not to eat of the tree, that God had not as yet made a woman for the man?

Have you ever noticed that the man—to whom God gave this command—was a physical male, and in his body, was a created seed that was a combination of a male (sperm) and female (egg)? (Genesis 1:27; Genesis 5:1-2; Genesis 2:19).

## Be Not Deceived

As the Genesis account continues; after God forbade Adam from eating of the tree that God then brought the animals to Adam to name them (Genesis 2:19-20). God had not yet made Adam's helper!

Only after Adam named all the animals did God make the woman for the man (Genesis 2:22). And to prove to man that God had given the man dominion over every living thing that moved upon the earth (Genesis 1:28), God left the responsibility of naming the woman to Adam. In Genesis 2:23 we read it was Adam who said,

> This is now bone of my bones, and flesh of my flesh: she shall be called Woman because she was taken out of Man.

## When the Woman Ate

Let's fast-forward to Genesis 3:15. Along came the serpent that tempted the woman. You know the story: she disobeyed God; she ate then "gave to her husband, and he did eat" (Genesis 3:6c). Now, the Bible says that the woman ate because she was deceived (1 Timothy 2:14). But what was the cause of her deception? The Bible says in Genesis 3:4-5 that the serpent told her that if she ate of the tree, she would become as gods:

4 And the serpent[5175] said[559] unto[413] the woman,[802] Ye shall not[3808] surely die:[4191] [4191]

5 For[3588] God[430] doth know[3045] that[3588] in the day[3117] ye eat[398] thereof,[4480] then your eyes[5869] shall be opened,[6491] and ye shall be[1961] as gods,[430] knowing[3045] good[2896] and evil.[7451]

## What Was the Truth?

The truth was that the woman did not have to eat of the tree to become something that she already was—and neither did the man! Why?

Because God created a spirit-man in His image and that spirit-man was a spirit-seed that was both male and female (Genesis 1:27; 5:1-2). God did not create a human! Throughout the Bible, the only other time that the phrase "image of God" is used is when it refers to Jesus Christ, God's only begotten Son (2 Corinthians 4:4; Hebrews 1:3; John 1:14). In all creation, man alone bore the image of God (Genesis 1:27) and of that image, in its perfect state, there were only three: There was Adam who was created or spoken into existence; there was Eve whom God made; and there was Jesus Christ, in His office as the man Christ Jesus, who was taken out-of-the-bosom of God (Genesis 1:27; John 1:18; Hebrews 13:8).

When Eve then Adam yielded their members to the serpent, effectively they changed the truth of God into a lie. God created them (male and female) in His image (Genesis 1:27). That was the truth. The lie was that they believed the serpent when he said they had to eat of the tree to become as gods (Genesis 3:1). Wrong! They already bore God's image (Genesis 1:27). They did not have to eat of any tree to get it. But, when they did, they proceeded to worship and serve the creature more than the Creator (Romans 1:25; Romans 6:16). Because of their sin, both became servants of sin (John 8:34); and because of Adam so too did all mankind become servants of sin. That's why the Bible says, "all have sinned, and come short of the glory of God" (Romans 3:23).

## What About the Soul and Spirit?

Remember now, God created man (Genesis 1:27); God blessed man (Genesis 1:28); God named the man Adam (Genesis 5:1-2); and then the Bible says in Genesis 2:7a,

> 7 And the LORD[3068] God[430] formed[3335] [853] man[120] of the dust[6083] of[4480] the ground,[127] and breathed[5301] into his nostrils[639] the breath[5397] of life;[2416] and man[120] became[1961] a living[2416] soul.[5315]

So, what is a living soul? Here's my definition: A living soul is a sinless human being in whose body the Spirit of God resided. Remember now; God created man. That man was a male-female spirit-seed. That spirit-man was alive even though he did not yet have a body. Once God made a body for the created spirit-man, that man became a human being.

Then, when God breathed into Adam's nostrils, Adam now had two spirits that were alive in his body—the one was God's spoken or creative Word that made man into God's image; the other was God's breath (Genesis 2:7b), which made man "in the likeness of God" (Genesis 5:1c). That likeness made the man Holy because God is Holy. God's breath became the soul of the man. And since the woman was taken out of the man after God had breathed into the nostrils of the man, then it means that the woman had to have had a soul (or the breath of God in her) as well.

## When Spiritual Death Came

Over and over preachers have preached that sin caused man to become separated from God spiritually. I believe that to be a true statement. However, if it took sin to separate man from God, what is it that connected man spiritually to God in the first place?

### The Penalty Applied

After Adam and Eve sinned, two things happened. First, the man and the woman were expelled from the Garden. In other words, God put them out of the spot where his presence was. Secondly, and this is something that has gone unnoticed: God removed His presence from within (the bodies of) both the man and the woman. You could say that God withdrew His breath—that was the same breath that He breathed into Adam's nostrils.

As I understand it, everyone who accepts Christ is empowered to say: "Greater is He that is in me, than he that is in the world" (1 John 4:4). Who is the "He that is in me"? He is the spirit of power, and of love, and of a sound mind (2 Timothy 1:7). Now, is it conceivable that God would choose to let His Spirit live in the bodies of known sinners, and not have caused it to live in Adam's body when He was sinless? Not possible!

### The Finished Man

When God had completed creating and making the man, I am saying that the finished man was a human being with two spirits living in him. Those two spirits were:

1. The spoken word or spirit called man (Genesis 1:27) who lived in his body (Genesis 2:7a) and gave him life; and
2. The God-breathed spirit (Genesis 2:7b) that made him into the likeness of God and gave to the man the ability to communicate with God in spirit and in truth.

The fact that God's Spirit resided in Adam's body meant that Adam's created spirit-man was always in God's presence, and it is that fact that made that first human a "living soul." When Lucifer was in God's presence, he was just a soul. To be a living soul, you must be human, you must be sinless, and God's Spirit tabernacle with you or must live in your body. (2 Corinthian 5:4)

Sin changed the condition of Adam's soul. Before he sinned, he was holy. After he had sinned, he became unholy. When Adam sinned, God vacated his (Adam's) body and the satanic spirit of the "god of this world" took up residence within. Because of sin, when Adam and Eve bore children, Satan's spirit was transferred from Adam to all his children, and hence to every human being through his blood.

So, when the Bible says, "in Adam all die" (1 Corinthians 15:22), this is how we were all born spiritually dead (Ephesians 2:1a). It is imperative that we grasp that the death we died in Adam was a death that was a one hundred percent spirit-man death. Physically, Adam was alive; spiritually, he was one hundred percent dead or separated from God.

In the book, *Pentateuch and Haftorahs* by the late Dr. J. H. Hertz, Chief Rabbi of the British Empire for over thirty years, it states,

> Man alone ... is endowed with both a *Yetzer tob* (a good inclination) and a *Yetzer ra* (an evil inclination) whereas animals have no moral discrimination or conflict.... Man alone, is a citizen of two worlds; he is both of earth and of heaven.[5]

Apparently, Dr. Hertz was right; because it should be clear that we got our good inclination from God, and we got our evil inclination from the God of this world. Also, this interpretation that "man alone is a citizen of two worlds" is consistent with Scripture. In 1 Corinthians 15:45-50 we read,

> (45) And so it is written, The first man Adam was made a living soul; the last Adam was made a quickening spirit. (46) Howbeit that was not first which is spiritual, but that which is natural; and afterward that which is spiritual. (47) The first man is of the earth, earthy: the second man is the Lord from heaven. (48) As is the earthy, such are they also that are earthy: and as is the heavenly, such are they also that are heavenly. (49) And as we have borne the image of the earthy, we shall also bear the image of the heavenly. (50) Now this I say, brethren, that flesh and blood cannot inherit the kingdom of God; neither doth corruption inherit incorruption.

In the text above, the "image of the earthy" refers to our sinful nature and our bodies of flesh and blood. The "image of the heavenly" refers to our new nature and our resurrected bodies, which will be like the body of the risen Christ. He had flesh and bone, but no blood (Luke 24:39).[6]

- When Jesus was baptized, He received the Holy Spirit and was led by him into the wilderness to do battle with the Devil (Mark 1:9-12).
- When Jesus sent out His disciples, "he breathed on them" and they received the Holy Spirit (John 20:22). They were thus empowered to overcome the devil (Luke 10:17).
- On the Day of Pentecost, everyone in the upper room received the Holy Spirit and were filled with power (Acts 1:8; 2:1-2).
- And every believer knows that without the Holy Spirit, they don't dare tackle the devil.

My position is, therefore, if God gave His Holy Spirit to Jesus and if He gives His Holy Spirit to born-again believers to combat the devil, then, He had to have done the same for Adam and Eve, because God is not a respecter of persons (Acts 10:34).

And the only place in the Bible that God could have given His Holy Spirit to Adam was when God breathed into the nostrils of the first human being (Genesis 2:7b).

Therefore, I conclude that the breath of God was and is the soul of man. Now if I am right that God divided man's soul and spirit in the Garden, do you know for sure, what will happen to your "self" or your inner spirit-man when you die if you do not confess Jesus as Lord and Savior and invite Him back into your life?

Your place in eternity hangs in the balance based on your answer to that question. Eternity is a long time to be wrong.

CHAPTER 5

# WHO AM I?

## What Does The Scripture Say about man?
According to Scripture,

1. God created man in His image (Genesis 1:27).
2. then God called that created man ADAM (Genesis 5:1-2). Moreover
3. the *man* that God created was both male and female (Genesis 1:27; 5:1-2).

I believe that the "man" God created was an invisible spirit being (John 6:63) that was a seed (Luke 8:11) that was both male and female (Genesis 1:27) who was very much alive, perfect, and unseen when God created him (Mark 12:27; Deuteronomy 32:4). I believe that Romans 1:20, Psalms 33:6, Hebrews 11:3, Nehemiah 9:6, and John 6:63 will support and confirm my interpretation.

The idea or the concept of the created man being both male and female has been problematic for many Bible interpreters. It has been my experience that most, if not all of them, had interpreted the man whom God had created (Genesis 1:27) in human terms. However, when you understand that the man that God created was a spirit that was a seed that was both male and female who was spoken into existence with a word of God (Psalms 33:6; Luke 8:11; John 6:63), then the problem is removed.

I have researched no less than thirty-three online commentaries[7] and all but one of those that I have researched perceived that the man whom God created was a fully grown human being with all intelligence, physicality, and what have you.

The sole exception was Keil and Delitzsch's commentary on the Old Testament. They stated (and I believe rightly so) that "the breath of God became the soul of man."[8] By "breath" I believe they were referring to the "breath of life" as it states in Genesis 2:7b, where the Bible says that God

> 7 And the LORD[3068] God[430] formed[3335] [853] man[120] of the dust[6083] of[4480] the ground,[127] and breathed[5301] into his nostrils[639] the breath[5397] of life;[2416] and man[120] became[1961] a living[2416] soul.[5315]

It is my considered opinion that their interpretation fell apart when they added and thus inadvertently implied that man "therefore is nothing but the breath of God." What's wrong with that interpretation? It makes no provision for the man whom God spoke into existence with a creative word called "man" (Genesis 1:27) and which created man God named ADAM (Genesis 5:1-2).

Think about what Keil and Delitzsch said, and I quote: "The rest of the world exists through the word of God; man, through His own peculiar breath." So, what they're saying is, that God spoke everything into existence, but man was so special that God breathed him into existence. That is inconsistent with whom God is. Believe that, and I've got to tell you I have some beach front property in Montana to sell you.

Of all the parables that Jesus spoke, the one he placed most emphasis on was the Parable of the Sower and the seed. Of that parable, Jesus said to

His disciples, "Know ye, not this parable? And how then will ye know all parables?" (Mark 4:13. See also Matthew 13:18-40 and Luke 8:11.)

When, you understand what Jesus meant, then you'll understand that I am not saying that I have some beach front property just to be facetious. I say it only to make a point.

Here's what I believe is wrong with Keil and Delitzsch's interpretation: They make no provisions) for the inclusion of both Genesis 1:27 and Genesis 5:1-2 in their interpretation. They limit it to Genesis 2:7. The same is true for many other Bible commentators. Those two verses state specifically that God created man and that God named him ADAM in the day that he created him. God did not wait until the day that He took the dust and formed the man to give the created man his name.

When we omit Genesis 1:27 and Genesis 5 verses 1 and two from our interpretations, we do not have a created man. Period! When we include them, we have a created man that is one hundred percent spirit and one hundred percent male and female.

It is important that you note that when God creates, He speaks (John 6:63); He does not breathe (Genesis 2:7a; John 20:22). For instance, when God created "the heavens and the earth," He spoke (Genesis 1:1; Psalms 33:6).

However, when God took dust and formed (a body) for the created man (Genesis 2:7a), God was using recycled material, if you will. Remember now, in Genesis 1:1, God had created the earth and Isaiah. 45:18, and Genesis 2, verses 2 and 3, tells us that God had made the earth perfect. Genesis 1:2a, however, tells us that the earth had become void. And following that chaotic state of Genesis 1:2a, God, through the agency of His Holy Spirit, restored the earth (Genesis 1:2b-25; 1:10; 2 Peter 3:5-7).

What I have noted with the interpretations of most of the Bible commentators is that many of them have much that lines up with scripture—but then there is that little bit of leaven or misinterpretation that leavens the whole lump of clay and throws everything off.

As an example, when Keil and Delitzsch state that "The breath of God became the soul of man," I agree with them. However, when they state further that "this breath is the seal and pledge of our relation to God, of our godlike dignity," then I disagree with them because that statement is only almost true.

To be accurate, the word "is" must be changed to "was" because when we were born, there was not one of us who had any godlike dignity. The Bible is clear: "All have sinned" (Romans 3:23) and we were all born dead in trespasses and sin (Ephesians 2:1b). By interpretation, it means that when we were born, we were all separated spiritually from God.

## So, Who Am I?

I am a present-day manifestation of a procreated spirit called "man." Would you allow me to tell you why I believe that to be so? Here goes: I am procreated because God did not speak me into existence. When God speaks, He speaks words that are spirit and life. And while it is true that there is resident in my body a procreated spirit call man, the fact is that my life did not begin as a spirit; it began as a conceived seed or zygote that morphed into a procreated spirit during the nine months I was in my mother's womb.

For my birth to occur, it took the combined efforts of my dad, my mom, and God. My dad provided a seed; my mom provided an egg. Then, God caused my mom to conceive when He joined the seed and the egg together making them one. With that done, God proceeded to make a body for the seed that my mom carried in her body (1 Corinthians 15:38). I guess you could say that I was the seed of my mom, who, by the way, was a woman. All God required was that my dad had to be male (Genesis 2:24a), my mom had to be female (Genesis 2:24b).

Today, in medical terms, the conceived seed that I had become in my mother's womb, is called a *zygote*. In biology, a *zygote* is the cell that results from the union of an ovum and a spermatozoon. *Zygote* is a term coined in 1878 by German cytologist Eduard Strasburger from the Greek *zygotos* meaning "yoked."

Through a God-ordained process of fruitfulness and multiplication (Genesis 1:28) that required my mom and dad to be sexually intimate, I was born. My mom had supplied an egg and my dad supplied his seed, and God used dad's seed, mom's egg, and my mother's womb to form my body. The fact is, God did for me the same that He did for Adam and Eve. His methodology may have been different but in either case, it was God who made bodies for Adam, Eve, me, and you (Genesis 2:7a; 3:19).

## When Did Life Begin?

My birth certificate says that I was born on July 26, 1947. However, I know now, and I can prove experientially, that life for me did not begin on that day. No, Sir! Life for me began in the darkest recesses of my mother's womb at conception when none but God knew I was there. During any sexual encounter that my dad may have had with my mom, he may have deposited anywhere from 45 million to 300 million sperm, give, or take. And from that vast and insurmountable number, I was the one sperm, or gamete that was chosen by God to attach itself to the one egg, or the other gamete; that was in my mother's womb during the six-day period when she would have been ovulating. As I see it, I was a miracle baby. And so were you. But think about this: What if, before Mom conceived, she and dad had been trying for 18 or 20 years with no success? Wouldn't the sheer miracle of that conception be obvious to everyone?

Do you get the picture that every conception is a God-ordained miracle? If you do, then tell me: When my mom was carrying me in her womb, did I belong to her or did I belong to God? Wasn't God the one who was forming my body while I was yet in my mother's womb?

Didn't God use the Virgin Mary's womb to prepare a body for Jesus Christ, His only begotten Son? And wasn't that Son the Eternal Spirit and also the Lamb that was slain from the foundation of the world?[9]

If the above is true, then must it not also be true that long before God manifested in the flesh the Eternal Spirit that was His Son, that God's Son had to have been known as "The Man Christ Jesus" (1 Timothy 2:5)? Who is this man Christ Jesus you ask? That man Christ Jesus is none other than God's Son, minus His deity. He is the Son who was one hundred percent Eternal Spirit who "thought it not robbery to be equal with God and made himself of no reputation" (Philippians 2:6-8) and allowed the Virgin Mary to give birth to Him so He could become a human being.

Now, here's a question for you: When the Bible says that God created man in His own image (Genesis 1:28), in whose image did God create man? Did God create the first Adam in the image of God who is referenced Revelation 1, verse 18, or did God create Adam in the image of the Man Christ Jesus (1 Timothy 2:5) who (it is written in Philippians 2:6-7)

> being in the form of God, thought it not robbery to be equal with God: But made himself of no reputation, and took upon him the form of a servant, and was made in the likeness of men.

Obviously, it was the latter, and I believe that it is so important for us to make crystal the distinction that the image of God in which God created Adam, was an image of God's Son minus His deity.

As a human being, Jesus Christ (Matthew 1:21, 25; Luke 1:31) was God's Son who was the Eternal Spirit minus His deity (1 Timothy 2:5), who put on flesh and resided in a body that God made for Him. Now check this: Through the agency of the Holy Spirit, God provided the sinless seed of His Son called the man Christ Jesus; then, God made a body for His Son and Mary gave birth to him. But here's what's interesting, as Christ, He was still God's Son, but as Jesus, he was Mary's child a.k.a. son of Man. And that is so because the Spirit of Life that resided in His body was one hundred percent God. He may have come from Mary, but He did not belong to Mary.

Khalil Gibran was right. In his poem "On Children," he said,

> Your children are not your children.
> They are the sons and daughters of Life's longing for itself.

> They come through you but not from you,
> And though they are with you, yet they belong not to you.
> You may house their bodies but not their souls,
> For their souls, dwell in the house of tomorrow,
> which you cannot visit, not even in your dreams

## What is the Biblical Definition of Man?

In the Book of Genesis 4:1, the Bible says,

> 1 And Adam[121] knew[3045] [853] Eve[2332] his wife;[802] and **she conceived**,[2029] and bore[3205] [853] Cain,[7014] and said,[559] I have gotten[7069] a man[376] from[854] the LORD.[3068]

By contemporary definition, a "man" is an adult human male. Now you and I both know that Eve did not give birth to an adult male. She gave birth to a baby, the same as every mother has done since and does today. Therefore, if we accept the contemporary definition for this word "man," we must conclude that it is inconsistent with the Bible's definition of the man God created who was spirit. And we must go further and realize that the "man" that the Bible says that Eve got from the Lord was actually a human baby boy that was the manifested product that God formed over nine months, using Adam's seed and Eve's egg. The Bible says,

### Genesis 2:7

> 7 And the LORD[3068] God[430] formed[3335] [853] man[120] of the dust[6083] of[4480] the ground,[127] and breathed[5301] into his nostrils[639] the breath[5397] of life;[2416] and man[120] became[1961] a living[2416] soul.[5315]

### Genesis 4:1

> 1 And Adam[121] knew[3045] [853] Eve[2332] his wife;[802] and she conceived,[2029] and bore[3205] [853] Cain,[7014] and said,[559] I have gotten[7069] a man[376] from[854] the LORD.[3068]

## The "Man" Came from the Lord

Why must this be so? It must, because the Bible says that God is the ONLY one who makes a body for every seed (1 Corinthians 15:38). And we know that God did that because the Bible also says that the reason why Eve got a man from the Lord was because "Adam knew Eve his wife; and she conceived." Conception is key! And it took sexual intercourse between Adam, who was one hundred percent male and Eve who was one hundred percent female, for it to occur.

In the original language, the word translated "knew" is the word yâda'.[10] Of the many meanings of the word yâda', today we would say that Adam had sexual intercourse with his wife, and she conceived. So, what does it take for conception to occur and for life to begin?

## LIFE, In Any of Its Forms, Begins with a Seed

Anyone who has reached the age of reason would have learned that all life begins with a seed! Also, everyone would have learned that all life does three things: (1) it comes out of the ground (2) lives for a while, and (3) then it dies and returns to the ground. This is consistent with Genesis 3:19 where God told Adam that he was taken out of the ground, and he must return there. Now, for life to come out of the ground, there must first be a seed in the ground, and Jesus says that only after the seed is placed in the ground, then comes "the blade, then the ear, after that the full corn in the ear" (Mark 4:28).

So, let's go back to the Garden of Eden. God is present. Plants and animals are present and visible. How did that happen? The simple answer is, God spoke.

In Genesis 1:11, we read,

> 11 And God[430] said,[559] Let the earth[776] bring forth[1876] grass,[1877] the herb[6212] yielding[2232] seed,[2233] and the fruit[6529] tree[6086] yielding[6213] fruit[6529] after his kind,[4327] whose[834] seed[2233] is in itself, upon[5921] the earth:[776] and it was[1961] so.[3651]

How could the earth have brought forth plants had it not been for the fact that seeds had to have been in the ground? And if indeed they were, how did they get there?

### The "Seed" Is the "Word" of God

For the answer, let's go to the Bible. Luke 8:11 says,

> 11 Now[1161] the[3588] parable[3850] is[2076] this:[3778] The[3588] seed[4703] is[2076] the[3588] word[3056] of God.[2316]

What's interesting about God's Word is this: It comes to us in three forms; namely (1) Spoken, (2) Written, and (3) Living. The Bible is God's written word. Jesus is His Living Word, and when anyone speaks the words that are in the Bible, those are God's Spoken Words.

The Bible says in the second half of John 6:63 (in which "I" is God),

> 63 the[3588] words[4487] that[3739] I[1473] speak[2980] unto you,[5213] they are[2076] spirit,[4151] and[2532] they are[2076] life.[2222]

Therefore, when God took dust and formed a body for the created spirit-man Adam (Genesis 2:7a) that male-female spirit-seed (Genesis 1:27) had to have had within itself the potential to come alive once it had been placed in the dust. And that is what happened.

When God placed the spirit-seed named Adam (Genesis 5:2) in the dust (Genesis 2:7a), it died, then, it brought forth fruit, and the human Adam was born. When God breathed into Adam's nostrils (Genesis 2:7b), Adam was now "born again." Adam's physical birth was different to ours, but it was the first recorded human birth. Make no mistake, Adam was physically alive when God formed His body.

The teaching of some that God breathed life into a "lifeless lump of clay" is unbiblical. Matthew 22:32 states that "God is not the God of the dead, but of the living." Therefore, we must conclude that when the created-spirit-man

Adam became the Human-Adam, he had to have been both physically alive and spiritually alive. Physical, because he had a body; spiritual, because God's breath was present in his body.

### The Created MAN is Called ADAM.

It is so important that you DO NOT ignore the fact that the created man was called ADAM in the day that God created him. God did not wait until Adam had a body to name him! With my bolding, Genesis 5, verses 1 and 2 makes it clear that God

> 1 This[2088] is the book[5612] of the generations[8435] of Adam.[121] In the day[3117] that God[430] created[1254] man,[120] in the likeness[1823] of God[430] made[6213] he him;
>
> 2 Male[2145] and female[5347] created[1254] he them; and blessed[1288] them, and **called[7121 853] their name[8034] Adam,**[121] **in the day[3117] when they were created.**[1254]

### The Created Man Was a Spirit.

Before God's spoken-word-spirit-man Adam (Genesis 1:27) had a body (Genesis 2:7a), God had already given him his name (Genesis 5:2). God could do that because every creative word that He spoke was a word that was spirit and life (John 6:63). We have a responsibility is to accept God's Word as "It is Written" simply because He is God!

The formed man was a spirit in a dirt body. Then as now, we call that man a human being. Genesis 2:7 states,

> 7 And the LORD[3068] God[430] formed[3335 853] man[120] of the dust[6083] of[4480] the ground,[127]

That first human being was merely a "natural man" because, with only his spirit-man in a dirt body, there is no way he could have known the things of God (1 Corinthians 2:14). For instance, before God breathed into Adam's nostrils, Adam could never have known what name to give to each of the animals (Genesis 2:19).

Everything changed however, when God breathed the breath of life into Adam's nostrils. Genesis 2:7 continues:

> 7 and breathed[5301] into his nostrils[639] the breath[5397] of life;[2416] and man[120] became[1961] a living[2416] soul.[5315]

Adam became a living soul because God's spirit was now residing in his body. Note: A living soul is a sinless human being in whose body God has tabernacled. That's my definition.

### God's Prescription for Life: Speak the Word, Not Breathe the Word

If you believe that when God formed Adam's body that Adam was dead, then I must ask: Would God have put his proverbial lips on the nostrils of a corpse to bring it to life? Does God bring the dead to life by breathing into it? I don't think so. The Bible doesn't either.

To clarify this issue, I had a one-on-one conversation with Jesus. I spent time studying His Word and He spoke with me. You can have the same conversation with Him, anywhere and anytime. Just open the pages of His Book and start talking with Him. When I spoke with Jesus, He was standing in front of Lazarus' tomb. Lazarus had been dead four days, and Jesus spoke these words: "Lazarus, come forth," and Lazarus did (John 11:43). Note: Jesus did not breathe on Lazarus the Genesis 2:7 "breath of life" to bring him back to life. Jesus spoke!

Similarly, in Mark 5, verses 41-42, the ruler of the synagogue's daughter had died, and Jesus spoke to her corpse and brought her alive. He said, "Talitha cumi; which is, being interpreted, Damsel, I say unto thee, arise. And straightway the damsel arose and walked." The message is clear.

When God wants to bring things to life, He speaks to them. He does not breathe on them. As to the words He speaks, in John 6:63, the Bible says,

63 they are²⁰⁷⁶ spirit,⁴¹⁵¹ and²⁵³² they are²⁰⁷⁶ life.²²²²

Question: What was this "man" Adam before he became a living soul? When God took dust and formed a body for the man called Adam, was he alive or was he dead? If you say he was alive, then (1) What was it that would have made the man alive, even before God breathed the breath of life into his nostrils when he became a living soul? Also (2) What was the purpose of the breath of life that God breathed into the nostrils of that first man Adam when he became a living soul (Genesis 2:7b)?

### Whose Report Do You Believe?

If you would search every Bible Commentary for an answer to *What Is the Soul?* you will find many different answers. Similarly, if you ask any pastor, prophet, priest, teacher, evangelist, or member of any religious sect, Christian or not, the same would hold true. You would receive many different answers. However, let's not forget that Jesus asked one specific question. In Mark 8:36, He asked, "What shall it profit a man, if he shall gain the whole world, and lose his own soul?"

There are two parts to that question. First, God is speaking to a "man." Does that mean that He excluded women and children? If He didn't, can we include them under the heading "man"? We need to answer that question. Second, God asks the man, what would he have gained if he gained the whole world, yet lost his own soul? God makes the soul personal to each man. And John 3:17 states that

> God sent not his Son into the world to condemn the world; but that the world through him might be saved.

### Let the Truth Set You Free

So, here's the deal: If God sent His One and Only Begotten Son, to save an entire world, and the entire world can be saved ONLY through that ONE SON, it tells me that this soul that Jesus came to save must be the same for each person. So, instead of relying on man's interpretation of *What Is the Soul?* What we need to do is search the scripture and find God's ONLY answer. When we do, shall find THE TRUTH, and it is that TRUTH that we find that will set us free indeed.

In John 8:36, Jesus said, "If the Son, therefore, shall make you free, ye shall be free indeed." So, I conclude, that saving our souls is directly connected to God's Son. Of this, there can be no doubt.

It is a faithful and true saying in 2 Corinthians 4:4 that

> the god of this world hath blinded the minds of them which believe not, lest the light of the glorious Gospel of Christ, who is the image of God, should shine unto them.

John 12:40b says,

> For if they did, then they would not see with their eyes nor understand with their heart; but they will be converted.

## From Where Did Adam's Seed Come?

For conception to occur, there must be a male sperm and a female egg. So, the question you should be asking is, from where or whom did Adam get his seed and Eve her egg?

1. Was Adam's seed to be found in the breath of life that God breathed into Adam's nostrils (Genesis 2:7d)? If you say yes, then your answer would be inconsistent with the Bible's, which says that in Luke 8:11 that

    > 11 The[3588] seed[4703] is[2076] the[3588] **word**[3056] of God.[2316]

    It does not say it is the breath of God!

2. Secondly, was Adam's seed to be found in the dust? Again, if you say yes, then I must ask you, how did the seed get in the dust in the first

place? Who put it there? Certainly, it could not have been Adam. God was still engaged in the process of making or forming him. The word translated "formed" is the Hebrew word ⬚*yâtsar*. It means "to mold" as when the potter molds the clay.

When God decided to form a body for the created-man (Genesis 2:7a), God had not yet breathed the breath of life into his nostrils (Genesis 2:7b). And since God and Adam were the only two who could have been present, the only logical answer is that it was God who was responsible for Adam to have seed with which to impregnate Eve.

So, I ask again: From whence cometh Adam's seed? As you search for an answer, may I tell you that the Bible is very clear that before a seed can bring forth fruit, it must first fall to the ground and die. John 12:24 says,

> 24 Verily,[281] verily,[281] I say[3004] unto you,[5213] Except[3362] a corn[2848] of wheat[4621] fall[4098] into[1519] the[3588] ground[1093] and die,[599] it[846] abideth[3306] alone:[3441] but[1161] if[1437] it die,[599] it bringeth forth[5342] much[4183] fruit.[2590]

When speaking of plants, the Bible says in Genesis 2:9, (with my bolding), that

> **the LORD God caused to grow out of the ground** every tree that is pleasant to the sight and good for food.

So now I ask, Is it not true that before a tree can grow out of the ground, that a seed must be placed in the ground and that seed must first die?

If yes, that what's the origin of the seed?

As you search for an answer, think about this: When speaking of animals, the Bible says in Genesis 2:19 (with my bolding) that it was

> 19 And **out of**[4480] **the ground**[127] **the LORD**[3068] **God**[430] **formed**[3335] every[3605] beast[2416] of the field,[7704] and every[3605] fowl[5775] of the air;[8064]

and brought⁹³⁵ them unto⁴¹³ Adam¹²¹ to see⁷²⁰⁰ what⁴¹⁰⁰ he would call⁷¹²¹ them: and whatsoever³⁶⁰⁵ ⁸³⁴ Adam¹²¹ called⁷¹²¹ every living²⁴¹⁶ creature,⁵³¹⁵ that¹⁹³¹ was the name⁸⁰³⁴ thereof.

When speaking of Adam, the Bible says in the first part of Genesis 2:7 (with my bolding added) that

> 7 And the LORD³⁰⁶⁸ God⁴³⁰ formed³³³⁵ ⁸⁵³ man¹²⁰ of the dust⁶⁰⁸³ of⁴⁴⁸⁰ the ground,¹²⁷

The point I am making is that God formed both beast (Genesis 2:9a) and man (Genesis 2:7a) out of the same ground. Nowhere in the Bible does it say that God breathed into the nostrils of the animals to make them alive.

But we know that they are. How come?

Other than speaking creative words that were spirit and life what else could God have done to bring forth life? John 6:63 says,

> 63 It is²⁰⁷⁶ the³⁵⁸⁸ spirit⁴¹⁵¹ that quickeneth;²²²⁷ the³⁵⁸⁸ flesh⁴⁵⁶¹ ³⁷⁵⁶ profiteth⁵⁶²³ nothing:³⁷⁶² the³⁵⁸⁸ words⁴⁴⁸⁷ that³⁷³⁹ I¹⁴⁷³ speak²⁹⁸⁰ unto you,⁵²¹³ they are²⁰⁷⁶ spirit,⁴¹⁵¹ and²⁵³² they are²⁰⁷⁶ life.²²²²

## Even Kids Know the Truth

In the year 2021, it is possible that every fourth grader knows that it takes three things for conception to occur. They are: (1) the seed of a male (2) the egg of a female, and (3) the right environment. They know also that the right environment for the male seed and the female egg to conceive is a woman's body; no other will do. They may not know much else about the processes of copulation and conception, but at least they know that daddy must be male, and mommy must be female.

Now when we read man's interpretation of how God created man, more often than not, we refer to the Bible, to the Book of Genesis 2:7, which reads as follows:

7 And the LORD³⁰⁶⁸ God⁴³⁰ formed³³³⁵ ⁸⁵³ man¹²⁰ of the dust⁶⁰⁸³ of⁴⁴⁸⁰ the ground,¹²⁷ and breathed⁵³⁰¹ into his nostrils⁶³⁹ the breath⁵³⁹⁷ of life;²⁴¹⁶ and man¹²⁰ became¹⁹⁶¹ a living²⁴¹⁶ soul.⁵³¹⁵

## What God Has Joined Together

It is indeed a true saying that "what God has put together, let not man put asunder" (Mark 10:9). Until recently we have always applied God's prescription for marriage to one male and one female.

Today, there are some who endorse and condone same-sex marriage. As I see it, same-sex marriage is not what God intended, because biologically, it is impossible for the parties involved in same-sex marriages ever to have babies the way God intended.

And in Genesis 1:28, God commanded His created seed that He called man to be fruitful and multiply. The inability of a same-sex couple to have babies between themselves makes their union anything but a marriage. No matter what anyone calls it you can be sure God that does not recognize it. In Romans 1, verses 26, 27, and 28, God describes such behavior as "unseemly" i.e., inappropriate. God's prescription for marriage was, is and ever shall be: one male and one female.

Here is what God said in His Word: "Therefore shall a man (i.e., a male) leave his father and his mother, and shall cleave unto his wife (i.e.: a female): and they shall be (i.e., become) one flesh" (Genesis 2:24). The one flesh they become is their offspring who may be baby boy or baby girl.

Do you know that to everything that God created and made He gave to them the ability to reproduce after their kind? There is not a plant, a bird, a fish, an insect, or any other creature that God created and made, that does not reproduce after its kind. When we violate God's instructions for natural reproduction, we end up with a product that is unnatural. To everything that God created He gave to them the command to be fruitful and multiply.

With humankind, God specified that for reproduction to occur there must be one male and one female. Romans 1:20-32, Leviticus 18:22, Leviticus 20:13; Deuteronomy 22:5; and Proverbs 5:18-19 they all confirm that God is opposed to same-sex marriages. Should you need further explanation, my best recommendation is that you talk one-on-one with God's Holy Spirit for final revelation for, in the end, He is the one who judges, not me.

Now, getting back to Mark 10:9, "What God has put together, no man can put asunder," think about this: in Genesis 2:18, the Bible says,

> The LORD$^{3068}$ God$^{430}$ said,$^{559}$ It is not$^{3808}$ good$^{2896}$ that the man$^{120}$ should be$^{1961}$ alone;$^{905}$ I will make$^{6213}$ him a help$^{5828}$ meet for him.$^{5048}$

Now, why did God say it is not good that the man should be alone?

I believe that before God created man, He knew that, for that man to reproduce "after his kind," that man would need a male (sperm) and a female (egg). Also, God knew that the male and female would have to come together sexually before they could produce another life.

To accomplish this, God put Adam to sleep and removed a rib. Then, God used the rib to make a female helper for Adam. This helper was bone of Adam's bone and flesh of his flesh. In verses 21 to 23, the Bible describes the process by which God made the helper for the male-man who was called Adam. When Adam's helper was made, Adam was given the privilege of naming her. He called her "Woman"—i.e., a female version of the male man that he was—because she was taken out of his body and was indeed bone of his bone and flesh of his flesh.

Ecclesiastes 4:12 says, "A threefold cord is not quickly broken."

Now in Genesis 2:24 God prescribed the formula for the marriage covenant. He said, "Therefore5921 3651 shall a man376 leave5800 853 his father1 and his mother,517 and shall cleave1692 unto his wife:802 and they shall be1961one259 flesh1320." From that day, the dynamics between the male and the female changed forever.

From that day, the woman's body would produce only eggs and the man's body only sperms. And (and this is an important "and") for a female to give birth, it would take just one egg of one female and one seed or sperm of the male. With God's help, the body for the newborn always is formed by God (1 Corinthians 15:38), and that's how the two (i.e., the seed and the egg) becomes one flesh (Genesis 2:24). This ability, of the male being able to produce only sperm and the female, only eggs went unnoticed for quite a while. Here's what I mean:

Per medical research, "At 20 weeks, a female fetus has a fully developed reproductive system, replete with six to seven million eggs."[11] But "Boys do not produce sperm until puberty"; once they begin to produce sperm, they produce "an average of 200 million sperm each day."

From millions of sperm and one egg, here I am. And if you are reading this, there you are. Who else but God could have done this? Try as anyone might, there is not a single person who can separate the sperm from the egg once one has been attached to the other and return each to its former state without causing death to both. Why is this so? It is so because the Bible says in Ecclesiastes 4:12,

> a threefold$^{8027}$ cord$^{2339}$ is not$^{3808}$ quickly$^{4120}$ broken.$^{5423}$

In this case, the threefold cord is the seed of the male, the egg of the female, and the handiwork of God. No "man" (i.e., no hu-man being) can do that! But God can! Ask Lazarus—dead for four days, yet God reunited Lazarus' spirit to his decomposed body (John 11:43-44). Ask *Talitha cumi* (Mark 5:41-42).

## The Two Shall Become One Flesh

When a woman conceives, no one can separate the seed and the egg without causing death to both. That's why, when my mother conceived, it was just a matter of time before I became a "one flesh" representative of my mom and dad (Genesis 2:24; Matthew 19:4-5). After my father had known my mom the way that Adam knew Eve (Genesis 2:24), conception occurred (Genesis 4:1), and nine months later I was born.

It is a fact that I am the natural offspring of my mom and dad and in my body dwell some if not many, of the traits and mannerisms of both my mother and father. The fact that very often I have been called "the spitting image of my parents" confirms this.

It took the medical profession many thousands of years since God had created the heavens and the earth before it invented a piece of High-Tech equipment called the sonogram. That tool now allows members of the medical profession to peer into the womb to observe fetal development.

But even doctors with their sonograms have their limitations. At best, they are unable to confirm pregnancy earlier than three to four weeks after a missed menstrual cycle.

And yet, from the very nanosecond my mom conceived, God knew that my mom was pregnant and that for me, my everlasting life had begun! When I say me, I am referring to my procreated spirit-man who lives in my body, and he is both male and female. So, biologically, even though I am a male person, there is residing in my body an invisible inner spirit-man that is both male and female. If you are female, then in you there is a spirit-man, that is both male and female. That spirit-man is an offspring, many times removed from the spiritual Adam whom God created (Genesis 1:27) and called Adam (Genesis 5:2).

Let's be very clear: For me, there may have been a time when my procreated spirit-man was not; that would be before my Mom conceived me; but once mom conceived, she set in motion the reality that there never will be a time when my inner spirit-man will not be; my inner spirit-man will be alive forever, somewhere. If the Bible is right, and I believe it is, the only options available for me when my body dies, are heaven and hell. The same options are available to you. What's good about this, is that you get to choose. I can tell you most assuredly that Hell is not an option for me, because on May 27, 1999, I made Jesus Christ my Lord. When I die, I know where my spirit-man is going. I am under no illusions. My eternal destination is settled in heaven.

When mom conceived, my spirit-man did not have a body. It would take approximately eighteen days before my heart would start beating; then, another nine months for God to make my body. But, through it all, this much was true: my inner spirit-man was very much alive from the day mom conceived. It was alive naturally yet separated spiritually from God. This is so because when the male sperm and the female egg fused and became a zygote, the result was that my soul that was dead in trespasses and sin, was pro-created. It was pro-created because it took the combined efforts of my dad who sowed a seed, my mom who supplied an egg and God, who gave increase (Ephesians 2:1; 1 Corinthians 15:38).

## I Was a Seed on a Shelf

Both the Bible and medical science will verify that my life began at conception. None but God knew the nanosecond that my mom conceived. For sure, my mom didn't. She would have been doing whatever it was she did, then one day, she would have missed something, and it was not her pocketbook. Period! When dad learned that mom was pregnant, he knew then that the seed that he sowed during intercourse had united with Mom's ovum and my natural life had begun. Over the next nine months, give or take—please hear me—my mom watered or nourished it, but through it all, it was God who gave increase to that seed that would later manifest itself as me in human form.

## So, Who Am I Today?

I started this chapter saying, "I am a present-day manifestation of a procreated spirit called "man." Whether you are male or female, the same is true for you. Per the Bible, that spirit-man was born dead in trespasses and sin

(Ephesians 2:1). The Bible also says that there is ONLY one way that our spirit-man can return into right-standing with God and that is through His only begotten Son, Jesus Christ.

When it comes to making it right with God, what is extremely important to note is this: The only time we can make it right with God is while we are alive. Let me say that another way: The only time we can make it right with God, is between the day we're hatched and the day we're dispatched. The Bible says, "the living know that they shall die: but the dead know not anything" (Ecclesiastes 9:5). The spirit-man of anyone who dies without restoring his broken relationship with God shall be damned for all eternity. That's Bible.

If you have already accepted Jesus Christ as your Lord and Savior, God bless you. It means your name is written in the Lamb's Book of Life (Luke 10:20; Philippians 4:3; Revelation 3:5) and you have the assurance of spending eternity with God when you die. I was 50 years old when I accepted Jesus Christ, and because I did, I know that I know that the same is true for me. All it took for me to seal the deal, was my confession of faith in the finished work of the Cross.

Once I did that, my pro-created inner spirit-man with which I was born became crucified with Christ, and he is now "hid with Christ in God" (Romans 10:9; Colossians 3:3). His new citizenship is in heaven (Ephesians 2:6). And the Spirit of the Risen Christ now lives in me (1 John 4:4). It took my faith in God for me to accept that, but once I internalized that sequence of events, it blew my mind. To think that all it took for me to guarantee my spending eternity in heaven with God, was for me to call on the name of His Son Jesus Christ. That's way past amazing. The instant I did, I became positionally sanctified. Between then and now, with the help of God's Holy Spirit, I have been working on my spiritual condition. And God assures me in His Word, that once I remain faithful to Him, the day will come when I shall see him as He is because I shall be like Him. What a glorious day that will be!

## Who Are You?

If you have already accepted Jesus as your Savior, Congratulations! You too will get to spend eternity in heaven with God. If you have not, I invite you to do so now. As it says in Romans 10:9-11, 10:13,

> confess, with your mouth the Lord Jesus, and ... believe in your heart that God hath raised him from the dead, [and] you shall be saved.

> For the scripture saith, whosoever shall call upon the name of the Lord shall be saved.

Thus, saith the Word of God. As you continue to read, I pray that you shall be blessed!

CHAPTER 6

# WHO MADE ME?

**Bible Verses**

The Bible says that "to every seed, God gives it a body" (1 Corinthians 15:38). So, though I was in my mother's womb, I did not belong to her; she was just allowing God to use her body to make my body for me.

I am fearfully and wonderfully made! I know this because the psalmist says in Psalm 139:13-16 (where "God" is rendered as "thou"),

> 13 For[3588] thou[859] hast possessed[7069] my reins:[3629] thou hast covered[5526] me in my mother's[517] womb.[990]
>
> 14 I will praise[3034] thee; for[5921 3588] I am fearfully[3372] and wonderfully[6395] made: marvelous[6381] are thy works;[4639] and that my soul[5315] knoweth[3045] right well.[3966]
>
> 15 My substance[6108] was not[3808] hid[3582] from[4480] thee, when[834] I was made[6213] in secret,[5643] and curiously wrought[7551] in the lowest parts[8482] of the earth.[776]

16 Thine eyes⁵⁸⁶⁹ did see⁷²⁰⁰ my substance, yet being unperfect;¹⁵⁶⁴ and in⁵⁹²¹ thy book⁵⁶¹² all³⁶⁰⁵ my members were written,³⁷⁸⁹ which in continuance³¹¹⁷ were fashioned,³³³⁵ when as yet there was none³⁸⁰⁸ ²⁵⁹ of them.

## No Different from the Prophet Jeremiah

In a very real sense, I was not, and neither were you any different from the prophet Jeremiah 1:5, of whom the Bible records God saying to him:

Before²⁹⁶² I formed³³³⁵ thee in the belly⁹⁹⁰ I knew³⁰⁴⁵ thee; and before²⁹⁶² thou camest forth³³¹⁸ out of the womb⁴⁴⁸⁰ ⁷³⁵⁸ I sanctified⁶⁹⁴² thee, and I ordained⁵⁴¹⁴ thee a prophet⁵⁰³⁰ unto the nations.¹⁴⁷¹

The word translated "knew" is *yâda'* (Strong's 3045). It is the same word that was used when the Bible (Genesis 4:1) says,

1 And Adam¹²¹ knew³⁰⁴⁵ ⁸⁵³ Eve²³³² his wife;⁸⁰² and she conceived.²⁰²⁹

It denotes genuine intimacy. That means, there had to have been a time when the inner spirit-man of every human being had to have been very intimate with God. And the only time that could have been was when all men were spirit-seeds in the loins of the created spirit-man named ADAM (Genesis 5:2). How long did our intimacy with God last? It lasted from the day when God created spirit-man Adam (Genesis 1:27) and it ceased the nanosecond that the human Adam (Genesis 2:7a) sinned (Genesis 3:6b).

## My Daddy Reaped What He Sowed

Because of this, I am convinced that at when I was born, I was the fruit of the seed my father sowed. Galatians 6:7 says, "whatsoever a man sows, that shall he also reap." If my dad were a drug addict, I might have been born with a drug addiction. If he had AIDS, I might have been born with AIDS. If he had been an alcoholic, I might have been born with an addiction to alcohol.

Thankfully, none of that happened. My dad sowed; my mom watered; God made my body (1 Corinthians 15:38). Over sixty-plus years, I molded the body that God made me into whatsoever shape and condition it is today.

If I had abused my body, then my body would be displaying the signs abuse. Thankfully, that is not so. But I do have many aches and pains. Could these pains be hereditary? I believe so. My dad had his share of aches and pains; so, does my son and daughter. What can I say? I am one apple that fell very close to the tree. Like father, like son.

## God Made My Body; He Did Not Create It!

The Scripture confirms that God made my body while I was yet in my mother's womb (1 Corinthians 15:38; Psalms 139:13-16). The Scripture is also clear that when God creates, He speaks (Psalms 33:6; Genesis 1:1). And, though there are many things of which I am not certain, I am certain that God did not speak me into existence! If I know nothing else, I know that my everlasting life and my natural life began after a sexual act between my mom and my dad. That truth is not negotiable.

About the sexual act what's interesting is this: Old age is not a disqualifier. If my dad were an octogenarian and my mom a teenager, God would still have made a body for me. The same would have happened if they were both teenagers. The only requirements God needed to get busy were (1) my dad had to let his seed fall to the ground that was my mother's womb (2) and my mom had to water that seed. As long as they did their part, God would give the seed increase.

God's formula for reproduction is simple. All that He requires is the seed of male and the egg of a female. If mom and dad were either both males, or both females, then it is certain that I would not be here. Apparently, God knew something that most of our leaders have yet to learn. This idea of same-sex marriage is something that was so foreign to God that in Genesis 19, verses 1 to 28, Moses wrote God's response to that behavior. In Genesis 2:24 gave us his formula for reproduction.

**24** Therefore[5921][3651] shall a man[376] leave[5800][853] his father[1] and his mother,[517] and shall cleave[1692] unto his wife:[802] and they shall be[1961] one[259] flesh.[1320]

In Strong's Concordance, the word "be" (Strong 1961)[12] can also mean "become." So, the phrase "be one flesh" would mean "become one flesh," which is what happens when a woman gives birth. The offspring becomes the product of the male sperm and the female's egg.

Regardless of anyone's sexual persuasion, I am, and you are the product of that one-flesh concept that God commanded. And I am ever so thankful that my mom was pro-life and not pro-choice and that I was born way before *Roe vs. Wade*. Had that decision been in effect, who knows what may have happened?

## God Created Spirits

You ask, if God did not create me, who did? To that, I say, no one because I am not a created being. With help from my mom and dad, God procreated me. When God creates, He works alone. When He created Adam, no one was there (Genesis 1:27, 5:2). That created Adam was a male-female spirit; that was the image of God. The image that was Adam, would have been the image of the Man Christ Jesus who is also Spirit. And, the Man, Christ Jesus, was the uncreated image of God's ONLY begotten son, minus His deity (1 Timothy 2:5; Philippians 2:6-8).

Already stated but being repeated for clarity, God created one man. The 7.9 billion people who alive today, plus all who have died and are yet unborn, came from that one man named Adam. Now here's a revelation for you: God never created any human being. He made them. Using Adam as our example, we see that God created a spirit-man and called him Adam; then, God took dust and built a body for Adam. The combination of the spirit with dust changed the created man from being a one hundred percent spirit-man to being a one hundred percent human being who was a mix of the invisible spirit and dust.

Now please hear me: I am not saying that God did not create ADAM. Genesis 1:27 and 5:1-2 confirms that he did. However, when the first Bible interpreters presented the created man as a human being, they erred. They missed the fact that the created Adam was a spirit, that was a seed, that God spoke into existence and was both male and female (Genesis 1:27; Luke 8:11; Genesis 1:1; Genesis 5:1-2).

Also, the interpreters missed the fact that God gave the name Adam to the spirit that was both the male and the female. Genesis 5:2 states that God called "their" name Adam. The Bible is explicit. It does not say that God called "his" name Adam even though the human Adam must have had the physique of a male person. Getting you to accept that the created man (bâ râ ') was a male-female spirit will take some doing, but doing it is mandatory if ever you're to interpret scripture accurately.

I give to you the Bible text to support my position from Genesis 5:1-2:

> 1 This[2088] is the book[5612] of the generations[8435] of Adam.[121] In the day[3117] that God[430] created[1254] man,[120] in the likeness[1823] of God[430] made[6213] he him;
>
> 2 Male[2145] and female[5347] created[1254] he them; and blessed[1288] them, and called[7121] [853] their name[8034] Adam,[121] in the day[3117] when they were created.[1254]

## A Comparison of Translations

Let's compare Genesis 5:1 in both the King James Version (KJV) and the New International Version (NIV). Note that in the NIV, the word "Adam" has been replaced with the word "mankind" (Genesis 5:1-2, NIV).

> This is the written account of Adam's family line. When God created mankind, he made them in the likeness of God. He created them male and female and blessed them. And he named them "Mankind" when they were created.

Were we to accept the NIV's translation then, to be consistent, we would have to extend that interpretation in the New Testament so that when the Bible says in 1 Corinthians 15:22 in the KJV,

> 22 For¹⁰⁶³ as⁵⁶¹⁸ in¹⁷²² Adam⁷⁶ all³⁹⁵⁶ die,⁵⁹⁹ even²⁵³² so³⁷⁷⁹ in¹⁷²² Christ⁵⁵⁴⁷ shall all³⁹⁵⁶ be made alive.²²²⁷

consistency would demand that the translation in the NIV should read: "For as in Mankind all die." But it doesn't say that does it?

No. It says, "For as in Adam all die, so in Christ all will be made alive."

Bottom line: God *creates* spirits. He *makes* humans.

Making this distinction is important because the Bible commands us to "rightly divide" God's Word (2 Timothy 2:15)! When anyone's interpretation conflicts with God's intent, the result is error. My approach (to interpretation) is simple—unconventional—but simple. I choose to believe before I understand. And then, I ask God for wisdom (James 1:5) and I ask the Holy Spirit to teach me and reveal to me the things Jesus had said and meant (John 14:26).

Now, as for the human Adam, who is the person with whom we identify and on whom we've been blaming the Fall of man, I am saying that God formed only Adam's body out of the dust. Adam's inner spirit-man was created or spoken into existence.

When we read Genesis 2:3, we are told

> 3 And God⁴³⁰ blessed¹²⁸⁸ ⁸⁵³ the seventh⁷⁶³⁷ day,³¹¹⁷ and sanctified⁶⁹⁴² it: because³⁵⁸⁸ that in it he had rested⁷⁶⁷³ from all⁴⁴⁸⁰ ³⁶⁰⁵ his work⁴³⁹⁹ which⁸³⁴ God⁴³⁰ created¹²⁵⁴ and made.⁶²¹³

What this verse conveys is that there were two processes that God used to bring the human Adam, into existence. First, there was a creating phase, and then there was a making phase. In phase one, Adam was a spirit. In phase two when God took the dust and made a body for the spirit, Adam became a human, i.e. a spirit in a dirt body.

Once you accept that, you've now got to include in your interpretation that in phase one the created man was a male-female-spirit, and in phase two the male-female spirit-man became hu-man, i.e. a combination of the spirit-man plus dust (Genesis 1:27 and Genesis 2:7a).

When these distinctions are crystal, you should realize that for all the time that we've been blaming a human, Adam, for the Fall of man, there is a very real possibility that we've been accusing him wrongfully. I say that because the Bible says that the "wages of sin is death" (Romans 6:23). It says also that it is the soul that sins, dies (Ezekiel 18:20).

I am not aware of anyone who denies that Adam's physical death was not immediate. The Bible records that he lived 930 years (Genesis 5:5)! So, if we believe God's Word, then we must accept that the day Adam sinned, he died. We must also accept that his death had to have been instantaneous and spiritual since he did not die physically. The effect of Adam's sin was his spiritual separation from God. Sin does that! It separates us from God. And for Adam to have died spiritually, he first had to have been spiritually alive. And if he were spiritually alive, it is incumbent upon us to identify with specificity what it was that made him spiritually alive. Wouldn't you agree? Of course, you would.

## Let's Rightly Divide

So, let us now examine the various texts concerning the creating and the making of man (Genesis 1:27; 2:7; 5:1-2) and let's use the Polyglot Bible, King James Version and see what turns up. May we do that?

### Phase 1: God Creates a Spirit Called Man

Genesis 1:27 tells us,

> So, God created man in his own image, in the image of God created he him; male and female created he them.

Already, we have established that when God creates, He speaks. As a young kid growing up in Catholic school, my teachers taught me that when God created the heavens and the earth, He created them out of nothing. If I were to take a poll, I believe that many people would hold the same to be true. Yet, what is the truth? The truth is, that "God created the heavens and the earth out of nothing ... but His self!

When we omit "but His self," we err.

Colossians 1, verses 16 and 17 make it very clear that:

> 16 For$^{3754}$ by$^{1722}$ him$^{846}$ were all things$^{3956}$ created,$^{2936}$ that$^{3588}$ are in$^{1722}$ heaven,$^{3772}$ and$^{2532}$ that$^{3588}$ are in$^{1909}$ earth,$^{1093}$ visible$^{3707}$ and$^{2532}$ invisible,$^{517}$ whether$^{1535}$ they be thrones,$^{2362}$ or$^{1535}$ dominions,$^{2963}$ or$^{1535}$ principalities,$^{746}$ or$^{1535}$ powers:$^{1849}$ all things$^{3956}$ were created$^{2936}$ by$^{1223}$ him,$^{846}$ and$^{2532}$ for$^{1519}$ him:$^{846}$
>
> 17 And$^{2532}$ he$^{846}$ is$^{2076}$ before$^{4253}$ all things,$^{3956}$ and$^{2532}$ by$^{1722}$ him$^{846}$ all things$^{3956}$ consist.$^{4921}$

## Phase 2: God Named That Created Spirit-Man, ADAM

In Genesis 5:1-2, we read

> 1 This$^{2088}$ is the book$^{5612}$ of the generations$^{8435}$ of Adam.$^{121}$ In the day$^{3117}$ that God$^{430}$ created$^{1254}$ man,$^{120}$ in the likeness$^{1823}$ of God$^{430}$ made$^{6213}$ he him;
>
> 2 Male$^{2145}$ and female$^{5347}$ created$^{1254}$ he them; and blessed$^{1288}$ them, and called$^{7121}$ $^{853}$ their name$^{8034}$ Adam,$^{121}$ in the day$^{3117}$ when they were created.$^{1254}$

Note that in the verse above, the man was called ADAM in the day that God created him. Note also that both the male and the female were called ADAM. The scripture says, God "called their name Adam" (Genesis 5:2).

## Phase 3: God Makes a Body out of Dust for Spirit-Man Adam

In Genesis 2:7, we read

> 7 And the LORD[3068] God[430] formed[3335] [853] man[120] of the dust[6083] of[4480] the ground.[127]

Note that in the day that God formed a body for the man (the opening of Genesis 2:7a), that He had created nor for the human that He had formed out of dust.

> but for Adam[121] there was not[3808] found[4672] a help[5828] meet for him.[5048]

Making a helper for the man would NOT happen until Genesis 2:22. Therefore, we must conclude that resident in the body of that first human being was a seed or God-spoken word (Luke 8:11) that was the combination in spirit form of what we now know as a male sperm and a female egg (Genesis 1:27; John 6:63). But, as a human-being, Adam was one hundred percent male! He was not bisexual neither was he transgender. Later, when God made Eve, she was one hundred percent female. Whereas by divine design, Adam's body would house both the "X" and "Y" chromosomes, Eve, being female, would house ONLY the "X" chromosome.

## The Truth Revealed

That being the case, it must mean that resident in everyone's body is a seed that is a combination of a male seed and a female egg. Today, we call that seed a zygote. It is the name given to the combination of the seed you got from your dad and the egg you got from your mom. Regardless of which gender you identify with, if you did not have both seed and egg within your body, you would never be born. But don't blindly accept my word. Do a Strong's Concordance study of Genesis 1:27, 2:7a, and 5:1-2. Then, if you feel that my interpretation is wrong, please, send me an email and let me know how you came to your conclusion. I'll appreciate that.

But, if I am right, then in answer to my question: Who am I? I must tell you that in the final analysis, I am just one of many billions of offspring of that first invisible-male-female-spirit-man, whom God created then named Adam (Genesis 1:27-28; 2:24; 5:1-2). Recently I was asked a question: From whence cometh all the races and all the colors? Only one answer I have, and it is biblical. Here it is: God has "made of one blood all nations of men" (Acts 17:26). Translation: Every human being—regardless of color, class, creed, race, ethnicity, sexual persuasion, or political affiliation—is a descendant of fallen Adam (Genesis 3:6b).

It may be that I am many generations and thousands of years removed from Adam, but these two things I know: (1) my spirit-man was procreated, and (2) God formed my body. When the Psalmist says that he was "conceived in sin and shapen in iniquity" (Psalms 51:5) he was letting us know that when he was born, he was a perfect replica of a fallen or sinful Adam because his inner spirit-man became alienated from God. And, and so too was yours (Matthew7:17-18; Luke 6:43).

Your inner spirit-man and mine are separated from God because when Adam sinned, the sin condition embedded itself in Adam's blood and it is through the blood that sin has been transferred to every human being who is alive, ever lived or is yet to be born (Genesis 3:6b; Genesis 5:3; Romans 3:23). Because we have an inner-spirit man, and because God is Spirit, we still maintain the spirit image of God; however, God is holy. We are not. There is not one of us who bears the likeness of God. No matter how good we may think we are, God sees our sinful condition because we bear the likeness of sinful Adam.

### God Blessed Man to Multiply Before He Made Him a Body.

In Genesis 1:28, we read that the very first command that God gave to the male/female man after He had created him was this:

> 28 And God[430] blessed[1288] them, and God[430] said[559] unto them, Be fruitful,[6509] and multiply.[7235]

Two simple commands: *Be fruitful and multiply*. What's interesting is this: When God gave those commands to the man God had not yet taken dust and formed a body for the man. In other words, the man was not yet a human being (Genesis 2:7a). He was just a spirit. Also, God had not yet taken a rib from Adam's body and made the woman (Genesis 2:21-23).

Let me say that another way: When God gave the man the command to be fruitful and multiply the man was a one hundred percent male-female spirit-man, that was a seed in which there was life. There was life in Him because God spoke him into existence (John 6:63). Now, what you've got to sink-your-teeth-into is this: Every human being whether dead, alive, or unborn is a descendant of that original spiritual seed named Adam (Genesis 1:27; 1:28; 5:1-2).

As I did my research for this book, I discovered that many people blame Adam for committing the first sin. That's not biblically accurate. The Bible is clear that it was the woman who ate first (Genesis 3:6a). Since she did, then it was she who was the first sinner in our human race. However, God imposed the penalty for sin on Adam because Adam was the progenitor of our entire human race. Adam was the first human. And when the first became corrupt, every spiritual seed that was resident in Adam's loins, became corrupt with him and in him (Matthew 12:33).

Because of Adam's sin, the Bible says that "all have sinned and come short of the glory of God" (Romans 3:23). Now here's the deal: If we have all come short of the glory, and we all came from Adam, does it not mean that before Adam sinned, he had to have had this glory? It stands to reason that if Adam never had God's glory, then there is no way he could have lost it. Our challenge, therefore, is to identify this glory.

## What Is the Glory?

I have two possible explanations. Let's see how they fit:

Firstly, I see the glory as being the Genesis 2:7b "breath of God" that God breathed into Adam's nostrils. The Bible records that when God breathed into Adam's nostrils, Adam "became a living soul."

What is a living soul?

My definition of a living soul is "a sinless human being in whose body God lives or cohabits with the spirit-man of that person."

While Adam was sinless, he possessed God's glory. When God made the woman, she too possessed God's glory because like Adam she was sinless. However, the minute she sinned she became a lost soul and when Adam followed suit, the entire human race, though yet unborn, became lost souls because the glory of God had departed from Adam.

This is captured in Romans 3:23.

> 23 For[1063] all[3956] have sinned,[264] and[2532] come short[5302] of the[3588] glory[1391] of God.[2316]

To say it another way: When Adam sinned, I believe it was then that the Word of God divided the Soul and the Spirit according to Hebrews 4:12. Sin had entered Adam's blood. The Bible says that the "life is in the blood." I conclude, therefore, that sin caused Adam's blood to become sin-contaminated. Once his blood became contaminated with sin, it meant also that his body which was the temple of God's Holy Spirit also became contaminated. God would no longer live in a sin-infected house, so instantly, God removed His presence or His glory from within Adam's body.

Romans 5:12 states: "by one man sin entered into the world, and death by sin; and so, death passed upon all men, for that, all have sinned." The Bible also says, "without (the) shedding of blood is no remission" of sin (Hebrews 9:22b).

Every time a baby is born, you need to understand that whatever blood or blood type s/he has, s/he got from his/her parents who got theirs from their parents, etc. And we all got our blood from Adam. The Bible says, God "has made of one blood all nations of men for to dwell on all the face of the earth" (Acts 17:26). Since we all possess Adam's blood, then we all possess a sinful nature because Adam and Eve had no children when they were in the Garden of Eden and without sin.

Here is what's really important for you to note: The moment that Adam sinned, Romans 6:16 became real for Adam directly, and indirectly it became real also, for the entire human race that was as yet unborn and still resident in Adam's loins. That verse states in part: "whom ye yield yourselves servants to obey, his servants ye are to whom ye obey; whether of sin unto death."

When Adam disobeyed, he dethroned God directly, and by default, and through deception Satan became the "God of this world" (2 Corinthians 4:4). When that happened, all humans, who were still unborn or unconceived seeds in Adam's loins, had become servants of Satan. The space in the heart of man where God resided was now occupied by one who entered the sheepfold, not through the door or "through the womb of a woman," but came in like a thief and a robber through another way, that is through the body of the serpent (John 10:1, paraphrased). I believe that deception was the key that opened the door that gave Satan access to the hearts of every human being who were but unborn seeds in Adam's loins.

If you can accept that when Adam sinned, he became spiritually separated from God (Genesis 3:6c), then it must follow that every seed of the billions of seeds that were yet resident in Adam's loins had to have suffered the same fate. Beginning with Cain and Abel and continuing up to the present time. Adam's sin caused everyone to be born with a procreated spirit-man that is born dead in trespasses and sins (Ephesians 2:1).

Of this condition the Bible says, "There is none righteous, no not one" (Romans 3:10). As cute as a newborn may be, God's Word declares that he is born in sin. How is this possible? It's possible because his blood is sin-infected. And it is sin-infected because the glory that was the breath of God, had departed when Adam sinned.

Secondly, I see the glory as a future event that will become manifest in the resurrected body that each believer shall receive when Jesus returns. Of His coming, the Bible says that it is then that "our vile body ... may be fashioned like unto his glorious body" (Philippians 3:21).

When speaking of that glorious body the Apostle Paul tells us in Colossians 1:26-27 that it is a

> mystery which hath been hid from ages and from generations, but now is made manifest to his saints: To whom God would make known what is the riches of the glory of this mystery among the Gentiles, which is Christ in you, the hope of glory.

Now, check this out:

## Lucifer's Fall

Ezekiel 18:4 states: "The soul that sinneth, it shall die." Ezekiel 28:16 establishes that Lucifer was the first sinner. When Lucifer sinned, God expelled him from the mountain of God. With my bolding, the verse states:

> By the multitude of thy merchandise, they have filled the midst of thee with violence, and **thou hast sinned**: therefore, I will cast thee as profane out of the mountain of God: and I will destroy thee, O covering cherub, from the midst of the stones of fire.

Now, since it is true that the soul that sins dies, then by God's definition, Lucifer had to have been a soul and, more importantly, he had to have been the first soul that sinned. Here's confirmation from 1 John 3:8 (with my bolding):

> He that commits sin is of the devil; for the devil sinneth **from the beginning**. For this purpose, the Son of God was manifested, that he might destroy the works of the devil.

And in Luke 10:18 Jesus says, "I beheld Satan as lightning fall from heaven."

Satan's fall from heaven was the result of Lucifer's sin. His fall was physical proof that he had become separated from God. Before he sinned, Lucifer's home was God's garden in heaven called Eden. With my bolding, Ezekiel 28:13-14 says,

> Thou (Lucifer) hast been in Eden the garden of God; every precious stone was thy covering, ... thou wast upon the holy mountain of God; thou hast walked up and down in the midst of the stones of fire.

After Lucifer had sinned, God cast him out of heaven, and he fell to earth. There, Lucifer became Satan, God's arch enemy number one.

Ezekiel 28:15-17, with my bolding added says,

> Thou wast perfect in thy ways from the day that thou wast created, till iniquity was found in thee. By the multitude of thy merchandise, they have filled the midst of thee with violence, and **thou hast sinned**: therefore, I will cast thee as profane out of the mountain of God: and I will destroy thee, O covering cherub, from the midst of the stones of fire. Thine heart was lifted up because of thy beauty, thou hast corrupted thy wisdom by reason of thy brightness: I will cast thee to the ground.

## Adam's Fall

When Adam sinned, he was on earth in a garden that God planted and called Eden (Genesis 2:8). And it was in that garden that God placed the first human being whom He had created and then formed out of the dust (Genesis 1:27; 5:2; 2:7). In his book, *The Purpose and Power of Praise and Worship*, the late Dr. Myles Munroe states that "Eden was the one place where God's presence dwelt on the earth. It was the Garden of His presence, the spot of His pleasantness, and that was precisely where God placed Adam."[13] The word *eden* or *ayden* (Strong's H5731, H5730) is best translated as the "garden of delight."[14]

Adam and Eve's penalty for sin was the same as Lucifer's. God expelled them from Eden. In Eden God cohabited with them just as He cohabits with every believer. God's presence was in their bodies. Out-of-Eden they were placed in an environment of thorns and thistles. They had lost intimacy with God. Their expulsion from Eden was physical proof that their created spirit-man (Genesis 1:27) had become separated from God. They had lost God's glory. It is important for us to note that spiritual death for the human race did not occur when the woman ate; rather, it happened when the woman "gave also unto her husband with her; and he did eat" (Genesis 3:6c). I firmly believe that if Adam did not eat of the fruit that the woman gave to him, books on this topic might never have been written.

CHAPTER 7

# SELF-EXAMINATION

## Bible Verses

**Mark 4:13**

Jesus had just finished sharing the parable of the Sower with His disciples and they understood it not. So, He asked them: "Know ye not this parable? and how then will ye know all parables?"

**1 Corinthian 15:36-38**

> 36 Thou fool, that which thou sowest is not quickened, except it die:
>
> 37 And that which thou sowest, thou sowest not that body that shall be, but bare grain, it may chance of wheat, or of some other grain:
>
> 38 But God giveth it a body as it hath pleased him, and to every seed his own body.

## Interpretation

Your body was made for you by God while you were being formed in your mother's womb.

Your inner spirit-man—which was and is your daddy's seed and your mother's egg—was procreated.

## What Happens When I Die?

Have you ever asked yourself the question, "What will happen to me after I die?"

Since the death of the body is inevitable, wouldn't you want to know what will happen to you when you die? I know that many books have been written, on death and dying.

And, unfortunately, there are so many differing opinions that you are challenged to decide which author's opinion is right and which is wrong.

So, now that we have explored our subject matter of *What Is the Soul?* I would like you to perform a very simple exercise.

There are two parts to this exercise: (1) You must accept that your soul was dead in sin when you were born. Also (2) you must understand and accept that there is ONLY one thing that you can do, that God will accept, to make your soul come alive again (Ephesians 2:1).

The exercise is simple. In this exercise, I want you to position yourself in front of a mirror and have a conversation with your "self"—or should I say with your "inner" self. During this conversation, you would ask your reflection in the mirror four simple questions. They are these:

1. What have you done with your body?
2. What have you done with the attributes that God gave to you?
3. What happens to your body when it dies?
4. What happens to your "self" when the body dies?

Just so you'd know, your "self" is your reflection or your image in the mirror with which you will be having the conversation. So, turn the page and let's begin.

## What Have You Done with Your Body?

Step 1: Say to yourself: "Self, this body that you have, God gave it to you on the day you were born (1 Corinthians 15:38). What have you done with it?"

Obviously, if you are slim, trim, and full of vim, you give yourself a pat on the back and say to yourself, "Self, you've done well with what God gave you."

If, however, all is not well—and being not well could be anything from being overweight to being bulimic to even being addicted to substances, whether it be for medical reasons or not—then I want you to say to yourself, "Self, from today we're going to fix that."

The purpose of this part of the exercise is to get you to take responsibility for whatever the state of your body. Your "why" is irrelevant. What is relevant is that you must commit to doing whatever it takes to become healthier.

Oh, and by the way, the word *commitment* means that you will do the thing you said you would do, long after the mood you said it in had left you. So, don't make a New Year type resolution where you set your goals, and by the end of the first week in January, you have discarded them. That's not acceptable. Clear? Let's begin. Of your health, the Bible says, in 3 John 1:3,

> 2 Beloved,[27] I wish[2172] above[4012] all things[3956] that thou[4571] mayest prosper[2137] and[2532] be in health,[5198] even as[2531] thy[4675] soul[5590] prospereth.[2137]

That verse is included because I want to let you know that God wants you to prosper, and He wants you to be healthy. Yours is the responsibility to make them both happen. The "how" and "when" is up to you.

## What Have You Done with Your Attributes?

In Step 2, now say to yourself, "Self, when your mom conceived you, you did not know, but the moment you were, God equipped you with at least seven attributes or gifts or talent. Then, He left it up to you to develop them and do what you will with them.

These seven attributes are

1. your mind,
2. your will,
3. your emotions,
4. your memory,
5. your imagination,
6. your conscience, and
7. your heart.

Note: When the Psalmist says, "Create in me a clean heart, O God; and renew a right spirit within me" (Psalms 51:10), please understand that he was NOT speaking about his heart that pumped his blood; he was referring to that inner, albeit invisible or spiritual part of his self of which the Bible says, "The heart is deceitful above all things, and desperately wicked: who can know it?" (Jeremiah. 17:9).

Now ask yourself, "Self, what have you done with your attributes?" As you ask, be aware that when God deposited them into your body, they were in an undeveloped state. The day you were born, you entered this physical arena called life with nothing but the ability to cry, sleep, eat, and poop.

As a child, you relied on your parents or caretakers to meet your every need one hundred percent of the time. After three to six months of this reliance, you recognized their voices first, then their faces. From that point, you recorded everything you experienced, good, bad, and indifferent.

So, as you go through this part of the exercise, follow the same protocol as you did in Step 1, and make a commitment to take whatever is wrong and make it right.

For instance, if you have a proclivity for blaming others for the circumstances in your life that don't measure up to what you would have liked them to be, then promise yourself that you will no longer play the blame game.

Promise yourself that you will begin to take full responsibility for all your actions, regardless of what they may be and then do that. Why would you want to do that?

You would because the cost of awareness is responsibility. In other words, once you have been made aware, moving forward the responsibility for fixing it is yours. You are not allowed to make an excuse like, "I didn't know."

Now, repeat the process for all seven attributes and don't stop until you have resolved all issues and made a commitment to make right whatever is wrong.

## What Happens to Your Body When It Dies?

For Step 3, say to yourself, "Self, whether you believe it or not, there is coming a day when you will have to leave this body that you see standing in front of you. The exact cause or reason you will leave your body may yet be unknown. For instance, Self, you could leave your body because of sickness, accident, or just plain old age. But listen to this, Self: While the why, when, and how you may leave is as yet unknown, I need to let you know that the certainty of your leaving your body is not open for debate. It is an absolute certainty that your body is going to die; it will be buried or cremated, and it will return to dust! Of your body, the Bible says your body shall return to dust!

"Did you get that, Self? Let me repeat that: your body shall return to dust!"

Of the body of the first human being, whom God created (Genesis 1:27) and made (Genesis 2:7a), the Bible says in Genesis 3:19,

> Thou shalt return unto the ground; for out of it wast thou taken: for dust thou art, and unto dust shalt thou return.

For you and me, and for every other human being already dead, presently alive, or yet to be born, the Bible says in 1 Timothy 6:7,

> We brought nothing into this world, and it is certain we can carry nothing out.

## What Happens to Your "Self" When the Body Dies?

For an answer to this last question, I invite you to hear the words of Jesus Christ as He hung on the cross on Calvary. The crucifixion was over. And just before He died, the Bible (in John 19:30) says that Jesus said,

> It is finished: and he bowed his head, and [He] gave up the ghost.

Luke 23:46 records it this way:

> 46 And[2532] when Jesus[2424] had cried[5455] with a loud[3173] voice,[5456] he said,[2036] Father,[3962] into[1519] thy[4675] hands[5495] I commend[3908] my[3450] spirit:[4151] and[2532] having said[2036] thus,[5023] he gave up the ghost.[1606]

What is important to note is that when death came upon the body of Jesus, though He was still on the Cross, He commended His spirit that was resident within His body for thirty-three years into the hands of God, His Father, who lives in heaven.

Of Jesus' body, the Bible says in the first half of 2 Corinthians 5:19,

> 19 To wit,[5613] that[3754] God[2316] was[2258] in[1722] Christ,[5547] reconciling[2644] the world[2889] unto himself,[1438]

And of God, the Bible says in John 4:24:

> 24 God[2316] is a Spirit:[4151] and[2532] they that worship[4352] him[846] must[1163] worship[4352] him in[1722] spirit[4151] and[2532] in truth.[225]

In the original language, *spirit* is translated as *pneuma*. It is the same word that Paul used in Ephesians 1:13 and 4:30 and is used in 1 Thessalonians 4:8. And that word *pneuma* refers to the Holy Spirit.

It would seem to me, therefore, that while you were having that conversation with yourself in the mirror, the reality is that your body was having a conversation with your inner spirit-man, which is and was a procreated spirit offspring of Adam (Genesis 3:6b). And as you know Adam had sinned and your spirit-man inherited his sin condition.

In Jesus' case, the Bible says that He was without sin (2 Corinthians 5:21; Hebrews 4:15; 1 John 3:5; John 19:4; Isaiah 53:9; 1 Peter 1:18-19). Why? Jesus said that He was not of this world (John 8:23). In other words, his spirit-man was not of this world. John 3:16 confirms that. It says, "God sent his son." Don't ever make the mistake of confusing the human Jesus with the man Christ Jesus. One is Spirit in a dirt body; the other is one hundred percent un-created Spirit, and He has a glorified body.

Now that you know, you must realize that on the cross when Jesus commended His Spirit into the hands of God His Father and gave up the ghost (Luke 23:46), it could only mean that Jesus' Spirit was a sinless Spirit. Why? Because when Lucifer sinned, God kicked him out of heaven. Neither sin nor sinner is allowed in heaven.

## What Will Happen to Your "Self" When You Die?

The next question asks, What will happen to your "self" or your inner spirit-man when you die? According to the Bible, it will go either to heaven or hell. The Bible offers no other option. The moment death strikes, you breathe no more, and your procreated spirit leaves your body. Moments later, the coroner will issue a death certificate and, on that certificate, will be a time that denotes the exact moment that you stopped breathing.

Now, I've got to confess: I searched the Internet for a definition of the word *death*, and I failed to find any that defines death clearly. Merriam-Webster's Dictionary provides us with the medical definition. It has assigned to death, "a permanent cessation of all vital functions: the end of life."[15] Albert Einstein, one of the wisest men who ever lived, said that death is "The distinction between the past, the present, and the future is only a stubbornly persistent illusion."[16]

Another source defines death as a "mystery." It says, "The mystery of death is so profound that, despite the millennia of religious doctrine, mythology, scientific research, and the many theories and explanations that exist on the subject, people today are more confused than ever about it."[17] To which I say, "Really?"

## Death: The Great Equalizer

When speaking of death, I believe that Jesus demonstrated clearly that physical death to the body is a state that occurs when your inner spirit-man leaves your body. As to the exact moment that death strikes, only God knows.

I can name the names of countless people who died. Some were family; others were friends, and most were people who were well known. In all likelihood, you probably can as well. If you're over sixty, then it would not be uncommon for either one or both of your parents to have passed from life to death. But beyond that, you must know the names of many people who died but made such an impact on humanity as a whole that we remember them by their first names.

For instance, we remember Muhammad, Frank, Dean, Sammy, Peter, Joey, Big John, Whitney, Michael, Liz, Joan, Richard, Freddie, Red, and Robin. Then there were others whom we remember by their last names; names such as Ali, Kennedy, Khrushchev, Lincoln, Ford, Roosevelt, Reagan. They were all very famous, maybe even powerful, while they lived. But, when they died, their bodies were all returned to the dust from whence they were taken.

Make a note of this: Death does not discriminate. It is the great equalizer. It levels the playing field. Death affects us all. It affects the rich as it affects the poor; it affects the wise as it does the not-so-wise and the otherwise. It affects black, white, brown, blue, pink, or polka dot. No one is exempt. It matters not if any of those famous people mentioned above or any of the people you know was born with royal blood, blue blood, AIDS-infected blood, or just plain, old, ordinary blood. Death occurs when the blood stops flowing. Leviticus 17:11 states that "the life of the flesh is in the blood" and then it says that "it is the blood that maketh an atonement for the soul."

## Don't Fear Death; Prepare for It!

Now, since we must all face the inevitability of death, I believe that it is not something that we should fear, but rather it is something for which we should all prepare. Like it or not, believe it or not, want it or not, death is coming. When he comes, you need to be very sure that it is well with your soul. And I will let you in on a little secret: Worrying about death only speeds up the process. So, don't! Instead, "Live as if Christ died yesterday, rose this morning, and is coming back tomorrow." Those words were spoken by Martin Luther.

So, what is death? For my answer, allow me to take you to the Bible, to the Book of James, Chapter 4:14. Once there, we'll see that not only does James ask a question, but also, he gives us the answer.

James asks: "For what is your life?" Then in the same verse, he defines it. He says, It is even a vapor that appears for a little time, and then vanishes away" (James 4:14). Interpretation? Life is but a breath!

The closest I've come to forming a mental picture of this "vapor" of which James speaks is when I revisit the Big Apple and mentally focus my attention on the effect that the cold temperature had on my warm breath as they collided head on with each other on a wintry day. I saw smoke, but there was no fire. My breath just vaporized.

I believe that on the sixth day of creation when God spoke a word called "Man," His breath turned to vapor (Genesis 1:27). The Bible confirms that when God speaks, He speaks words that are "spirit and life" (John 6:63). And the Bible affirms that God spoke a word called "man" (Genesis 1:27 and Genesis 5:1-2). I conclude therefore that the spirit-man named ADAM was but a breath of God. If I am right in saying that Adam's life was but a breath, then the same must be true for every human being. The only thing that separates the one who is alive and one who is dead is the latter's inability to breathe. When we take our last breath, life ceases.

The Bible says God's Word abides forever. It also says that His Word does "not return to Him void and that it accomplishes that which He pleases. Further, it says that God's Word always "prospers in the thing whereto He sent it" (1 Peter 1:25; Matthew 24:35; 2 Corinthians 4:18; Isaiah 40:7-8 and Isaiah 55:11).

When God sent forth His word called "Man," He sent it to

> 28 Be fruitful,⁶⁵⁰⁹ and multiply,⁷²³⁵ and replenish⁴³⁹⁰ ⁸⁵³ the earth.⁷⁷⁶

Between then and now, we now have over 7.9 billion people on planet Earth. Conclusion: God's Word has always prospered and always will prosper in the thing He sent it to do.

Now, do you recall that when God gave the command (Genesis 1:28) to the man to be fruitful, that the man was still a spirit and did not as yet have a body?

So, since God gave the command to be fruitful to a spirit that He created with His breath, could there be any doubt that when Adam sinned, it was that same spirit called man who fell from grace and got spiritually separated from God? Think about it: Spirit and flesh are two different substances. One is invisible; the other is not. In 2 Corinthians 4, verses 16-18, Paul confirms this.

He states,

> Though our outward man [i.e., our bodies] perish, yet the inward [or procreated spirit] man is renewed day by day. For ...we look not at the things which are seen, but at the things which are not seen: for the things which are seen are temporal; but the things which are not seen are eternal.

In the next chapter, Paul continues (2 Corinthians 5, verses 1-2 and 4-6).

> For we know that if our earthly house of this tabernacle were dissolved, we have a building of God, a house not made with hands, eternal in the heavens. For in this we groan, earnestly desiring to be clothed upon with our house which is from heaven: ... For we that are in this tabernacle do groan, being burdened: not for that we would be unclothed, but clothed upon, that mortality might be swallowed up of life. Now he that hath wrought us for the selfsame thing is God, who also hath given unto us the earnest of the Spirit. Therefore, we are always confident, knowing that, whilst we are at home in the body, we are absent from the Lord:

In the above text, Paul compared our earthly house, our body which must die or be dissolved, with our heavenly body which we will receive when Jesus returns. So, he begs us to not lose faith but remain confident in the knowledge that as long as we are in our bodies, we are absent from the Lord.

### The Finality of Bodily Death

What I glean from the above verses is that when a believer dies, his inner spirit-man goes home to be with the Lord. But whether you are a believer or a non-believer, death of the body has the same effect on all men: their inner spirit-man leaves the body and when it does that body breathes no more. So, whereas life is but a breath, death, is the absence of breath. That's it!

If you're lucky as some have been, you may get a chance to say a few words before your spirit-man leaves your body. If you are, I recommend that you choose your last words wisely. Here are a few last words from a few famous people:

1. According to Steve Jobs' sister Mona, the Apple founder's last words were, "Oh wow. Oh wow. Oh wow."[18] Did he get a glimpse of glory? I don't know.

2. Blues singer Bessie Smith died saying, "I'm going, but I'm going in the name of the Lord."[19]
3. Actress Joan Crawford yelled at her housekeeper, who was praying as Crawford died. Crawford said, 'Damn it! Don't you dare ask God to help me."[20]
4. "Frank Sinatra died after saying, "I'm losing it."[21]

When Frank was alive, many called him Old Blue Eyes. Many remember him for his song, "My Way." In that song, he claimed to have lived his life his way. In others, he went all the way both night and day. At the end of the day, however, Frank had to go. Old Blue Eyes could not stay. Death does not discriminate.

But get this: When Frank spoke his last words, he said, "I'm losing it." Do you know? It was not his flesh that spoke; it was his procreated spirit-man that was resident in his body and gave him his natural life for some eighty-plus years. When his body died, the proof that his body was dead was that his procreated spirit had gotten up and left this arena that we call life.

### The Body Without the Spirit Is Dead

The Apostle James was right. He said, "Just as faith without works is dead, so too the body without the spirit is dead" (James 2:26).

Commenting on this verse, Bible commentator Barnes in Bible Hub says,

> The meaning here is the obvious one, that the body is animated or kept alive by the presence of the soul, and that when that is withdrawn, hope departs. The body has no life independent of the presence of the soul.[22]

CHAPTER 8

# SPIRITUAL DISCONNECT

## Bible Verses
### Genesis 3:8b and 3:23-24

> 8 And Adam and his wife hid themselves from the presence of the LORD God amongst the trees of the garden.
>
> 23 Therefore the LORD God sent him forth from the Garden of Eden.... 24 So he drove out the man.

### Romans 6:16

> Know ye not, that to whom ye yield yourselves servants to obey, his servants ye are to whom ye obey; whether of sin unto death.

## Each of Us Has a Soul

To appreciate Barnes's comment at the end of the previous chapter and to keep his comment in context, you need to understand that both believers and unbelievers have souls. Every human being is a tripartite being who was born with a body, a soul, and a spirit. The body is the flesh. The spirit begins its' life as a seed and egg on over nine months morphs itself into spirit or invisible form. The soul once was the breath of God, and was alive; but when Adam sinned, his soul died; then God vacated Adam's body, and the god of this world took up residence in the bodies of all humanity.

You've got to understand that when a woman conceives, the everlasting life of a soul begins, and because of Adam's sin, that soul is at enmity with God (Romans 8:7). When the baby is born, Romans 3:23 and Ephesians 2:1 kick in. Romans 3:23 says all have sinned and come short of the glory, and Ephesians 2:1 says that the inner spirit-man of all humans was born dead in trespasses and sin.

Before Adam sinned, he was body, soul, and spirit. His soul, which was the breath of God, was alive and connected him directly to God.

Though he lived on earth, it was the fact that God resided in his body that made him a living soul. As a living soul, Adam had intimacy with God.

When he sinned, he remained body, soul, and spirit, but with one key difference: with sin, came death to Adam's soul. It was at this point that the Word of God, that is sharper than a two-edged sword, divided Adam's soul and spirit. God removed His Spirit from Adam's body. God's Glory had departed.

When God left, Satan established residence in the space that once belonged to God. Because of sin, Adam became Satan's servant.

Man, whom God had designed to be immortal, had now become mortal. In due course, the physical death of Adam's body would follow the death of his soul. Sin was the culprit that caused both to happen.

### The Difference: Before Sin and After Sin

Before Adam sinned, he was connected spiritually to God (Genesis 2:7b). God resided in Adam's body. After Adam sinned two things happened:

1. He became spiritually disconnected from God (Genesis 3:8b, 23-24) and,

2. He became spiritually connected to Satan because he yielded his self to Satan (Romans 6:16).

## Another Way to See the Disconnect

One of the ways to look at this soul-disconnect-from-God relationship is to compare the soul to a cable TV converter box. When you order cable service, the company installs a converter box in your home that will allow you to watch all your favorite TV shows, providing of course, that you pay your bill.

Should you become delinquent, your cable company simply flips a switch from a remote location and turns off your service. From that moment until you pay your bill, the converter box remains in your house, but your TV service remains disconnected. No more TV.

## Spiritual Reconnect

But watch what happens when you pay your bill. Doesn't the TV Company restore your service? Of course, they do. And, through it all, the converter box was never taken out of your home.

The same is true for the sin condition in all humans. When Adam sinned, the bloodline which is the life source of all humanity became sin-infected. Concurrent with Adam's sin, the entire human race as yet unborn, became spiritually separated from God (Romans 3:23; Ephesians 2:1b) and spiritually connected to Satan (Romans 6:16).

However, when a person confesses with his lips and believes in his heart (Romans 10:9) that Jesus Christ is God's Son and Lord of all, from that moment, his confession of faith in the finished work of the Cross has the same effect as the payment of his past due TV bill. When he paid his TV bill, he gave the TV company the go-ahead to restore his service.

Similarly, when a person confesses Jesus Christ as his Lord and Savior, God is then empowered restore the broken relationship without violating His

Word, which He holds higher than His name. Adam's sin spiritually disconnected us all from God. When we use our mouths to verbalize our confession of faith in the finished work of the Cross, we fulfill God's requirements, and He reconnects us to his self through Jesus Christ.

## Only One Way

When Jesus says, "I am the way, the truth, and the life: no man cometh unto the Father, but by me" (John 14:6), I believe that the "one way" to which He referred was our confession of faith in the work He finished on the cross.

Sadly, many have failed to identify clearly "the way" that Jesus specified. This failure stems from misinterpreting the scripture. When Jesus said, "no man cometh"—apparently many assumed that He was speaking about flesh and blood humans. But what is the truth? The truth is, Jesus was speaking directly to the spirit-man that resides in the body of each human being that is responsible for the life that each person enjoys.

Medical scientists and others agree that life begins at conception, in our mother's womb, but how many of them understand that it is God who makes our bodies for us while we are in her womb? How many understand that it is God who is the architect that selects the male seed and female egg and from them, brings forth life? I don't have a number, but should the day come when all men realize that life is precious and that life is indeed a gift from God, then and only then do I believe that the heinous practices that violate human life while yet in the womb, would cease. The scripture says, we perish for lack of knowledge—of God's Word. It says, also:

"What therefore God hath joined together, let not man put asunder" (Matthew 19:6b).

## Life and Death in the Power of the Tongue

When Adam sinned, he used his tongue to defy God. First, he ate of the tree; then when God questioned him, he lied. When anyone wants Jesus to save his soul from eternal damnation, it is imperative that he use his tongue to confess Jesus Christ and make Him his Lord and Savior. Adam used his tongue to sin, and he died. The believer uses his tongue to confess Jesus, and he lives. When the Bible says that "life and death are in the power of the tongue" (Proverbs 18:21), it was not referring to your physical life. It was referring to the eternal life of your inner spirit-man.

Understanding this concept is crucial. And, when you understand that with your confession of faith in the finished work of the Cross, the eternal life you save shall be your own, you are way ahead of everyone who chooses to not confess.

When anyone dies, the minute he takes his last breath his soul and spirit depart. Once the spirit-man leaves this arena we call life, the body dies. It becomes a corpse. The Apostle James says, "the body without the spirit is dead" (James 2:26). The final destination of the body is well known; it goes back to the dust. But what about the spirit and soul that were resident in the body while it was alive? Where do they go?

As per the Bible, there are only two choices: Heaven or Hell. If you confessed Jesus while you were alive, your spirit-man would go to heaven. If you didn't, then Hell is your eternal destination. That's Bible!

The scripture says, "you were (i.e., your inner spirit-man was) born dead in trespasses and sins" (Ephesians 2:1b). To be born dead in trespasses and sin means that your inner spirit-man was born separated from God. When was your spirit-man separated from God? Answer: When Adam sinned! Romans 3:23 states, "all have sinned and come short of the glory of God." "All" exempts no one and includes everyone.

Here's what Jesus said, "I am the resurrection, and the life: he that believeth in me, though he were dead, yet shall he live" (John 11:25).

And John 1:12, states: "As many as received him to them gave He the power to become sons of God" (John 1:12). "Him" would be the eternal Spirit of the Risen Christ.

It would appear to me therefore that belief in Jesus is good and probably sufficient; however, when you believe and receive that puts you in the driver's seat. Now your salvation is sure. In the Old Testament, "Abraham believed God, and it was imputed unto him for righteousness" (James 2:23). In Abraham's case, faith, or belief in the promise of God was sufficient because Jesus Christ had not yet shed His blood on Calvary's Cross. But after Jesus shed His blood, then receiving Him as Lord and Savior became God's sole standard by which all people can be saved.

Luke 3:38 says that Adam "was the son of God." As a son of God, Adam was connected spiritually to God. When Adam sinned, a spiritual-disconnect occurred between God and man and hence between heaven and earth.

Adam's sin caused God to flip the disconnect switch through which all spiritual blessings flow. The Word of God divided man's spirit and soul. Our confession of faith in the finished work of the Cross obligates God to restore that service to all who comply with Romans 10:9-10. As I stated earlier, the Apostle James was right. He said that "just as faith without works is dead, so too the body without the spirit is dead" (James 2:26).

### Natural Death Defined

So here another definition of death that I came up with: Death is that lifeless state that occurs to the body of every human being when the inner spirit-man—that animated his body for however long he lived—vacates the premises or his earthly house, either because of old age, sickness, or accident.

## What About Spiritual Death?

The question you need to answer is this: When your inner spirit- man leaves your body, would you be able to do as Jesus did and commend your spirit into the hands of God our Father who lives in heaven? If you accepted Jesus as your Savior, you can. If you did not, then you do not have that option. John 14:6 says Jesus declared,

6 Jesus²⁴²⁴ saith³⁰⁰⁴ unto him,⁸⁴⁶ I¹⁴⁷³ am¹⁵¹⁰ the³⁵⁸⁸ way,³⁵⁹⁸ the³⁵⁸⁸ truth,²²⁵ and²⁵³² the³⁵⁸⁸ life:²²²² no man³⁷⁶² cometh²⁰⁶⁴ unto⁴³¹⁴ the³⁵⁸⁸ Father,³⁹⁶² but¹⁵⁰⁸ by¹²²³ me.¹⁷⁰⁰

What's important about John 14:6 is this: The Jesus who spoke and said, "I am the way," is functionally different from the Jesus that Joseph of Arimathea placed in the tomb. The Jesus who went in the tomb was a living soul; the one who rose on the third day was the quickening Spirit of the risen Christ who now sits in heaven making intercession for us.

Because he died on the cross and shed His blood, He is now also known as the man Christ Jesus, the one mediator between God and men (1 Timothy 2:5). According to Revelation 1:18, He is the same Jesus who now lives and was dead; and is alive for evermore.

Now, when Jesus said, "no man" comes to the Father, did you notice that He did not specify male, female, or child. He said simply, "no man." So, who is this man? That man can refer only to your inner spirit-man because the Bible says 1 Corinthians 15:50 that

50 Now¹¹⁶¹ this⁵¹²⁴ I say,⁵³⁴⁶ brethren,⁸⁰ that³⁷⁵⁴ flesh⁴⁵⁶¹ and²⁵³² blood¹²⁹ cannot¹⁴¹⁰ ³⁷⁵⁶ inherit²⁸¹⁶ the kingdom⁹³² of God;²³¹⁶ neither³⁷⁶¹ doth corruption⁵³⁵⁶ inherit²⁸¹⁶ incorruption.⁸⁶¹

Why can't flesh and blood inherit God's kingdom? Because Job 21:26 says

26 They shall lie down⁷⁹⁰¹ alike³¹⁶² in⁵⁹²¹ the dust,⁶⁰⁸³ and the worms⁷⁴¹⁵ shall cover³⁶⁸⁰ ⁵⁹²¹ them.

So, since your mortal corrupted body shall not go to heaven, how can your inner spirit-man ascend to the Father through His Son Jesus Christ?

## Let's Go Back to the Garden of Eden

In the Garden, the Bible says that God took the dust and formed the man (Genesis 2:7a). Then, it says that God commanded the man to give "names to all cattle, and to the fowl of the air, and to every beast of the field" (Genesis 2:20). After Adam did so, in the next verse, Genesis says God then put Adam into a deep sleep, opened up his side, took out a rib, made the woman, and immediately thereafter,

> 21 closed up[5462] the flesh[1320] instead[8478] thereof.

What should we learn from that verse? We should learn that from one created male-female spirit named Adam, God made two independent human beings—one male and one female. Also, we should learn that those two humans are responsible for the reproduction of the seven to ten billion people that are alive today, and that God made bodies for each one of them. (1 Corinthians 15:38).

Add to that the billions of people who died since God created man and it is mind-boggling to grasp that no matter who you are, or where you're from, we all came from the one-man Adam. So, when we discriminate against another for whatever reason, we do so and perish because of a lack of knowledge of the Word of God.

The Bible says in the first half of Hosea 4:6,

> 6 My people[5971] are destroyed[1820] for lack[4480 1097] of knowledge:[1847]

### Let's Go Forward to Calvary

Now, let's fast-forward to Calvary. Jesus was on the cross. The soldiers were preparing to break the legs of those crucified. The Apostle John tells us in Chapter 19, verses 34 and 36, that when they came to Jesus and saw that He was already dead,

> 34 But[235] one[1520] of the[3588] soldiers[4757] with a spear[3057] pierced[3572] his[846] side,[4125] and[2532] forthwith[2117] came there out[1831] blood[129] and[2532] water.[5204]

36 For¹⁰⁶³ these things⁵⁰²³ were done,¹⁰⁹⁶ that²⁴⁴³ the³⁵⁸⁸ Scripture¹¹²⁴ should be fulfilled,⁴¹³⁷ A bone³⁷⁴⁷ of him⁸⁴⁶ shall not³⁷⁵⁶ be broken.⁴⁹³⁷

Did you get that? The soldier pierced Jesus' side. Now He had a hole in his side, and when He rose from the grave, the hole was still there. Not so with Adam. God closed the hole in Adam's side (Genesis 2:21). Why?

## Let's Go to the Upper Room

Fast-forward once more to Resurrection Sunday at evening time. Jesus fulfilled prophesy and rose from the dead. He saw Mary and asked her to notify the disciples. Then later that day He appeared in the Upper Room and showed Himself to His disciples as they were cowering in fear of the Jews (John 20:1-20).

When He showed them the holes in His hands and side, and later showed them again to Thomas, both Thomas and the disciples were glad. With my added bolding, John 20:20-22 says,

> 21 Then³⁷⁶⁷ said²⁰³⁶ Jesus²⁴²⁴ to them⁸⁴⁶ again,³⁸²⁵ Peace¹⁵¹⁵ be unto you:⁵²¹³ as²⁵³¹ my Father³⁹⁶² hath sent⁶⁴⁹ me,³¹⁶⁵ even so send I²⁵⁰⁴ ³⁹⁹² you.⁵²⁰⁹
>
> 22 And²⁵³² when he had said²⁰³⁶ this,⁵¹²⁴ he breathed on¹⁷²⁰ them, and²⁵³² saith³⁰⁰⁴ unto them,⁸⁴⁶ **Receive**²⁹⁸³ **ye the Holy**⁴⁰ **Ghost:**⁴¹⁵¹

Let's make a note of two important things that happened in the Upper Room, as described in John 20.

## One: The Disciples' Souls Were Redeemed

When Jesus breathed on His disciples, I believe His breath was the equivalent of the Genesis 2:7 breath of life that God breathed into Adam's nostrils, which caused Adam to "become" a living soul. Take away God's breath and all we have is an invisible spirit-man named Adam, who lived in a body that

God made from dust for him. God had placed the spirit in the dirt and gave human form to a non-human thing. In other words, God made the invisible visible (Romans 1:20).

In the Upper Room, however, when Jesus breathed on His disciples, I believe that it was then that their souls were redeemed. Jesus had shed His blood. Because He did, he had paid God's price for the remission of Adam's sin. So, when Jesus breathed on His disciples, their spiritual relationship with God was restored instantly. Their body, soul and spirit were now sanctified and would be preserved until Jesus comes.

> 23 And[1161] the[3588] very[846] God[2316] of peace[1515] sanctify[37] you[5209] wholly;[3651] and[2532] I pray God your[5216] whole[3648] spirit[4151] and[2532] soul[5590] and[2532] body[4983] be preserved[5083] blameless[274] unto[1722] the[3588] coming[3952] of our[2257] Lord[2962] Jesus[2424] Christ.[5547]

In Greek, "spirit and soul and body" would have been written as *pneuma*[4151], *psuchē*[5590], and *sōma*[4983].

### Two: The Souls of Believers Are Redeemed

Now, I want to share with you another observation, and that is that Jesus retained the hole in His side. In Adam's case, if you recall, once God had taken out the rib and made the woman, God closed up Adam's side. In Jesus' case, however, God did not. God left it open. The question is, Why? Why did God leave open the hole in Jesus' side?

I believe God left it open to allow anyone—also known as "any wild olive branch"—who confesses Jesus Christ as Lord and Savior, to be grafted into the family of God (Romans 11:16-24). In biology, the verb *graft* means "to unite (a shoot or bud) with a growing plant by insertion or by placing it in close contact."[23]

When a graft is successful, the engrafted shoot derives its nourishment from the root of its host and flourishes just as any original branch would.

When I interpret spiritual grafting, I have a mental picture of the Risen Christ. I see Him seated in heaven at the right hand of God, just waiting with open arms to receive the confessions of faith of the spirit-man of each person who calls on the name of Jesus, and then I see Him taking the spirit-words of each person's confession and inserting them or grafting them into the open wound in His side.

Remember now, the Bible says, "death and life are in the power of the tongue" (Proverbs 18:21). As I see it, the life being referenced is the eternal life of our inner spirit-man. Romans 10:9 says,

> He that believeth on the Son hath everlasting life: and he that believeth not the Son shall not see life; but the wrath of God abides on him.

This means, our confession positions us to lay claim to the scripture that says in part "if any man" (meaning, any spirit-man) "be in Christ, he is a new creature" (2 Corinthians 5:17). Permit me to give you another interpretation of that verse. "If any man be in Christ … a New Creation … then he is a new creature."

Let's go back to Genesis 1:1, God created the heavens and the earth. In Genesis 2:1 and in Colossians 1:16, we read, "and all the host(s) of them." Then, "God created great whales, and every living creature" (Genesis 1:21). And finally, God created man in his own image (Genesis 1:27). Genesis 2:2 says,

> 2 And on the seventh[7637] day[3117] God[430] ended[3615] his work[4399] which[834] he had made;[6213] and he rested[7673] on the seventh[7637] day[3117] from all[4480 3605] his work[4399] which[834] he had made.[6213]

When God rested, Father, Son, and Holy Spirit were in heaven. Adam was on earth. After Adam sinned (Genesis 3:6c), there came a day when God sent his Son to earth to be born of a woman and be clothed in a body of flesh. Of that event, the scripture says that "God was in (the body of) Christ, reconciling unto himself, the world." However, the reconciliation process could not begin until God's Son had been crucified, buried, risen, and "ascended, far above all heavens, that he might fill [fulfill] all things" (Ephesians 4:10). The reality of Christ being in heaven with a body that looks human yet is "incorruptible" (1 Peter 1:23) is something that heaven had never seen before. Only Abraham had gotten a glimpse of the ascended Christ, and the Bible says he "was glad" (John 8:56).

While on earth, God's Son had a physical body (1 Corinthians 15:44), just as you and I have. In heaven, He now has a spiritual body (1 Corinthians 15:44) that has flesh and bone (Luke 24:39), yet it has no blood. He shed His blood for our sin. And what is important is this: In His side, there is an open wound that was made by a soldier's spear. That open wound is there, so when you confess and make Christ your Lord and Savior, your spirit-man can be placed, in Christ.

As human beings, we all came out-of-Adam. We were all born spiritually dead. And we are all destined to die physically. When we die, we will breathe no more and our inner spirit-man will leave our bodies. Its eternal destination is either heaven or hell. God's desire for the entire world is that "all would come to repentance" (2 Peter 3:9) and "believe on the Lord Jesus Christ" (Acts 16:31). Only those who do are destined to become new creatures, in the New Creation that is Jesus Christ.

With my bolding, the Scripture says,

> 4 But[1161] God,[2316] who is[5607] rich[4145] in[1722] mercy,[1656] for[1223] his[848] great[4183] love[26] wherewith[3739] he loved[25] us,[2248]
>
> 5 Even[2532] when we[2248] were[5607] dead[3498] in sins,[3900] hath quickened us together[4806] with Christ, by[5547] (grace[5485] ye are[2075] saved;)[4982]
>
> 6 And[2532] hath raised us up together,[4891] and[2532] made us sit **together**[4776] **in**[1722] **heavenly**[2032] **places in**[1722] **Christ**[5547] **Jesus:**[2424]
>
> 7 That[2443] in[1722] the[3588] ages[165] to come[1904] he might show[1731] the[3588] exceeding[5235] riches[4149] of his[848] grace[5485] in[1722] his kindness[5544] toward[1909] us[2248] through[1722] Christ[5547] Jesus.[2424]

CHAPTER 9

# SURROGACY VS GESTATIONAL SURROGACY

## Bible Verses

### Hebrews 2:3, 2:10

[3] How shall we escape, if we neglect so great salvation, which at the first began to be spoken by the Lord and was confirmed unto us by them that heard him.

[10] For it became him, for whom are all things, and by whom are all things, in bringing many sons unto glory, to make the captain of their salvation perfect through sufferings.

### 1 Peter 4:16-18

[16] Yet if any man suffers as a Christian, let him not be ashamed; but let him glorify God on this behalf.

[17] For the time is come that judgment must begin at the house of God: and if it first begins at us, what shall the end be of them that obey not the gospel of God?

[18] And if the righteous scarcely be saved, where shall the ungodly and the sinner appear?

## The Truth About Surrogacy

### Jesus Had None of Mary's Blood

Interestingly, even though Mary gave birth to baby Jesus, the baby Jesus obviously had none of Mary's blood. Take every human being since Adam who has been born or is yet to be born, and of them, the Bible says that they have all "sinned and come short of the glory of God" (Romans 3:23).

Surrogacy has been around for centuries. The most commonly known case would probably be when Sarah could not bear children and had her husband, Abraham, conceive a child with her maidservant Hagar (Genesis 16). In the United States, the first formal agreement for surrogacy was in 1976. Since then, it has been evolving with a great number of legal issues involved.[24] It is now becoming more commonplace around the world. The word is that if you're a woman, and for whatever reason you are unable to carry a child to term, you can always get a surrogate mom. Gestational surrogacy defined.

Traditional surrogacy occurs via *in vitro* fertilization (IVF), through which the mother is artificially inseminated with embryos created from her own eggs that were fertilized outside of the womb. However, in medicine today, the procedure called gestational surrogacy occurs when a doctor implants a female with a fertilized embryo that is not her own but from another woman.[25]

My research on this topic revealed that every year at least 750 babies are born using gestational surrogacy.[26] My wife and I know one woman personally, an African-American woman who has given birth to Caucasian twins.

God's preference, of course, is that the male and female involved should be husband and wife (Genesis 2:24) and that they should "know" or "*yâda☒*" each other, as Adam knew Eve when she conceived (Genesis 4:1). But the interesting thing about any fertilized seed is that it will grow and bring forth the fruit of the womb, be it baby girl or baby boy, whether or not the male and the female are married.

### God's Prescription for Reproduction

The Bible specifies that, for conception to occur, there must be the seed or sperm of a male and the egg of a female. Therefore, when pregnancy occurs, whether through natural or IVF means, as long as those two conditions are met, God steps in and forms a body (1 Corinthians 15:38) for the conceived zygote. Then, when the baby is born, we recognize that it became the one flesh offspring of the father who had to be male and the mother who had to be female.

Genesis 2:24 states: "What therefore God hath joined together, let not man put asunder." Since God is the one who joins the male seed with the female egg and then forms its body, I believe that whether you are male or female, God never intended for anyone to undergo a sex-change; neither did He intend for members of the same sex to copulate. Romans 1, verses 26 to 32 documents God's position very plainly. Read it.

There are many people who were born physically challenged. Time and again history proves that when they surrender their lives to serving God, God calls them with all their imperfections, and He uses them to do good works that bring Him glory (Matthew 5:16; Romans 8:28).

Nick Vujicic from New Zealand comes to mind. He was born with no arms and no legs, yet today he lives a life with no limits.[27] Helen Keller is another; blind and deaf from her youth, yet she impacted world leaders. And may I tell you? If God, did it for the physically challenged, he would do it also for the sexually challenged. All they've got to do is give their life to Jesus and He'll fix them. With God, nothing shall be impossible (Luke 1:37).

Back to gestational surrogacy: Using IVF, an OB/GYN implants a fertilized egg into the uterus of a gestational surrogate, aptly called a surrogate mom. When the baby is born, DNA tests can prove that, even though the surrogate mom carried the baby to term, she has no genetic ties to the baby, because as surrogate, she did not use her eggs.

## No Genetic Ties in Gestational Surrogacy

Geneticist Julie Ganka said the following:

> The bottom line is that once an egg is fertilized, the woman carrying the fertilized egg does not contribute a significant amount of DNA to the fetus.[28]

## What's So Important About Gestational Surrogacy?

In Genesis 17:9-12, God commanded Abraham to circumcise baby boys on the eighth day of their lives.

> 9 And God[430] said[559] unto[413] Abraham,[85] Thou[859] shalt keep[8104] [853] my covenant[1285] therefore, thou,[859] and thy seed[2233] after[310] thee in their generations.[1755]
>
> 10 This[2063] is my covenant,[1285] which[834] ye shall keep,[8104] between[996] me and you and thy seed[2233] after[310] thee; Every[3605] man child[2145] among you shall be circumcised.[4135]
>
> 11 And ye shall circumcise[4135] [853] the flesh[1320] of your foreskin;[6190] and it shall be[1961] a token[226] of the covenant[1285] between[996] me and you.
>
> 12 And he that is eight[8083] days[3117] old[1121] shall be circumcised[4135] among you, every[3605] man child[2145] in your generations,[1755] he that is born[3211] in the house,[1004] or bought[4736] with money[3701] of any[4480] [3605] stranger,[1121] [5236] which[834] is not[3808] of thy seed.[4480] [2233]

## What Did God Know that We Didn't?

Why day eight? What did God know that we would not become aware of until 1935? Was there any medical or scientific reason for specifying day eight? The answer is an emphatic yes!

In 1935, Professor H. Dam proposed the name "vitamin K" for the factor in foods that helps prevent hemorrhaging in baby chicks. We know now that vitamin K is responsible for the production (by the liver) of the element known as prothrombin. If vitamin K is deficient, there will be a prothrombin deficiency and hemorrhaging may occur. Oddly, it is only on the fifth through the seventh days of the newborn male's life that vitamin K (which is produced by bacteria in the intestinal tract) is present in adequate quantities. Vitamin K, coupled with prothrombin, causes blood coagulation, which is important in any surgical procedure.[29]

I interpret that to mean that any baby boy who gets circumcised before day eight, could potentially bleed to death. I could be wrong with my interpretation, but, to me, it sounds logical.

I find comfort in what John 17:17 says: "Thy word is truth."

Now get this. It took our medical practitioners 1,935 years after Jesus was born to find out a Biblical truth that God gave to Moses some 7,000 years before. Why so long? The simple answer is, as I stated earlier on in this book, "We learn nothing from the books we don't read."

And please know that the eighth-day circumcision is not the only truth in the Bible. There are many others.

## Prophecy Fulfilled

Let's look at Isaiah 7:14. It reads as follows:

> 14 Therefore[3651] the Lord[136] himself[1931] shall give[5414] you a sign;[226] Behold,[2009] a virgin[5959] shall conceive,[2029] and bear[3205] a son,[1121] and shall call[7121] his name[8034] Immanuel.[6005]

Imagine, 700 years before Jesus was born, the Lord sent His word through a prophet named Isaiah; and 2,000 years ago, when the fullness of time had come, every word that Isaiah spoke came to pass. Why? It is because God's Word is truth and whenever God speaks or sends forth His word, His word always accomplishes the purpose for which God sent it (Isaiah 55:11).

### Gestational Surrogacy Is Not New

Therefore, when the Bible said that a "virgin shall bring forth a child and you shall call His name Jesus," what you need to understand is that even though Mary gave birth to the baby Jesus, the baby Jesus had none of Mary's blood. Ask any surrogate mom and they will tell you that their surrogate baby had none of their blood. This is so because the surrogate baby gets its blood from the zygote that the doctor implanted in the womb of the surrogate mom.

### The Virgin Mary, the First Surrogate Mom; Jesus Christ, the First Surrogate Son

Based on the preceding discussion, it is my position that the Virgin Mary was the first surrogate mom, and the baby Jesus was the first surrogate Son. When Jesus was born, He had nothing from His birth mother and everything from His eternal Father. As such, when Jesus said in John 10:30,

> 30 I$^{1473}$ and$^{2532}$ my Father$^{3962}$ are$^{2070}$ one.$^{1520}$

what He meant was the Eternal Spirit that resided in His body was one with, that is in total unison with, the Spirit of His Father who lives in heaven.

## About the Blood

### The Blood of Jesus

As we had just seen with gestational surrogacy, when Jesus was born, He had neither Mary's DNA nor Mary's blood. The question, therefore, is this: From where could the human Jesus have gotten His blood? Based on what we know now, I am sure you'll agree that the ONLY place Jesus blood could have come from would be from within his self! Why? John 1:4 tells us

> 4 In$^{1722}$ him$^{846}$ was$^{2258}$ life.$^{2222}$

And remember, before the Christ Jesus (who was Spirit) was made flesh, He was (1) the Creator of Colossians 1:16; (2) the Maker of all things of John

1:1; (3) the Creator of Genesis 1:1; (4) the one hundred percent Eternal Spirit of Hebrews 9:14; and (5) equal with His Father, in every way (John 10:30; 5:18).

Even though the human Jesus took the form of a servant and was made in the likeness of men (Philippians 2:7), the Spirit that resided in His body, animated Him, and gave Him life as we know, it was still the eternal Spirit of God's only begotten Son (John 1:18) who was The Logos of John 1:1, minus His deity, *a.k.a.* The Man Christ Jesus (1 Timothy 2:5).

### The Blood of Adam

Now, as for the first human whom God named Adam, it is my position that his blood had to have come from the same Word of God that gave Jesus His blood, with one exception: In Adam's case, Adam's spirit-man was a word that God spoke into existence (Genesis 1:27). The fact that God spoke Adam into being, is what made Adam a "created" being.

### Adam's Spirit Was Created

As further proof that Adam was a created being, let's read the Book of Genesis, Chapter 5, verses one and two. It reads as follows:

> 1 This[2088] is the book[5612] of the generations[8435] of Adam.[121] In the day[3117] that God[430] created[1254] man,[120] in the likeness[1823] of God[430] made[6213] he him;
>
> 2 Male[2145] and female[5347] created[1254] he them; and blessed[1288] them, and called[7121] [853] their name[8034] Adam,[121] in the day[3117] when they were created.[1254]

### God's Spirit Is Uncreated

With the man Christ Jesus, however, (1 Timothy 2:5) because He was the Lamb that was slain from the foundation of the world (Revelation 13:8) and because He was taken out of the very bosom of God (John 1:18), those two facts made the inner spirit-man of the human Jesus an uncreated being and God's only begotten son.

## God Made Bodies for the Spirit in Humans

God did not create humans. He created spirits and made bodies for them.

It is important to note that in either case, whether with Jesus or with Adam, God was and is, the one who made a both for them. Note also that God is the one who makes bodies for every newborn baby and also makes bodies for every animal, bird, fish, insect, and plant (1 Corinthians 15:38).

Here's God's formula:

Human or Humus-man = God's Spoken Spirit-word + Dust (Genesis 1:27; 2:7a)

Living Soul = Humus-man + Breath of God (Genesis 1:27; 2:7a; 2:7b)

Somewhere in the mix God was able to take the dust and His spoken work and make a body that has blood, flesh, and bone. Nothing is too hard for God. (Jeremiah 32:27; Genesis 18:14; Matthew 19:26)

## Man's Blood

So, how did God take His word that He called man, place it in dust, and produce a human being with somewhere around six quarts of blood and forty quarts his weight of water? Quite frankly, I don't know. But I know that He did. And I'm cool with that.

One thing that pleases God is when we believe His Word, as It is Written. I choose to believe before I understand; and even when I don't. Will I ever understand how an iron axe can swim (2 Kings 6:5-6)? I think not. Will I ever understand how God "opened the mouth of the ass" (Num. 22:28)? I know I won't. But the Bible said it. I believe it. And for me, that settles it! Now, let's get back to the bloodline.

## Blood Container

After God had completed creating, forming, and empowering Adam as only God could, Adam had within his body about six quarts of blood and three-quarters of his weight in water. We know this because today that's about what any adult male or female has.

Now, I'd like you to see Adam's body as a wineskin or a container for holding liquids, which it was, and which is what it did. Also, I'd like you to see God putting Adam to sleep and then see God opening Adam's side and taking out a rib and making a helper suitable for Adam (Genesis 2:18, 21-23).

When God made Adam's helper, only two humans were then alive—Adam who was one hundred percent male and Eve who was one hundred percent female. Now it's important for you to note that whereas God took dust and made a body for Adam, in Eve's case, God did not go back to the dust. God went into the male and divinely removed a rib that He then used to make a body for the female. Also, it is important to note that when God was finished making a body for the woman, God closed up Adam's side (Genesis 2:21).

Now, between Adam's time and the year 1905, no one knew about sex chromosomes. But today, thanks to everyone's global "Professor Google" for anyone who is willing to do a little web research, s/he can learn of Nettie Stevens and Edmund Beecher Wilson. Google credits these two with independently discovering, in 1905, the chromosomal XY sex-determination system. Because of their discovery, it is now a matter of public knowledge that if you are a male, it is because you have the XY sex chromosomes and if you are female, then you have the XX sex chromosomes. We know also that if you have only one of the chromosomes, either X or Y, then you just would not be, because under any condition, it takes the two, X and Y, coming together, to produce a third and by divine design that third, always is and ever will be either XY or XX; that third always is either one hundred percent male or one hundred percent female. Now, I didn't make that up. I am merely repeating what God said in the first book of the Bible. Let's read Genesis 2, verses 24 and 25.

> Therefore, shall a man leave his father and his mother, and shall cleave unto his wife: and they shall be one flesh. And they were both naked, the man and his wife, and were not ashamed.

May I tell you? When a man and his wife are naked and not ashamed, they are not getting ready to watch reruns of a TV show. I think it is safe to say they've got other plans. They got naked for a purpose. And normally, that purpose is intimacy. As to the type of intimacy, God was so specific that He left no room for misinterpretation. He specified that the male and female should cleave to each other and when they do, then the one flesh or new birth is produced some nine months later.

I must tell you that, because of Nettie Stevens and Edmund Beecher Wilson's discovery, I have no problem accepting as fact that the "male and female" that God created were not two independent human beings, nor two independent spirit-beings, but rather, the male and female in Genesis 1:27, referred to—the "X" chromosome and the "Y" chromosome that we find in each zygote. Today, medical science has established that to produce life, the female must supply the X, and the male may supply either the X or Y sex chromosome before the baby comes.

### First, There Was One; and from the One, Two

Knowing this, it must follow, that if the male (Adam) had flesh, bone, blood, and water in his body, then the female (Eve) had to have had the same. The only difference between the two was each person's sexual make up. Adam was one hundred percent male. He had the (XY) chromosomes; and Eve was one hundred percent female because she had the (XX) chromosomes. Resident, in spirit-form, in Adam's body was a created seed that was a spoken Word of God and since God did not speak a second time, in Eve's case her spirit-man was a procreated seed. In Adam was a spirit-seed that had the (XY) or male combination; in Eve was the (XX) or female equivalent. This must be so because God did not speak the woman into existence. God spoke once and created ONLY ONE man. And, from Adam, came ALL men, including Eve, and including you and me.

## Procreation: The Process

We need to understand that, since Adam and Eve were the prototypes, the process through which God created and made Adam, and procreated and formed Eve, was unique to only the two of them. But, for every other human being who has since been born, the process has been the same: A male supplies a sperm (XY) and a female provides an egg (XX); and when conditions are ideal, God intervenes and produces a fertilized embryo or zygote that is either (XY) or (XX) (1 Corinthians 15:38).

So, here's the deal: Whether you have male or female genitals, the reality is that some nine months before you were born your daddy sowed a seed; that seed fertilized an ovum that was supplied by your mother; and over the course of the next nine months, it was God who made a body for you while you were in your mother's womb (1 Corinthians 15:38).

The scripture says, "God gives a body to every seed, as it pleases Him" (1 Corinthian 15:38). It says also, "Jesus, in his preincarnate state as the Logos, or the eternal Spirit, is the Word of God who made everything" (John 1:3). Now take a deep breath and stand in front of a mirror and say to yourself (whichever applies):

> I am a male (or I am a female). And within my body is my father's seed and my mother's egg. Together these two united and formed my inner spirit-man that is both male and female. Biologically, however, I am one hundred percent male (XY) (or female (XX)). My mother did not make my body for me; God did (1 Corinthians 15:38), and God did so for His predestined purpose. Whenever I deviate from God's predestined purpose for my life, whether through reconstructive surgery or unnatural acts or behavior, I subvert God's procreative plan for me, and God sees that as an abomination (Leviticus 20:13; Romans 1:26-32).

## So, Who Is the Eternal Spirit?

The "eternal," of course, would be the Spirit that was the Lamb of God (Revelation 13:8). That Lamb was the Word that was God (John 1:1c), who was made flesh (John 1:14). In the flesh, the Spirit of God that was Christ was now resident in the human body of the person that the people who lived in the first century identified as Jesus Christ. In John 14:6, Jesus Himself said of that person,

> 6 Jesus[2424] saith[3004] unto him,[846] I[1473] am[1510] the[3588] way,[3598] the[3588] truth,[225] and[2532] the[3588] life:[2222]

In each of the above references, the same word "zō ē" is translated as "life." What we've been missing in the translation of John 14:6 is that when Jesus says, "I am the way, the truth, and the life," most definitely He was not speaking of the human representation of whom He had become, but rather He was referring to the Him, or to that eternal Spirit, who is the Great "I AM," who was now resident in His human body.

## The Son of God Was Called Jesus

The son of God, who was Spirit and became one hundred percent human, was called Jesus. It is extremely important for us to note that physically, Jesus Christ was just as one hundred percent human as any other person. The Bible says of Him that though He "was in all points tempted like as we are," yet He was "without sin" (Hebrews 4:15). In John 8:23, Jesus said of Himself that He was not of this world, that He was from above. And Luke tells us that the Holy thing to which Mary gave birth was called the Son of God (Luke 1:35).

## He Was Full of Glory

However, the Son of God was different. He "was made flesh and dwelt among men." The Apostle John said that "we beheld his glory, the glory as of the only-begotten of the Father, full of grace and truth" (John 1:14). In other words, when God sent His only begotten Son into the world, God did not send a human Jesus. Rather, God sent the Eternal Spirit who was His Son, that is the man Christ Jesus (1 Timothy 2:5) whom God the Father had taken out of His very bosom (John 1:18).

### He Came from the Bosom of God

Unlike ADAM, whom God spoke into existence (Genesis 1:27; 5:1-2), the Son of God was NOT. This fact that God spoke Adam into existence is what made the spirit-man Adam, a "created being."

But, when God's Son came to earth, apart from coming to seek and to save that which was lost (Luke 19:10) and apart from coming to destroy the works of the devil (1 John 3:8), the Apostle John tells us that He came to declare God our Father to us (John 1:18).

Further, John specified that this Son came out-of-the-very bosom of the Father (John 1:18). Timothy calls him "the man Christ Jesus" (1 Timothy 2:5). And the apostle John referred to him as the Lamb who was slain from the foundation of the world (Revelation 13:8).

Further, John 1:18 says,

> 18 No man$^{3762}$ hath seen$^{3708}$ God$^{2316}$ at any time;$^{4455}$ the$^{3588}$ only begotten$^{3439}$ Son,$^{5207}$ which is$^{5607}$ in$^{1519}$ the$^{3588}$ bosom$^{2859}$ of the$^{3588}$ Father,$^{3962}$ he$^{1565}$ hath declared$^{1834}$ him.

### Jesus Is Uncreated and Eternal

To suggest that God spoke the human Jesus into existence is to misinterpret Scripture. The fact that The Man Christ Jesus (1 Timothy 2:5) was taken out-of-the-bosom-of-God (John 1:18) is what makes Him an uncreated being. It also is what makes Him eternal (John 8:58) and also one with the Father (John 10:30).

For Jesus to become a human being, the Holy Ghost had to span time and space and retrieve the Lamb that was slain (Revelation 13:8)—which was the Man Christ Jesus (1 Timothy 2:5) who was also, the seed of God (Luke 8:11)—and then bring that seed from "out-of-this-world" and deposit it into Mary's womb. That process is what qualified the eternal Spirit (Hebrews 9:14) who was the Son of God and also God, to be born without the Adamic stain of sin (Hebrews 4:15).

### Jesus Brought Within Him His Own Blood

What you need to understand is that when Jesus was born, He was born sin-spotless, because He Had brought within Himself—which is to say within the Eternal Spirit that He is—His own blood, His own water, and His own Glory.

The Apostle John says it beautifully in John 1:14.

> 14 And[2532] the[3588] Word[3056] was made[1096] flesh,[4561] and[2532] dwelt[4637] among[1722] us,[2254] (and[2532] we beheld[2300] his[846] glory,[1391] the glory[1391] as[5613] of the only begotten[3439] of[3844] the Father,)[3962] full[4134] of grace[5485] and[2532] truth.[225]

## If Only Adam Had Not Sinned

Correct biblical interpretation demands that you see the woman as being the first to disobey God (Genesis 3:6a), hence the first to have sinned; hence the first to have died a spiritual death (Genesis 2:17). Think about this: If Adam had not eaten, we would not be having this conversation because the man would not have sinned, and humans would not have perished. Why is this so? It is so because God took the female out of the male. Hence, apart from the male, the female's actions could not have affected anything that was in the male's body.

### By the Sin of One Man, Adam

But, when Adam ate of the tree, the dynamics changed drastically. Adam's blood instantly became sin-contaminated and since the life of all flesh is in the blood (Leviticus 17:11), it meant that the instant Adam ate the life of every unborn seed in his loins also became sin-contaminated.

Remember what I said about seeing the body as a wineskin. Well, now I want you to see your blood and water as milk, which is pure white. Got the picture? Now imagine that sin is black, and I believe it is. Imagine also that the fruit of the forbidden tree produces a black juice. Can you now see, that when the woman ate of the fruit, it released its black juice into her wineskin that contained the pure white milk that is the Word of God?[30] What do you think happened to the milk in Eve's body? It turned black, didn't it?

Let's read Genesis 3:6a, then you decide.

> 6 And when the woman[802] saw[7200] that[3588] the tree[6086] was good[2896] for food,[3978] and that[3588] it[1931] was pleasant[8378] to the eyes,[5869] and a tree[6086] to be desired[2530] to make one wise,[7919] she took[3947] of the fruit[4480] [6529] thereof, and did eat,[398]

At this point, the woman had not yet given any of the fruit to her husband. The blood in her body was the only blood that had become sin-contaminated because up to that point she was the only one who had sinned. She disobeyed because she was deceived (1 Timothy 2:14). But then disaster struck. The Bible says in Genesis 3.6b that she (Eve)

> gave[5414] also[1571] unto her husband[376] with[5973] her; and he did eat.[398]

### That Was the Day Man Died!

What a sad day that was for every unborn human who was still resident in seed form in Adam loins! Sin contaminated all the blood that was in Adam's wineskin and because it did, all unborn humans inherited Adam's sin-nature. While it is true that Adam maintained his spirit-man-image of God, it is certain that he lost God's Glory, which I believe is one and the same with the Genesis 2:7b breath of God. And he lost also God's likeness or holiness of Genesis 5:1. Had Adam and Eve not eaten of the forbidden tree, what a different world we would have today!

## Whatsoever a Man Sows

The Bible is very clear. Galatians 6:7 says,

> 7 Be not³³⁶¹ deceived;⁴¹⁰⁵ God²³¹⁶ is not³⁷⁵⁶ mocked:³⁴⁵⁶ for¹⁰⁶³ whatsoever³⁷³⁹ ¹⁴³⁷ a man⁴⁴⁴ soweth,⁴⁶⁸⁷ that⁵¹²⁴ shall he also²⁵³² reap. ²³²⁵

In Genesis 4:1, the Bible says that Adam *knew* Eve and she conceived. Birth followed conception so when Cain and Abel were born, because their parents' blood was sin-contaminated, their blood also was. The sin that had entered their parents' blood was transferred to their children, and since every human being is a descendant of that first man, Adam, we should have no problem embracing God's Word when it says that "all have sinned and come short of the glory of God" (Romans 3:23).

Now consider this: Hebrews 9:22, says "without the shedding of blood there's no remission of sin." Then, Matthew 7:18 and Luke 6:4 both say that "a corrupt tree cannot bring forth good fruit." For this to make sense, you must see Adam as the tree and his offspring as the fruit. Also, you must see that if Adam was sin-contaminated, then his offspring had to have been sin-contaminated as well.

When God had finished creating, forming, and empowering Adam, the Bible says in that Adam became a living soul (Genesis 2:7b), He became a living soul because God's presence or God's breath was living in his body. But Luke 3:38 tells us that Adam was the son of God. This means that God had removed his presence from Adam's body. God's Word, which is so sharp (Hebrews 4:12), had divided Adam's soul and spirit. Had it not been for sin, all of Adam's children would have borne the sinless and perfect image God. But, because of sin, every human being now bears the image of a fallen and sinful Adam. As spirit-beings, we maintain the image of God but because of sin, we no longer bear God's likeness because not one of us is holy. Only God is!

## The Penalty Applied

The Bible records in Genesis 5:3 that, unlike Adam who was made in the likeness of God, Adam's son Seth was made in the likeness of (sinful) Adam.

> 3 And Adam¹²¹ lived²⁴²¹ a hundred³⁹⁶⁷ and thirty⁷⁹⁷⁰ years,⁸¹⁴¹ and begot³²⁰⁵ a son in his own likeness,¹⁸²³ after his image;⁶⁷⁵⁴ and called⁷¹²¹ ⁸⁵³ his name⁸⁰³⁴ Seth:⁸³⁵²

Therefore, if Seth bore the image of sinful Adam, must it not follow that every human being since born, must bear the same Adamic image? How could it be otherwise? If God is the one who makes a body for every seed (1 Corinthians 15:38) and every seed sown by a male is a sinful seed, mustn't the product of a corrupt seed also be corrupt? You need to understand that when God was in His creative mode, everything He created was perfect. But now, in these times, God in His making mode, and whatsoever the seed is, that is what God makes.

In my case, since I am the product of my daddy's seed and my mother's egg, I am certain that God did not create me. I know for a fact, that He made my body for me, because He did not speak me into existence. I am the product of a sexual act between a man and his wife. My daddy sowed; my mother watered, and God gave my body increase (1 Corinthians 3:6). When I was born, my image was that of a sinful man and that man was a descendant of a sinful Adam. The Bible confirms this. It says that my spirit-man was "born dead in trespasses and sins" (Ephesians 2:1b). And since I was, there is no way I could have been created in the image and likeness of a holy and sinless God. To be sure, I, was shaped in iniquity and in sin did my mother conceive me (Psalms 51:5). Now if that is true for me, I would assume that the same must also be true for you.

Deuteronomy 32:4 states that all God's works are perfect and if we were born sinful, it means that we are far from perfect. It matters not if we had one sin or many sins; with God, the small sin is penalized the same as the big sin. The Apostle James says, When you break any part of the law, you break the whole law (James 2:10). So let me repeat: If Seth was born in the image of sinful Adam, then so too has every human being who has since been born. No one is exempt. As a matter of fact, even Louise Brown, the first "test-tube baby"—a product of her father's sperm and mother's egg conceived in a test tube via IVF—had to have been born with that stain of sin.[31] The Bible is very clear: Adam's sin—that occurred when the woman "gave unto her husband with her and he did eat" (Genesis 3:6c),—forever stained humanity's spiritual DNA.

### Spiritually Separated? How Come?

In 1 Corinthians 15:22, the Bible says,

> 22 For[1063] as[5618] in[1722] Adam[76] all[3956] die,[599] even[2532] so[3779] in[1722] Christ[5547] shall all[3956] be made alive.[2227]

So, if it took sin to spiritually separate Adam from God, what was it that connected Adam spiritually to God in the first place?

- Was it the dust of Genesis 2:7a?
- Was it the breath of life of Genesis 2:7b?
- Was it the spoken word of Genesis 1:27?
- Why does the Bible say that we all died in Adam when the Bible is clear that it was the woman who ate of the tree first?
- Why did we not all die in Eve? Let us look at Genesis 3:6.

> 6 And when the woman[802] saw[7200] that[3588] the tree[6086] was good[2896] for food,[3978] and that[3588] it[1931] was pleasant[8378] to the eyes,[5869] and a tree[6086] to be desired[2530] to make one wise,[7919] she took[3947] of the fruit[4480] [6529] thereof, and did eat,[398] and gave[5414] also[1571] unto her husband[376] with[5973] her; and he did eat.[398]

How was it possible for the entire human race become spiritually separated from God, when as yet, there were no other humans alive save Adam and Eve? You've got to remember that when Adam sinned, he had not yet "known" his wife Eve, and Eve had not as yet given birth to Cain (Genesis 4:1).

## All Were Born Spiritually Dead

Ephesians 2:1b says that everyone was born "dead in trespasses and sins." Most Christians blame Adam for our sinful condition. Yet, for some reason they never hold Eve responsible even though she sinned first. Also, interesting is the fact that even God did not hold Eve responsible. Was God showing favoritism? After all, how was it possible for Adam to have become spiritually separated from God were it not for the fact that he first had to have been spiritually connected to God? And if he was, what was it that connected him spiritually to God?

CHAPTER 10

# THE LOST GLORY

## Bible Verses on the Glory

### Romans 3:23

For all have sinned and come short of the glory of God.

### John 1:14

And the Word was made flesh and dwelt among us (and we beheld his glory, the glory as of the only begotten of the Father) full of grace and truth.

### 2 Corinthian 4:6

For God, who commanded the light to shine out of darkness, hath shined in our hearts, to give the light of the knowledge of the glory of God in the face of Jesus Christ.

### Colossians 1:26-27

Even the mystery which hath been hid from ages and from generations, but now is made manifest to his saints: To whom God would make known what is the riches of the glory of this mystery among the Gentiles, which is Christ in you, the hope of glory.

**1 Corinthians 10:31**

Whether therefore ye eat, or drink, or whatsoever ye do, do all to the glory of God.

**Matthew 6:2**

For thine is the kingdom, and the power, and the glory, forever. Amen.

## Lost Glory

Romans 3:23 tells us that we "all have sinned and come short of the glory of God." It follows that, if we have come short, then it must mean that Adam came short as well. And yet, nowhere in the Genesis story are we told specifically that Adam had any glory. All we are told is that he became a living soul. So, could it be that when God breathed into Adam's nostrils that it was then that he received the glory of God? I am going to suggest to you that the glory of God that we have all come short of is the same glory that Adam and Eve had in the Garden of Eden (Genesis 2:7b).

1. That glory is the same glory that every believer regains access to when he or she confesses Jesus Christ as Lord and Savior (John 1:12; Romans 10:9).

2. That glory is wrapped up as the free gift of salvation that we receive and not because of any works that we may have done. The Bible says we are all saved by grace, through faith, and our salvation is the gift of God (Ephesians 2:8).

3. That glory is not a spirit of fear, as we read in 2 Timothy 1:7.

    7 For[1063] God[2316] hath not[3756] given[1325] us[2254] the spirit[4151] of fear;[1167] but[235] of power,[1411] and[2532] of love,[26] and[2532] of a sound mind.[4995]

It is important to note that for the person who believes, it is that person's confession of faith in Jesus Christ as Lord and Savior that grants him access to the lost glory. In John 14:6, Jesus said that He is "the way, the truth, and the life: no man cometh unto the Father," but by Him. That one way is the believer's confession of faith. That person's spirit-man must surrender and make Jesus Christ Lord and Savior of his life. No works are necessary, and none are accepted.

Here's what the Bible says in Hebrews 2:3,

> How shall we escape, if we neglect so great salvation; which at the first began to be spoken by the Lord, and was confirmed unto us by them that heard him?

And in Hebrews 2:10,

> For it became him, for whom are all things, and by whom are all things, in bringing many sons unto glory, to make the captain of their salvation perfect through sufferings.

A believer's faithfulness and obedience to God's Word is what guarantees him or her the assurance that when Jesus returns, he or she shall have that glory restored for all eternity, "and so shall we ever be with the Lord" (1 Thessalonians 4:17).

Until that time, according to 1 Peter 1:5, we

> are kept by the power of God through faith unto salvation ready to be revealed in the last time. And this salvation, is the salvation.

In 1 Peter 1:10,

> Of which salvation the prophets have inquired and searched diligently, who prophesied of the grace that should come unto you.

In Colossians, Chapter 1, verses 26 and 27, the Apostle Paul describes this glory as

> this mystery which hath been hid from ages and from generations, but now is made manifest to his saints: To whom God would make known what is the riches of the glory of this mystery among the Gentiles, which is Christ in you, the hope of glory.

So, as I wrap up this chapter, it is my position that the glory of God of which we've all come short is the glory that we regain when we accept Jesus Christ as Lord and Savior. That Glory is Christ in us, our hope of Glory (Colossians 1:27)!

Because He came into me and is now living in me, I can say with authority, that "greater is he that is in me, than he that is in the world" (1 John 4:4). If you've accepted Jesus Christ as Lord and Savior, you too, can say the same. That's enough to give God praise! Hallelujah!

## Sin and Mankind

### Those Imaginative Toddlers

Would you agree that toddlers who are just learning to speak have imaginations? Would you also agree that each has a memory and a conscience? Do you know of anyone who can be more imaginative than a toddler? Do you know of anyone who can tell a lie more sincerely and more innocently than a toddler? "Who took the cookie?" you ask. "Not me!" That's a common response, right? So, who taught him how to lie? Could it have been his parents?

I refuse to believe that any parent would intentionally teach his kids to lie. And yet kids do. Why? We live in a time when kids seem to be learning to lie younger and younger—almost as if lying were etched indelibly into their spiritual DNA. May I tell you? It is!

## What's the First Sin and When?

In Romans 3:23, the Bible says, "All have sinned and come short of the glory of God."

Do you know that when God confronted Adam and Eve, the very first sin they committed was lying? Disobeying God by eating of the forbidden tree was the first sin recorded, but when God confronted them, lying was their first sin. I wonder if that's why God hates liars (Proverbs 6:16-17).

The Bible account goes like this: God asked a question. The male blamed the female. The female blamed the serpent. And the poor old serpent didn't have a leg on which to stand. You can read the account in Genesis 3, verses 9-14. And incidentally, have you ever noticed that in addition to lying, most kids would disobey, and most kids would covet— "want"— what's not theirs?

## Seven Sins in the Garden

Think about this: Our children are born into this world with nothing but the ability to suck, cry, and poop; and then as they grow, instinctively, they all seem to do things that parents, and others despise. How is that possible? Who taught our children such a disgustingly bad habit as lying? May I tell you? It all started in the Garden. When Adam sinned, it was then that every member of humanity inherited the sin nature and we inherited not just one sin but at least seven!

Here's the scenario: Both Adam and Eve have just eaten of the forbidden tree. God showed up on the scene, and He questioned them. They displayed signs of the following:

1. **Fear.** The first thing that they did was go and hide. But of the believer, the Bible says that God has not given us a spirit of fear. My thinking is if God did not give us a spirit of fear (2 Timothy 1:7), then neither could He have given one to Adam and Eve. So where did fear originate?

2. **Lying.** Next, both Adam and Eve lied to God when He questioned them. The devil is the only creature of whom the Bible that he says was a sinner from the beginning (1 John 3:8). So, who influenced Adam and Eve to lie to God?
3. **Disobedience.** When the woman ate, she disobeyed God. When the man ate, he disobeyed as well (Genesis 3:6). However, when God commanded the man to not eat of the tree, He had not yet taken one of Adam's ribs and made the woman!
4. **Deception.** In the New Testament, the Bible says, that the woman was "deceived" yet the man sinned willfully (1 Timothy 2:14). Why did the man do that? We'll talk about that later.

In the meantime, be aware that Jesus tells us in 1 John 2:16 that all that's in the world are the

5. **The lust of the flesh**
6. **The lust of the eyes**
7. **The pride of life**

In addition to those seven sins that originated in the Garden of Eden, let's not forget the sin of iniquity. Chronologically, this is the first recorded sin and I have reason to believe that Lucifer committed that sin somewhere between Genesis 1:1 *when God created the heavens and the earth,* and Genesis 1:2 *when the earth became void.* Psalm 18, verses 7 to 15, and Jeremiah 4, verses 23 to 28 give us an account of what caused the earth to become void. Second Peter 3, verses 5 to 7, recorded the event, but in addition, he gave us advance notice of what's to come.

Speaking of Lucifer, Ezekiel 28:15 records that Lucifer was "perfect" when he was created, "till iniquity was found in him." 1 John 3:8 says that the devil (also known as Lucifer) "sinneth from the beginning." So, be assured that every newborn begins his life with the potential to commit those eight sins. This is so because the ability to sin is part of his nature. And that sin nature in embedded in his blood and ours.

Hebrews 9:22 says that "without (the) shedding of blood, there is no remission (of our sin)." What that means is, until we shed the blood which keeps us physically alive, we will never be rid of sin-nature or our ability to commit sin. It was to get rid of our sin nature and restore us into right standing with God, that "the Son of God was manifested, that he might destroy the works of the devil" (1 John 3:8b).

**Now This Is Important**

In addition to those seven sins, please do NOT overlook the fact that when Adam yielded his members to Satan, he became a servant of Satan. And, as you recall, before Lucifer had fallen to earth at which time he became Satan, he was the star performer in heaven. Of Lucifer, the Bible says that he (Lucifer) "was created perfect in all his ways until the day that iniquity was found" in him (Ezekiel 28:15).

Could this be why the Psalmist says in Psalms 51:5 that he "was shapen in iniquity; and in sin did (his) mother conceive (him)?" I think so.

**Born in Sin; Shaped in Iniquity**

Would you like to know why toddlers lie, disobey and are covetous, even though no one taught them how? It all started in the Garden. You must remember that when God placed Adam and Eve in the Garden, they were both perfect.

No one knows how long Adam and Eve existed in sheer perfection. All we know is that one day they sinned and the first two human beings who were perfect became imperfect. Because of that day the Bible says that "there is none righteous, no not one" (Romans 3:10).

Now before proceeding, I need to tell you one thing I learned about Bible interpretation. I learned that whatsoever is in the New Testament (NT) is the revealed Word of God and whatsoever is in the Old (OT) is the concealed Word of God. I learned, that if I saw something in the New Testament, I should search the Old Testament for a type and shadow of whatever it was I saw in the New.

## Personal Thoughts

So, would you allow me to share two things with you? I have no intention of making a doctrine out of what follows, but I would be very curious to know your thoughts. Here goes:

### Greater Love Has No Man

John 15:13 says,

> 13 Greater[3187] love[26] hath[2192] no man[3762] than this,[5026] that[2443] a man[5100] lay down[5087] his[848] life[5590] for[5228] his[848] friends.[5384]

Many Bible scholars and others believe that, when Adam sinned, every human being past, present, and future sinned in him, even though when Adam sinned, only he and Eve were alive, and as yet no other humans had been born (Romans 5:12, 19).

The Bible confirms that sin entered the entire human race when Adam ate of the tree (Genesis 3:6c), even though the record states that it was the woman who was the first to eat of the forbidden tree (Genesis 3.6a.

Now in Matthew 12:45 and Luke 11:26, Jesus stated that when the enemy comes and sees a house empty, he goes and gets seven of his friends then he invites them to occupy that empty house.

Let's return to the Garden. Eve and Adam have just eaten of the tree. What did God do? From my perspective the minute they sinned, God withdrew His Genesis 2:7 breath from within their bodies and Satan took up residence. If we view our bodies as the house for our spirit-man, and if we accept that there was a time when God tabernacled in that house with Adam, then what was the condition Adam's house, when God left?

Correct answer: The house would have become empty of God's presence because God's Spirit vacated Adam's house, and Satan moved in along with a few of his minions. Let's prove that.

## From God of Heaven to God of This World

As per Jesus, once a man's house becomes empty then it opens the door for the unclean spirit to move in and take up residence (Matthew 12:43-45). To be empty meant that Adam's house was devoid of God's spiritual protection and unprotected from spiritual invasion. Since God's Spirit was no longer a resident in Adam's body, the empty state of Adam's body paved the way for Satan and his seven devils to move in and occupy.

I believe this is what happened. I also believe that when Satan moved in and occupied, he brought with him the seven devils of Deception, Disobedience, Lying, Fear, Lust of the flesh, Lust of the eyes, and the Pride of life.

What you've got to come to terms with is the fact that when the God of heaven withdrew His presence from within the body of the human Adam (Genesis 3:6b), the space that God once occupied in the human heart did not just stay empty.

Once Satan saw Adam's house empty, I believe he acted very swiftly and took with him, "seven other spirits more wicked than himself, and they entered in and dwelled there" (Matthew 7:45).

Why do I believe this to be so? I believe it to be so because in Romans 6:16 the Bible says,

> Know ye not, that to whom ye yield yourselves servants to obey, his servants ye are to whom ye obey; whether of sin unto death or of obedience unto righteousness.

And although that verse appears in the New Testament, I believe it was Adam's sinful act (Genesis 3:6b) that caused God to inspire Paul to write that verse in the Book of Romans.

You know, I have always heard it said that we were born spiritually separated from God and apart from the sins of disobedience and deception no one that I know has ever enumerated the seven sins I mentioned above. But we all know that we do not have to teach babies to lie or covet or steal or lust.

Now God's Word clearly stated that: "the day you eat, you shall surely die" (Genesis 2:17). By interpretation, therefore, it can mean only one thing—and that is, that when the woman ate, she died spiritually. Greater love has no man.

So, when John 15:13 says that "greater love hath no man than to lay down his life for his friend" could Adam have been the man who laid down his life for his friend?

### Did Jesus Die for His Friends?

The record shows that on Crucifixion Day, Jesus had not one friend in the world. The cry of the day was "Crucify Him" (Mark 15:13-14). All His disciples had abandoned Him (Mark 14:50). If we want to take it to the extreme, on Crucifixion Day, not only did God abandon Him (Matthew 27:46) but so did everyone else. Romans 5:10 confirms that on Crucifixion Day, everyone was Jesus' enemy.

### Could This Be Love?

Many commentators have portrayed Adam as being a type of Christ, and I think he was. Because as I see it when Adam ate of the tree, effectively he had sacrificed spending eternity with God preferring instead to suffer spiritual death or spiritual separation from God just to be with Eve, who was the bone of his bone and the flesh of his flesh.

Now, if that is not what's called agape (*ag-ah'-pay*) or unconditional love, I don't know what is. But it makes you wonder, doesn't it? At least it should. But remember now, I'm not going to build a doctrine on that. Okay?

## Another Personal Thought

### While the Watchman Slept

Now, since I'm at it, let me throw you another curve ball: Jesus was in a parable-speaking mode. He said in Matthew 13:24-25: "The kingdom of heaven is likened unto a man which sowed good seed in his field: But while men slept, his enemy came and sowed tares among the wheat, and went his way." Luke 8:11 says that the "seed is the word of God." And Matthew 13:38 says, "The good seed are the children of the kingdom, but the tares are the children of the wicked one." So, here are some questions for you.

**Questions**

1. Could the Garden of Eden have been the field where the Sower sowed the good seed (Genesis 2:8)?
2. Could Adam and Eve have been the good seeds which were the children of the kingdom (Matthew 13:38)?
3. If that were true, then, when God had planted them in the Garden, what word did God sow in their hearts?
4. Did He not say, the day you eat you shall surely die (Genesis 2:16-17)?
5. What word did the enemy sow (Genesis 3:4-5)?
6. Did the enemy not say you shall not surely die (Genesis 3:4)?
7. In type and in shadow, is it not feasible to think that while the watchman Adam slept, the enemy, who is that old serpent the devil (Revelation 12:9; 20:2) moved in and deceived Eve (1 Timothy 2:14)?
8. And, if all that were true, then in type and shadow could we not interpret John 15:13 in such a way that we see Adam as the one who had the greater love to lay down his life for his friend, because she was "bone of his bone and flesh of his flesh" (John 15:13)?

I think we could. I do not think that such an interpretation is far-fetched at all. Remember now, on Crucifixion Day, Jesus had zero friends. Everyone had deserted Him. But if you recall in Matthew 5:46, He had counseled his disciples and told them to "bless them that curse you and pray for them which despitefully use you." Those words of His became manifest when He was on the cross because it was while He was on the cross, that He prayed for His enemies. He said in Luke 23:34, "Father, forgive them; for they know not what they do." I submit to you, that if you can bring yourself to see Adam as one who had the greater love and laid down his life for his friend, Eve, then you should have no problem embracing Jesus as one who had a love that was far greater than Adam's seeing that He (Jesus) laid down His life for His enemies. Remember now, the Bible does say that "when we were enemies (of God) we were reconciled to God by the death of his Son" (Romans 5:10).

Because of the precious blood of the lamb of God that was shed on Calvary's Cross, everyone has been given an opportunity to be reconciled with God.

## From Where Did Adam's Blood and Water Come?

So, here's a question for you: Where did Adam's blood and water come from? As we examine the creation story, we see that

1. God created man (Genesis 1:27).
2. God blessed man (Genesis 1:28).
3. God named man (Genesis 5:1-2).
4. God took dust and formed man (Genesis 2:7a); and finally
5. God breathed the breath of life into the nostrils of man and man became a living soul (Genesis 2:7b).

Search the Bible all you want; you will not find anything else that describes the process of how humans came to be. And yet, one does not have to be a heart specialist or a medical doctor to know that a person's body contains about five and one-half quarts of blood[32] and 60 percent or ten gallons of his weight in water![33]

So, my question is: From where or whom did Adam get his blood and water?

Let me tell you what I believe; and when I am through, I'll leave it up to you to agree with me or disagree, is that all right?

And by the way, let me share this with you: I owe this explanation to my brother Lawrence. He was the one who asked the question that crystallized my thinking and helped me come up with the answer you're about to read. Way to go, Bro. Jesus loves you. And God has a plan for your life. Here goes:

## When Cain slew Abel

Now, here's the deal: When Cain slew Abel, do you remember what God said, according to Genesis 4:10:

> 10 And he said,[559] What[4100] hast thou done?[6213] the voice[6963] of thy brother's[251] blood[1818] crieth[6817] unto[413] me from[4480] the ground.[127]

From that verse, we learn two things about blood: (1) blood has a voice and (2) blood can cry.

In the Book of Leviticus, chapter 17, Moses was laying down the ceremonial law concerning blood sacrifices, and he said in verse 11:

> 11 For[3588] the life[5315] of the flesh[1320] is in the blood:[1818] and I[589] have given[5414] it to you upon[5921] the altar[4196] to make an atonement[3722] for[5921] your souls:[5315] for[3588] it[1931] is the blood[1818] that maketh an atonement[3722] for the soul.[5315]

In the Old Testament, the blood sacrifice represented life and death. Also, it represented freedom from Pharaoh at the first Passover. In the New Testament, it represents remission (of sin). Hebrews 9:22 states "… almost all things are by the law purged with blood; and without shedding of blood is no remission."

Note: In the passage above (Leviticus 17:11) you will see that the Strong's concordance number for the word "life" and the words "soul" and "souls" is the same, #5315, which translates to the word nephesh.[34] "Nephesh" is the same word that the Bible uses when it says that "man became a living soul" (Genesis 2:7). So, Leviticus chapter 17:11 is clear. The life is in the blood.

Now that we know that the life is in the blood, let's answer the question: How did the blood and water get in Adam's body? The Bible records that (1) God created Adam with His spoken word (Genesis 1:27); (2) God used dust to form Adam's body; and He used His breath of life, to cause Adam to become a living soul. Nowhere in the creation story is either blood or water mentioned. So, How did the blood and the water get into Adam's body?

Here's my take: The Bible says that the mystery of godliness is great (1 Timothy 3:16); and, to understand this mystery, I asked God for wisdom, as is recommended in James 1:5.

> 5 $^{1161}$ If$^{1487}$ any$^{5100}$ of you$^{5216}$ lack$^{3007}$ wisdom,$^{4678}$ let him ask$^{154}$ of$^{3844}$ God,$^{2316}$ that giveth$^{1325}$ to all$^{3956}$ men liberally,$^{574}$ and$^{2532}$ upbraideth$^{3679}$ not;$^{3361}$ and$^{2532}$ it shall be given$^{1325}$ him.$^{846}$

Here's what He told the Apostle John to tell everyone who asks (John 1:4).

> 4 In$^{1722}$ him$^{846}$ was$^{2258}$ life.$^{2222}$

By referring to John 1:1, the "Him" in John 1:4 is the Eternal Spirit of God, who is the maker all things. In Colossians 1:16, "Him" is that same Spirit, only this time, in context, He is the Creator of all things.

> 16 For$^{3754}$ by$^{1722}$ him$^{846}$ were all things$^{3956}$ created,$^{2936}$ that$^{3588}$ are in$^{1722}$ heaven,$^{3772}$ and$^{2532}$ that$^{3588}$ are in$^{1909}$ earth,$^{1093}$ visible$^{3707}$ and$^{2532}$ invisible,$^{517}$ whether$^{1535}$ they be thrones,$^{2362}$ or$^{1535}$ dominions,$^{2963}$ or$^{1535}$ principalities,$^{746}$ or$^{1535}$ powers:$^{1849}$ all things$^{3956}$ were created$^{2936}$ by$^{1223}$ him,$^{846}$ and$^{2532}$ for$^{1519}$ him:$^{846}$

1 Timothy 2:5 represents God's Son as "the man Christ Jesus." And, as the man, He is the uncreated and sinless Spirit-man who is the ONE Mediator between God and Man. To say it differently, He is the equivalent of the Logos of John 1:1, minus His deity (Philippians 2:7).

When Jesus Christ as the "Word of God" was creating the universe in Genesis 1:1, the "man Christ Jesus" of 1 Timothy 2:5 had not as yet been made manifest as a human being.

Thousands of years would pass before that would occur and when it did, it was the Apostle John who got the privilege of telling us in John 1:14 that "the Word was made flesh."

According to Matthew, that son that God sent, and Mary conceived in her womb, was of the Holy Ghost. Galatians 4:4, informs us that "He was made of a woman, made under the law." Being made under the law and being born of a woman was necessary for Jesus because in Genesis 2:24, God established the process through which procreation must occur. And since God had given man DOMINION in the Earth, God could not violate His Word! Several Bible verses confirm this: Revelation 19:13; John 1:1, 1:3, 1:14; Colossians 1:16; 1 Timothy 2:5; Matthew 1:21; Mark 1:1; 1 John 1:2; Hebrews 10:5; Genesis 1:1; and Galatians 4:4.

And of that same Jesus, John said later (1 John 1:2,

> 2 For[2532] the[3588] life[2222] was manifested,[5319] and[2532] we have seen[3708] it, and[2532] bear witness,[3140] and[2532] show[518] unto you[5213] that **eternal**[166] life,[2222] which[3748] was[2258] with[4314] the[3588] Father,[3962] and[2532] was manifested[5319] unto us.[2254]

CHAPTER 11

# THE RESTORED GLORY

## Bible Verses

**1 Thessalonians 5:23**

23 And[1161] the[3588] very[846] God[2316] of peace[1515] sanctify[37] you[5209] wholly;[3651] and[2532] I pray God your[5216] whole[3648] spirit[4151] and[2532] soul[5590] and[2532] body[4983] be preserved[5083] blameless[274] unto[1722] the[3588] coming[3952] of our[2257] Lord[2962] Jesus[2424] Christ.[5547]

**Romans 10:9-10**

9 That[3754] if[1437] thou shalt confess[3670] with[1722] thy[4675] mouth[4750] the Lord[2962] Jesus,[2424] and[2532] shalt believe[4100] in[1722] thine[4675] heart[2588] that[3754] God[2316] hath raised[1453] him[846] from[1537] the dead,[3498] thou shalt be saved.[4982]

10 For[1063] with the heart[2588] man believeth[4100] unto[1519] righteousness;[1343] and[1161] with the mouth[4750] confession is made[3670] unto[1519] salvation.[4991]

## The Value of the Soul?

I define the soul as the Spirit of God that takes up residence in the body of each human who confesses Jesus Christ as His Lord and Savior. The soul was and is so valuable to God that even before Adam sinned, God had already set a predestined time to send His Only Begotten Son (John 3:16)—also known as the Man Christ Jesus (1 Timothy 2:5)—to redeem or buy back the souls of men so that every human being can have the opportunity to have the glory of God restored and become once again a son of God.

Remember, it was Adam's sin that caused a spiritual disconnect between God and man. And it is a believer's confession-of-faith in the finished work of the cross that restores that connection.

When we read 1 Thessalonians 5:23 what we see is that the Thessalonians were the first ones on record to whom Paul acknowledged that they had believed in the finished work of the cross and had accepted the risen Christ as their Savior. We know this because the Apostle Paul told them that they are body, soul, and spirit. What he meant was, that they were body, spirit, and redeemed soul. It should interest you to know that the Bible identifies only three groups of people in all creation. They are Jews, Gentiles, and the Christians who are belong to the Church that Jesus is building and against which the gates of hell shall not prevail (Matthew 16:18).

Those three groups are further subdivided into two other groups, namely (1) those who are in Adam, and (2) those who are in Christ.

In 1 Corinthian 15:22, the Bible says, "in Adam **ALL** die, even so in Christ shall **ALL** be made alive."[35]

Specifically, those in Adam include

1. The inner spirit-man of every person who is alive who has not yet accepted Jesus Christ as Savior.

2. The inner spirit-man of every person who lived and died and did not accept Jesus Christ as Savior; and
3. The inner spirit-man of every person yet to be born.

Ephesians 2:1b tells us that every person, whether male or female, is born physically alive yet spiritually dead in trespasses and sins.

Those in Christ would include everyone who has accepted Jesus Christ as Lord and Savior and has become spiritually alive; they now live in the hope of spending eternity in heaven with God.

## Getting into Christ: The Process

### Here Is How You Get into Christ

Romans 10:9-10 says,

> 9 That$^{3754}$ if$^{1437}$ thou shalt confess$^{3670}$ with$^{1722}$ thy$^{4675}$ mouth$^{4750}$ the Lord$^{2962}$ Jesus,$^{2424}$ and$^{2532}$ shalt believe$^{4100}$ in$^{1722}$ thine$^{4675}$ heart$^{2588}$ that$^{3754}$ God$^{2316}$ hath raised$^{1453}$ him$^{846}$ from$^{1537}$ the dead,$^{3498}$ thou shalt be saved.$^{4982}$
>
> 10 For$^{1063}$ with the heart$^{2588}$ man believeth$^{4100}$ unto$^{1519}$ righteousness;$^{1343}$ and$^{1161}$ with the mouth$^{4750}$ confession is made$^{3670}$ unto$^{1519}$ salvation.$^{4991}$

Now, I ask you this: How is it possible for the world's current population of 7.9 billion people and counting to all be born dead in Adam in trespasses and sins?

And how is it possible for only those who accept Jesus Christ as Lord and Savior to be made spiritually alive?

Obviously, for each person to have been born spiritually "dead in trespasses and sins" (Ephesians 2:1; Colossians 2:13), it must mean that there had to have been a time when everyone was spiritually alive? And that time could only have been when we were all spiritual seeds in Adam's loins.

## From Adamic Man, to Human, to Living Soul

In chapter one, I enumerated fifteen definitions of the soul. When I apply any one of those definitions to Adam, I conclude that a "living soul" is not something that Adam was but rather it was something that he became. In Genesis 2:7a, when

> the Lord God[430] formed[3335] [853] man[120] of the dust[6083] of[4480] the ground,[127]

Adam was just a sinless human being, and his body was a house for his inner spirit-man. But, then God

> breathed[5301] into his nostrils[639] the breath[5397] of life;[2416] and man[120] became[1961] a living[2416] soul.[5315]

Therefore, I am saying that when Adam received God's breath (Genesis 2:7b), it was then that he received the Holy Spirit, and in an instant just as it happens to every believer Adam's body became the Temple of the Holy Spirit according to 1Corinthians 6:19.

When we read the genealogy of Jesus in the Book of Luke, chapter 3, we need to note that in verse 38c, it says, "Adam,76 was the son of God.2316"

So, what was it about Adam that made him the son of God? We find the answer in the New Testament, in John 1:12-13, where John says,

> 12 But[1161] as many as[3745] received[2983] him,[846] to them[846] gave[1325] he power[1849] to become[1096] the sons[5043] of God,[2316] even to them that believe[4100] on[1519] his[846] name:[3686]
>
> 13 Which[3739] were born,[1080] not[3756] of[1537] blood,[129] nor[3761] of[1537] the will[2307] of the flesh,[4561] nor[3761] of[1537] the will[2307] of man,[435] but[235] of[1537] God.[2316]

### The Law of First Mention

There is in Scripture a principle called The Law of First Mention. That principle means that whenever a term appears for the first time, whatever meaning was applied to that term first, that meaning must remain constant for every successive interpretation.

In John 1:12, we find the first mention of what it takes to become a son of God. Now, I admit that the Book of John is in the New Testament. However, in this case, the principle of the Law of First Mention has to be applied retroactively.

The Bible does not tell us what God did to Adam for Him to call Adam the son of God; but we know this about God: God is no respecter of persons (Acts 10:34). What God does for one, He is obligated to do it for all! If He gives the Holy Spirit to all who believe, then he had to have done the same for Adam.

And if God, did it for Adam, then He had to have done the same for Jesus even if it were only for the benefit of all who were present. Here's the Bible verse that confirms this, Matthew 3:15-17. Jesus is speaking to John:

> 15 And$^{1161}$ Jesus$^{2424}$ answering$^{611}$ said$^{2036}$ unto$^{4314}$ him,$^{846}$ Suffer$^{863}$ it to be so now:$^{737}$ for$^{1063}$ thus$^{3779}$ it$^{2076}$ becometh$^{4241}$ us$^{2254}$ to fulfill$^{4137}$ all$^{3956}$ righteousness.$^{1343}$ Then$^{5119}$ he suffered$^{863}$ him.$^{846}$
>
> 16 And$^{2532}$ Jesus,$^{2424}$ when he was baptized,$^{907}$ went up$^{305}$ straightway$^{2117}$ out of$^{575}$ the$^{3588}$ water:$^{5204}$ and,$^{2532}$ lo,$^{2400}$ the$^{3588}$ heavens$^{3772}$ were opened$^{455}$ unto him,$^{846}$ and$^{2532}$ he saw$^{1492}$ the$^{3588}$ Spirit$^{4151}$ of God$^{2316}$ descending$^{2597}$ like$^{5616}$ a dove,$^{4058}$ and$^{2532}$ lighting$^{2064}$ upon$^{1909}$ him:$^{846}$
>
> 17 And$^{2532}$ lo$^{2400}$ a voice$^{5456}$ from$^{1537}$ heaven,$^{3772}$ saying,$^{3004}$ This$^{3778}$ is$^{2076}$ my$^{3450}$ beloved$^{27}$ Son,$^{5207}$ in$^{1722}$ whom$^{3739}$ I am well pleased.$^{2106}$

## Jesus Did Not Need to Be Baptized, But We Do

What I am saying is, Jesus did not need to be baptized to become something that He already was—God's only begotten Son. Yet, for our benefit, and to demonstrate for us the process that we need to follow to become sons of God, it is written in Philippians 2:6-8, Jesus

> 6 Who,$^{3739}$ being$^{5225}$ in$^{1722}$ the form$^{3444}$ of God,$^{2316}$ thought$^{2233}$ it not$^{3756}$ robbery$^{725}$ to be$^{1511}$ equal$^{2470}$ with God:$^{2316}$
>
> 7 But$^{235}$ made himself of no reputation,$^{2758}$ $^{1438}$ and took$^{2983}$ upon him the form$^{3444}$ of a servant,$^{1401}$ and was made$^{1096}$ in$^{1722}$ the likeness$^{3667}$ of men:$^{444}$
>
> 8 And$^{2532}$ being found$^{2147}$ in fashion$^{4976}$ as$^{5613}$ a man,$^{444}$ he humbled$^{5013}$ himself,$^{1438}$ and became$^{1096}$ obedient$^{5255}$ unto$^{3360}$ death,$^{2288}$ even$^{1161}$ the death$^{2288}$ of the cross.$^{4716}$

Baptism for Jesus was just a preliminary but necessary step on the way to the cross. It was necessary because through it He showed us what we needed to do to identify with Him and be accepted by God.

Colossians 2:12 puts it this way:

> 12 Buried with$^{4916}$ him$^{846}$ in$^{1722}$ baptism,$^{908}$ wherein$^{1722}$ $^{3739}$ also$^{2532}$ ye are risen with$^{4891}$ him through$^{1223}$ the$^{3588}$ faith$^{4102}$ of the$^{3588}$ operation$^{1753}$ of God,$^{2316}$ who hath raised$^{1453}$ him$^{846}$ from$^{1537}$ the$^{3588}$ dead.$^{3498}$

## If Us, Then Adam

Therefore, I submit, that if believers must receive Jesus Christ as Lord and Savior to become spiritually alive and eventually become a son of God then for Adam the same principle would have had to have held true, or God wouldn't be God.

Please note that today, because we were all born in sin when a person receives Jesus Christ as Lord and Savior, he is only given the power to become a son of God. He (that is his entire being) does not instantly become a son of God. Salvation, you see, is a threefold process.

My pastor, Dr. Amar Rambisoon, is very clear on this point. He says that when a person accepts Jesus Christ as Lord and Savior, three things happen, and they are progressive in nature.[36]

1. **The inner spirit-man of that person is saved from the penalty of sin.** He was born spiritually dead (Ephesians 2:1b). Now his confession of faith in the finished work of the cross restores him into right standing with God (Romans 10:9); and God forgives all sins committed up to that time. As a matter of fact, God takes them and buries them in the deepest ocean, and He remembers them no more (Micah 7:18-19).

2. **The inner spirit-man of that person is being saved from the power of sin.** Having confessed Jesus as Lord, then spiritually speaking the person receives the Spirit of the risen Christ (John 1:12; Colossians 2:6; 1 Corinthians 2:12) who comes and lives in him (1 John 4:4) along with the Spirit of the Holy Ghost (Acts 19:2), the Spirit of God (Romans 8:9, 14).

3. And finally, **the entire person shall be saved from the very presence of sin.** The first is immediate, the second is progressive daily, and the third is future and final. The third occurs when the rapture comes.

Be blessed as you read (1 Corinthians 15:50-58) and see what's in store for all who choose to believe:

> 50 Now[1161] this[5124] I say,[5346] brethren,[80] that[3754] flesh[4561] and[2532] blood[129] cannot[1410 3756] inherit[2816] the kingdom[932] of God;[2316] neither[3761] doth corruption[5356] inherit[2816] incorruption.[861]
>
> 51 Behold,[2400] I show[3004] you[5213] a mystery;[3466] We shall not[3756] all[3956] sleep,[2837] but[1161] we shall all[3956] be changed,[236]

52 In¹⁷²² a moment,⁸²³ in¹⁷²² the twinkling⁴⁴⁹³ of an eye,³⁷⁸⁸ at¹⁷²² the³⁵⁸⁸ last²⁰⁷⁸ trump:⁴⁵³⁶ for¹⁰⁶³ the trumpet shall sound,⁴⁵³⁷ and²⁵³² the³⁵⁸⁸ dead³⁴⁹⁸ shall be raised¹⁴⁵³ incorruptible,⁸⁶² and²⁵³² we²²⁴⁹ shall be changed.²³⁶

53 For¹⁰⁶³ this⁵¹²⁴ corruptible⁵³⁴⁹ must¹¹⁶³ put on¹⁷⁴⁶ incorruption,⁸⁶¹ and²⁵³² this⁵¹²⁴ mortal²³⁴⁹ must put on¹⁷⁴⁶ immortality.¹¹⁰

54 So¹¹⁶¹ when³⁷⁵² this⁵¹²⁴ corruptible⁵³⁴⁹ shall have put on¹⁷⁴⁶ incorruption,⁸⁶¹ and²⁵³² this⁵¹²⁴ mortal²³⁴⁹ shall have put on¹⁷⁴⁶ immortality,¹¹⁰ then⁵¹¹⁹ shall be brought to pass¹⁰⁹⁶ the³⁵⁸⁸ saying³⁰⁵⁶ that is written,¹¹²⁵ Death²²⁸⁸ is swallowed up²⁶⁶⁶ in¹⁵¹⁹ victory.³⁵³⁴

55 O death,²²⁸⁸ where⁴²²⁶ is thy⁴⁶⁷⁵ sting?²⁷⁵⁹ O grave,⁸⁶ where⁴²²⁶ is thy⁴⁶⁷⁵ victory?³⁵³⁴

56 ¹¹⁶¹ The³⁵⁸⁸ sting²⁷⁵⁹ of death²²⁸⁸ is sin;²⁶⁶ and¹¹⁶¹ the³⁵⁸⁸ strength¹⁴¹¹ of sin²⁶⁶ is the³⁵⁸⁸ law.³⁵⁵¹

57 But¹¹⁶¹ thanks⁵⁴⁸⁵ be to God,²³¹⁶ which giveth¹³²⁵ us²²⁵⁴ the³⁵⁸⁸ victory³⁵³⁴ through¹²²³ our²²⁵⁷ Lord²⁹⁶² Jesus²⁴²⁴ Christ.⁵⁵⁴⁷

58 Therefore,⁵⁶²⁰ my³⁴⁵⁰ beloved²⁷ brethren,⁸⁰ be¹⁰⁹⁶ ye steadfast,¹⁴⁷⁶ unmovable,²⁷⁷ always³⁸⁴² abounding⁴⁰⁵² in¹⁷²² the³⁵⁸⁸ work²⁰⁴¹ of the³⁵⁸⁸ Lord,²⁹⁶² forasmuch as ye know¹⁴⁹² that³⁷⁵⁴ your⁵²¹⁶ labor²⁸⁷³ is²⁰⁷⁶ not³⁷⁵⁶ in vain²⁷⁵⁶ in¹⁷²² the Lord.²⁹⁶²

And let's not forget 1 Thessalonians 4:15-17:

15 For¹⁰⁶³ this⁵¹²⁴ we say³⁰⁰⁴ unto you⁵²¹³ by¹⁷²² the word³⁰⁵⁶ of the Lord,²⁹⁶² that³⁷⁵⁴ we²²⁴⁹ which are alive²¹⁹⁸ and remain⁴⁰³⁵ unto¹⁵¹⁹ the³⁵⁸⁸ coming³⁹⁵² of the³⁵⁸⁸ Lord²⁹⁶² shall not³³⁶⁴ prevent⁵³⁴⁸ them which are asleep.²⁸³⁷

16 For³⁷⁵⁴ the³⁵⁸⁸ Lord²⁹⁶² himself⁸⁴⁶ shall descend²⁵⁹⁷ from⁵⁷⁵ heaven³⁷⁷² with¹⁷²² a shout,²⁷⁵² with¹⁷²² the voice⁵⁴⁵⁶ of the

archangel,⁷⁴³ and²⁵³² with¹⁷²² the trump⁴⁵³⁶ of God:²³¹⁶ and²⁵³² the³⁵⁸⁸ dead³⁴⁹⁸ in¹⁷²² Christ⁵⁵⁴⁷ shall rise⁴⁵⁰ first:⁴⁴¹²

17 Then¹⁸⁹⁹ we²²⁴⁹ which are alive²¹⁹⁸ and remain⁴⁰³⁵ shall be caught up⁷²⁶ together²⁶⁰ with⁴⁸⁶² them⁸⁴⁶ in¹⁷²² the clouds³⁵⁰⁷ to meet¹⁵¹⁹ ⁵²⁹ the³⁵⁸⁸ Lord²⁹⁶² in¹⁵¹⁹ the air:¹⁰⁹ and²⁵³² so³⁷⁷⁹ shall we ever³⁸⁴² be²⁰⁷¹ with⁴⁸⁶² the Lord.²⁹⁶²

When the above happens, and we are changed, it is only then that we who have accepted Jesus Christ as Lord and Savior shall be saved from the very presence of sin.

From the minute, we receive Jesus, we become a work in progress. And each person must begin and continue to work out his own salvation with fear and trembling (Philippians 2:12). As we work out our salvation, others should notice significant changes in our behaviors. More and more we should be becoming more like Christ. Why? Because He is our Lord; and as our Lord, He is our light and our salvation (Psalms 27:1). Therefore, Christ must increase, and we must decrease (John 3:30).

Receiving the Spirit of the Risen Christ through our confession of faith in the finished work of the Cross prepares us for a future transformation of what we shall become. Our mortal bodies will put on immortal ones; our corpses, which shall be buried or sown in corruption, shall be raised in *incorruption* (1 Corinthians 15:42); "and so shall we ever be with the Lord" (1 Thessalonians 4:17).

Remember now, before Adam sinned, there was no corruption in him. Had he not sinned, it is likely that he would have lived eternally sinless, and this conversation would be academic!

But the Bible says that Adam was (past tense) the son of God (Luke 3:38). What was it that made him the son of God? I submit that it was the very breath of life that God breathed into Adam's nostrils (Genesis 2:7b).

When God breathed His Spirit into Adam's nostrils, it was only then that Adam became spiritually connected to God and it was only then that the Bible says that Adam "became a living soul" (Genesis 2:7b).

Note also, that when God pronounced the blessing of fruitfulness upon the created man (Genesis 1:28), Adam was still a one hundred percent male-female spirit being. It wasn't until Genesis 2:7a that God made a human Adam; and not until Genesis 2:22 that God made a human Eve.

When God had finished making a body for Adam, Adam was a sinless human being, and he was alone. There was no one else like him. God had not yet brought the animals to Adam so he could name them, and, God had not yet made a helper for Adam, yet, the Bible says Adam was the son of God (Luke 3:38).

### How Does One Become a Child of God?

John 1:12-13 answers how one becomes a child of God.

> 12 But[1161] as many as[3745] received[2983] him,[846] to them[846] gave[1325] he power[1849] to become[1096] the sons[5043] of God,[2316] even to them that believe[4100] on[1519] his[846] name:[3686]
>
> 13 Which[3739] were born,[1080] not[3756] of[1537] blood,[129] nor[3761] of[1537] the will[2307] of the flesh,[4561] nor[3761] of[1537] the will[2307] of man,[435] but[235] of[1537] God.[2316]

The message is this: For you to become a son of God, you must believe in the finished work of the cross and receive Jesus Christ as Lord and Savior (Romans 10:9; John 1:12). That's the ONLY way. The Thessalonians did it. And as we'll see in a moment so too did the Ephesians.

## Thessalonians Connection

Many preachers have used 1 Thessalonians 5:23 in their preaching. It reads as follows:

23 And¹¹⁶¹ the³⁵⁸⁸ very⁸⁴⁶ God²³¹⁶ of peace¹⁵¹⁵ sanctify³⁷ you⁵²⁰⁹ wholly;³⁶⁵¹ and²⁵³² I pray God your⁵²¹⁶ whole³⁶⁴⁸ spirit⁴¹⁵¹ and²⁵³² soul⁵⁵⁹⁰ and²⁵³² body⁴⁹⁸³ be preserved⁵⁰⁸³ blameless²⁷⁴ unto¹⁷²² the³⁵⁸⁸ coming³⁹⁵² of our²²⁵⁷ Lord²⁹⁶² Jesus²⁴²⁴ Christ.⁵⁵⁴⁷

In this verse, the Apostle Paul states clearly that the spirit and soul and body are three independents, albeit tangible, components of the human being. And then again there are other preachers who claim that the soul is "the mind, will, and emotions." So, who is right? I believe that Paul is. And I believe that my definition of the soul explains why I believe Paul is right.

## The Ephesians Connection

The Book of Ephesians was written by the Apostle Paul to the Ephesians earlier than the Book of Thessalonians. The Ephesians too were a group of people who believed in the finished work of the cross and had accepted Jesus Christ as Lord and Savior. So, by association or reasonable deduction, we could say that Paul would have referred to them, as well, as having spirit and soul and body.

Here's what Paul says in Ephesians, chapter 2, verse 1: "And you hath he quickened, who were dead in trespasses and sins."

1. Who is the "he" that did the quickening?
2. Who are they who were dead in trespasses and sins?
3. How were they quickened?
4. What does it mean to be quickened?

Verses 2-5 give us the answers.

2 Wherein¹⁷²² ³⁷³⁹ in time past⁴²¹⁸ ye walked⁴⁰⁴³ according²⁵⁹⁶ to the³⁵⁸⁸ course¹⁶⁵ of this⁵¹²⁷ world,²⁸⁸⁹ according²⁵⁹⁶ to the³⁵⁸⁸ prince⁷⁵⁸ of the³⁵⁸⁸ power¹⁸⁴⁹ of the³⁵⁸⁸ air,¹⁰⁹ the³⁵⁸⁸ spirit⁴¹⁵¹ that now worketh¹⁷⁵⁴ ³⁵⁶⁸ in¹⁷²² the³⁵⁸⁸ children⁵²⁰⁷ of disobedience:⁵⁴³

3 Among¹⁷²² whom³⁷³⁹ also²⁵³² we²²⁴⁹ all³⁹⁵⁶ had our conversation³⁹⁰ in times past⁴²¹⁸ in¹⁷²² the³⁵⁸⁸ lusts¹⁹³⁹ of our²²⁵⁷ flesh,⁴⁵⁶¹ fulfilling⁴¹⁶⁰ the³⁵⁸⁸ desires²³⁰⁷ of the³⁵⁸⁸ flesh⁴⁵⁶¹ and²⁵³² of the³⁵⁸⁸ mind;¹²⁷¹ and²⁵³² were²²⁵⁸ by nature⁵⁴⁴⁹ the children⁵⁰⁴³ of wrath,³⁷⁰⁹ even²⁵³² as⁵⁶¹³ others.³⁰⁶²

4 But¹¹⁶¹ God,²³¹⁶ who is⁵⁶⁰⁷ rich⁴¹⁴⁵ in¹⁷²² mercy,¹⁶⁵⁶ for¹²²³ his⁸⁴⁸ great⁴¹⁸³ love²⁶ wherewith³⁷³⁹ he loved²⁵ us,²²⁴⁸

5 Even²⁵³² when we²²⁴⁸ were⁵⁶⁰⁷ dead³⁴⁹⁸ in sins,³⁹⁰⁰ hath quickened us together⁴⁸⁰⁶ with Christ, by⁵⁵⁴⁷ (grace⁵⁴⁸⁵ ye are²⁰⁷⁵ saved;)⁴⁹⁸²

These verses inform us that the Ephesians were a people who were spiritually dead. This means they were being ruled by the god (little "g") of this world; this means they were ruled by "the lusts of the flesh, the lust of the eyes, and the pride of life" (1 John 2:16), and that there came a time when they were quickened or made spiritually alive because they accepted Jesus Christ as Lord and Savior.

In Ephesians 2:2a, "ye" would be the Ephesians, but today, it applies to everyone (Romans 3:23).

In Ephesians 2:2b, "walked according to the course of this world, according to the prince of the power of the air," refers to the devil or Satan.

Ephesians 2:2c, "the spirit that now worketh in the children of disobedience," refers to the spirit of the devil.

**Question**: What is one indisputable difference between the one who believes in Jesus Christ and the one who doesn't?

**Answer**: Simply this and ONLY this: The one who believes has accepted the finished work of the cross and received by faith the Spirit of the Risen Christ (Romans 10:9; John 1:14). And the one who doesn't, hasn't.

**Question**: What happens when someone accepts the finished work of the cross?

**Answer:** The Spirit of God's only begotten Son comes and lives within the body of the believer. God tabernacles with your spirit-man. Of that phenomenon, the Bible says, "Greater is He that is in you, than he that is in the world" (1 John 4:4).

**Question**: And who is "He"?

- "He" is God's only begotten Son (John 1:14; John 3:16; Hebrews 5:5).
- "He" is the Word that was God (John 1:1c).
- "He" is the Word that was made flesh (John 1:14).
- "He" is the Lamb that was slain from the foundation of the world (Revelation 13:8).
- "He" is the Man Christ Jesus, the one mediator between God and man (1 Timothy 2:5).
- "He" is the only one who said and could say with authority (Revelation 1:18),

> I am he that liveth and was dead; and behold, I am alive for evermore, amen; and have the keys of hell and of death.

Because they had received the Spirit of the Risen Christ as their Savior, both the Ephesians and the Thessalonians thus became sons of God, and though they did not appear as what they shall later become, they knew that when Jesus returns, they shall be like him; for they shall see Him as He is (1 John 3:2). The same is true for everyone who believes (Romans 10:9) and everyone who receives Him (John 1:12).

## The Apostle Paul's Connection

When you study the life of the Apostle Paul, you can't help but notice that Paul was not always a follower of Jesus Christ. In fact, until his Damascus road experience, he was a persecutor par excellence of Christ's followers. After Damascus and after Jesus Christ Himself had worked on Paul, Paul would describe his conversion experience and acknowledge that he had seen, and he had received the risen Christ.

In 1 Corinthians 15:3-4 and 8-10, Paul says, with my bolding,

> For I delivered unto you first of all that which I also received, how that Christ died for our sins according to the scriptures; And that he was buried, and that he rose again the third day according to the scriptures.... **And last of all, he was seen of me also**, as of one born out of due time. For I am the least of the apostles, that am not meet to be called an apostle, because **I persecuted the church of God. But by the grace of God, I am what I am**: and his grace which was bestowed upon me was not in vain; but I labored more abundantly than they all: yet not I, but the grace of God which was with me.

In Paul's Epistle to the Galatians (1:11-12, 15-16, with my bolding), he also describes his conversion as a divine revelation, with God's Son revealing Himself in the body of Paul:

> But I certify you, brethren that **the gospel** which was **preached of me is not after man**. For I neither received it of man, neither was I taught it, **but by the revelation of Jesus Christ**.... But when it pleased God, who separated me from my mother's womb, and called me by his grace, **to reveal his Son in me, that I might preach him among the heathen; immediately I conferred not with flesh and blood**.

So, when we compare: (1) the Thessalonians, with (2) the Ephesians, and (3) the Apostle Paul, what do we have in common? Is it not the fact that all three had received Jesus Christ as Lord and Savior and the Spirit of God now lived in them?

If you would search the books of Acts, Luke, John, Ephesians, and Romans, you would see that the Bible does not come up short of information that proves that when anyone accepts Jesus Christ as Lord and Savior, the Spirit of God comes and lives in the physical body of that person, whosoever he or she may be.

First John 4:4 puts it this way: "Greater is he that is in you, than he that is in the world."

Now, I am sure that you may know people who claim to have accepted Jesus Christ and they act as if they had ... and then again, there are others whom you know who claim to have accepted Him and they behave as anything but believers in Christ!

How is it possible for two people to claim to have accepted Jesus Christ, yet act differently?

And why is it that one person does things that glorify both God and man and the other doesn't?

May I tell you?

For the one who does, I believe, he or she recognizes and feels the very presence of the Spirit of God in him, and he seeks to be holy because God is holy (1 Peter 1:16).

And the one who doesn't, hasn't yet experienced what it means to feel the Spirit of God's presence living inside his body. From a practical standpoint, the latter still hovers between two opinions (1 Kings 18:21) and has not yet come to the point where he can say, as did Joshua, "As for me and my house, we will serve the LORD" (Joshua 24:15).

Long story short, because Paul accepted Jesus Christ as Lord and Savior, he too received the Spirit of Christ that made him a son of God.

Therefore, as I see it, Paul had to have had a spirit, a redeemed soul, and a body. In other words, Paul's spirit-man was born again. Now if you can believe that as I do, then indeed, you are blessed, because having not seen, yet you believe (John 20:29, paraphrased).

And to that, I say, Amen.

## Galatians 1:11-12, 15-16

But I certify you, brethren that the gospel which was preached of me is not after man.

For I neither received it of man, neither was I taught it, but by the revelation of Jesus Christ

But when it pleased God,

who separated me from my mother's womb, and called me by his grace,

To reveal his Son in me,

that I might preach him among the heathen; immediately

I conferred not with flesh and blood.

## CHAPTER 12

# THE REJECTED GIFT, THE FOUR SONS OF GOD, AND THE RE-MEMBERED MAN

### Bible Verses

**Job 19:25-27**

25 For I[589] know[3045] that my redeemer[1350] liveth,[2416] and that he shall stand[6965] at the latter[314] day upon[5921] the earth:[6083]

26 And though after[310] my skin[5785] worms destroy[5362] this[2063] body, yet in my flesh[4480] [1320] shall I see[2372] God:[433]

27 Whom[834] I[589] shall see[2372] for myself, and mine eyes[5869] shall behold,[7200] and not[3808] another;[2114] though my reins[3629] be consumed[3615] within[2436] me.

**Luke 23:42-43**

42 And[2532] he said[3004] unto Jesus,[2424] Lord,[2962] remember[3415] me[3450] when[3752] thou comest[2064] into[1722] thy[4675] kingdom.[932]

43 And[2532] Jesus[2424] said[2036] unto him,[846] Verily[281] I say[3004] unto thee,[4671] Today[4594] shalt thou be[2071] with[3326] me[1700] in[1722] paradise.[3857]

## Luke 11:13

13 If[1487] ye[5210] then,[3767] being[5225] evil,[4190] know[1492] how to give[1325] good[18] gifts[1390] unto your[5216] children:[5043] how much[4214] more[3123] shall your heavenly[1537] [3772] Father[3962] give[1325] the Holy[40] Spirit[4151] to them that ask[154] him?[846]

## The Case of the Rejected Gift

If you've stuck with me this far, then I presume that you would not have kept on reading had it not been for the fact that as you read you were making conclusions that maybe, just maybe, some of what I've been saying makes sense.

Now I'm going to get a little heavy, but only because I must and because there is no other way to say what I'm about to say.

The story I am about to tell you is true. It happened. I'm going to summarize most of it, but you can verify it online. I call this story "The Case of the Rejected Gift." The internet calls it "United States v. George Wilson."[37]

Here's the deal:

On May 27, 1830, a man named George Wilson, who had committed violent felonies in November and December of 1829, was sentenced to die by hanging. (Actually, there were two men, but my interest is in George.)

The record states that some men of influence intervened on George's behalf and secured for him a presidential pardon.

A presidential pardon has the same effect in criminal justice as a "Get Out of Jail Free" card has in the game of Monopoly.

It tells all the players, even as it told George's executioner, that no matter what George did, George was forgiven. George's slate was wiped clean. It was as if George had never committed any offense.

But get this: George Wilson rejected the gift. The record indicates that George refused to accept the presidential pardon; and because he did this, his pardon became null and void. As a result, George Wilson was executed.

To say it another way—because George rejected the gift of the presidential pardon—George Wilson chose to die when he could have chosen to live.

## The Gift of Calvary

Now back up about 2,000 years to Calvary. Jesus Christ, God's only begotten Son in human form, had just shed every drop of His blood on Calvary's hill; and in so doing He paid the ultimate price that God demanded for sin and thus provided for all men, the FREE gift of a heavenly pardon, better known as the FREE Gift of Salvation.

That pardon that Jesus had secured with His blood had the power then, even as it does today, to restore all people into a right spiritual relationship with a holy and heavenly God. It matters not if they were or are black, white, pink, brown, blue, polka-dot; rich or poor; educated or uneducated; healthy or sick; straight or LGBT.

The fact of the matter is that in God's eyes, where sin is concerned, there is not any one person who is better than any other; because, as God sees it and without exception, every human, male or female, has within his or her body a procreated spirit-man that was born spiritually dead in trespasses and sins (Ephesians 2:1b).

From the very day that Adam sinned and was expelled from God's presence, God had but one desire: to redeem or otherwise buy back all people, so that all can spend eternity with Him in heaven.

The cost of entry into heaven was simple. It still is: Accept the FREE Gift of Salvation by calling on the name Jesus Christ, and your soul shall be saved (Acts 2:21). It is a gift (Ephesians 2:8). You cannot buy it nor negotiate for it. You cannot get it by any means other than through Jesus Christ, who now sits in heaven in a glorified body (Philippians 2:20-21) that was once human with flesh and blood even as yours and mine is.

Now, if you are one who has already accepted God's FREE gift, congratulations! God is pleased, and the day you did, all of heaven rejoiced (Luke 15:10).

On the other hand, if you have rejected God's FREE Gift of Salvation, the fact is whether you die naturally and end up spending eternity being spiritually dead and spiritually separated from God, or whether you confess and receive Jesus as Lord and become spiritually alive and spend eternity with Him in heaven, know this to be true: Your spiritual death and your spiritual life "are in the power of [your flesh and blood] tongue" (Proverbs 18:21, brackets added).

If you have already confessed Jesus Christ as Lord and Savior, then the life of the procreated spirit-man that you saved was your own (John 1:12). Alternatively, if you have rejected God's FREE Gift of Salvation, then according to the Word of God, your procreated inner spirit-man "shall die in your sins" (John 8:24) and be "cast into the lake of fire. This is the second death" (Revelation 20:14; see also verse 15).

For the record, the first death of your procreated spirit-man occurred when Adam sinned (Genesis 3:6b). The Bible says, "In Adam all die" (1 Corinthians 15:22). What that means is when you were born, even though your body was physically alive, your inner procreated spirit-man was already spiritually dead or spiritually separated from God.

When the Bible says in Hebrews 9:27,

> 27 And[2532] as[2596] [3745] it is appointed[606] unto men[444] once[530] to die,[599] but[1161] after[3326] this[5124] the judgment,[2920]

divide it or interpret it rightly (1 Timothy 2:15) and you will see that the inner spirit-man of every human being died because of the sin of one spirit-man named Adam (Genesis 6:3b; Romans 5:12, 5:19, 5:17a).

This is so because, at the time that Adam sinned, the inner spirit-man of every human being (both male and female) were but spiritual seeds in Adam's loins. This means that when your procreated spirit-man was born, it was already spiritually dead. It did not know God (Ephesians2:1).

What your birth did for you is that it gave your procreated spirit-man a second chance at bat. It gave him a chance to get right with God.

In His omniscience, God knew that when Adam sinned, the procreated spirit-man that would eventually reside in the dirt body of every human being was as yet in seed form in Adam's loins. So even though the penalty of death (which was spiritual separation from God) was applied to spiritual Adam, the reality is that as an act of mercy, God intervened and provided a way for us to be redeemed. And I am certain that God must have said to His only begotten Son: "Let's give everyone, even the unborn procreated spirits, a second chance."

Here's a hypothetical conversation based on Ephesians 2:8-9 that could have happened between God and His Son Jesus. And what's important about this conversation is that, had it taken place, it would have taken place before the foundation of the world. In other words, when Adam sinned, God was not taken by surprise. He already had a solution.

The conversation would have gone like this: God is speaking, and he says, "Son, let's be generous. Let's make the gift of salvation FREE for each and every member of humanity regardless of race, color, class, creed, religion, ethnicity, sexual orientation, or political affiliation. All that is required is for anyone to confess with his lips and believe in his heart that Jesus is Lord, and he shall be saved by grace through faith. This is our gift to them; they do not have to work for it nor can they. This is so that no human or pastor or priest or preacher or evangelist should boast. Salvation will be one hundred percent FREE!"

It was for such a time as Adam's sin (Genesis 3:6b) that the Lamb was slain from the foundation of the world (Revelation 13:8). It was for such an event that God sent the eternal Spirit that was His only begotten Son, the man Christ Jesus (1 Timothy 2:5), to become a human, to be born of a virgin, and be obedient even unto death (Philippians 2:8). It was thus so that whoever believes on the name and the power and the authority of the Spirit of the risen Christ shall not perish but have everlasting life (John 3:16).

If you have accepted Jesus Christ as Lord and Savior, then you have done well, and you need not fear the second death.

The Bible states that when the time comes, your procreated spirit-man shall be "absent from the body and ... present with the Lord" (2 Corinthians 5:8). And you know it will because you would have confessed with your lips and believed in your heart that God raised from the dead the eternal Spirit that resided in the human body of Jesus Christ for some thirty-three years.

## The Second Death

But on the other hand, if you have *not* accepted Jesus Christ as Lord and Savior, then the second spiritual death for your inner man shall occur at the very instant you close your eyes for the last time.

At the exact moment when your physical body has died and your procreated spirit-man has left the arena of life, without a body your procreated spirit-man shall be eternally separated from God.

Here are the facts:

You were born once physically alive but spiritually dead (Ephesians 2:1b). For you to enter bodily into the kingdom of heaven, you need to be born again (John 3:3; Ephesians 2:1a; 1 Peter 1:23).

A created or procreated spirit is born when it has a body (Genesis 1:27; 2:7a; 4:1). A procreated spirit is born again when it has a new body. In either case, the body for the spirit, whether "created" or "pro-created," MUST, repeat MUST, be made by God (1 Corinthians 15:38).

When you were born physically, you had no say in the matter. Your daddy planted a seed; your mom watered it, and God gave the increase (1 Corinthians 3:6).

For your procreated spirit-man to be born again, you do have a say. As a matter of fact, for your procreated spirit-man to be born again, it is imperative that you confess as your Lord and Savior the eternal Spirit of the risen Christ (Romans 10:9). If you don't, then according to the Bible, your procreated spirit-man will die twice. But it doesn't have to be that way.

The Bible says that "whosoever shall call on the name of the Lord shall be saved" (Acts 2:21).

How do you know this to be true? The Bible states, "that flesh and blood cannot inherit the kingdom of God" (1 Corinthians 15:50).

Long before God's only begotten Son came in the flesh and dwelt among men in the person of Jesus Christ, the prophet Job prophesied of His coming in Job 19:25-27. Job said,

> 25 For I[589] know[3045] that my redeemer[1350] liveth,[2416] and that he shall stand[6965] at the latter[314] day upon[5921] the earth:[6083]
>
> 26 And though after[310] my skin[5785] worms destroy[5362] this[2063] body, yet in my flesh[4480] [1320] shall I see[2372] God:[433]
>
> 27 Whom[834] I[589] shall see[2372] for myself, and mine eyes[5869] shall behold,[7200] and not[3808] another;[2114] though my reins[3629] be consumed[3615] within[2436] me.

Abraham, the father of faith, "believed God, and it was imputed unto him for righteousness: and he was called the Friend of God" (James 2:23; see also Galatians 3:6; Romans 4:3; Hebrews 11:8-10). But that was then. That was Old Testament.

Today mere faith alone will not stop your procreated spirit-man from going to hell.

If faith is to believe and not doubt what God has said, just remember that the Bible says the devils also believe and they tremble (James 2:19).

Today what God requires is confession with your mouth and a belief in your heart that God raised Jesus from the dead (Romans 10:9). That's it.

In John 1:12-13, the Bible says,

> As many as received him, to them gave He the power to become the sons of God, even to them that believe on his name: Which were born, not of blood, nor of the will of the flesh, nor of the will of man, but of God.

My prayer for you, is that you are one who has.

## The Four Sons of God

Have you ever known anyone who professed to be a Christian, also known as a follower of Jesus Christ, yet when you look at his lifestyle it is anything but Christlike? I know I have. And the way I know is because I look at his fruit. I look at the way he lives. I look at the things he does and says.

Sure, many people go to church, and many pay their tithes, and so on; but then many engage in so many other practices that God forbids that no one can tell the difference between the believer (1 John 5:2; Philippians 4:8) and the unbeliever (1 Corinthians 6:9; Galatians 5:21; 2 Timothy 3:1-7; Philippians 3:18-19).

At least when the unbeliever does something that God forbids, you could say, "Okay, he doesn't know any better." But the unbeliever looks at some who profess to be Christians and sees them as hypocrites or actors, if you will. Because even though the one who believes may be on his way to heaven, the reality is he may live like more hell than some unbelievers.

So, how can you tell who is and who is not? I ask that question because I have identified at least four categories of sons of God in the Bible.

They are:

- Son #1 is a group, the angelic beings as recorded in Job 1:6; 2:1; 38:7; and Genesis 6:2, 6:4. Lucifer was the chief of these beings, and I call him the heavenly son who was cast out of the place. He was in the garden of God in Eden when Eden was in heaven (Ezekiel 28:13).
- Son #2 was Adam, who was created in the image of God and made into His likeness (Luke 3:38; Gen 1:26, 1:27, 2:7, 5:1). He too was in Eden (Genesis 2:8), yet he fell from grace (3:6b). As a result of this, he caused every single one of his spiritual sons, who as yet were unborn and were but spiritual seeds in his loins, to come short of the glory of God (Romans 3:23).
- Son #3 is Jesus Christ: This Son was called "The man Christ Jesus" (1Timothy 2:5). He is, He was, and He ever shall be God's only begotten Son (Hebrews 13:8). He stayed on the case even until his death on the cross (Philippians 2:8).[38]
- Son #4 is the born-again believer. He is the redeemed son who must finish the race. He resides in the body of every believer, whether male or female (Philippians 2:15; 3:13-14, 3:20-21).[39] And, to finish the race, all he needs to do is call on the name Jesus and he shall be saved (Acts 2:38).

Of these four sons, no human being can be or ever has been an angel (son #1), neither can any human being be Jesus Christ, God's only begotten Son (son #3). This means that every human being is either son #2, which means he was born into Adam, he has a sin-nature and from birth his pro-created spirit-man was on its way to hell. Or he is son #4, which means he has received Jesus Christ as Lord and Savior (John 1:12) and his name is written in the Lamb's Book of Life (Revelation 13:8).

Son #4 knows that between now and when Jesus returns, he must work out his salvation with fear and trembling (Philippians 2:12), because he knows that the more Christlike, he becomes (John 3:30), the more he will be persecuted (John 15:20). Yet, Son #4 is unperturbed because he knows that his God shall supply all his needs according to his riches in Glory, in Christ Jesus (Philippians 4:19). Furthermore, like Abraham, Son #4 staggers not at the promises of God because he is confident that whatsoever Jesus promised, Jesus is also able to perform (Romans 4:21).

The challenge of every believer is this: If we say that we belong to Christ, we should let our light so shine that men will come to see our good works and glorify our Father who lives in heaven (Matthew 5:16). That light that must shine refers to the Spirit of the Risen Christ who comes and lives in the body of every believer (1 John 4:4; John 1:12).

The problem we have is that when a believer does not let the Christ-light shine in him, then that believer sends the wrong message to the world. It was Gandhi who said, "I like your Christ. I do not like your Christians. Your Christians are so unlike your Christ."[40]

When the day comes when everyone will be able to distinguish between a Christian and a non-Christian, "the people that do know their God shall be strong, and (they shall) do exploits" (Daniel 11:32).

According to Mark 11:23, they shall be able to

> say unto this mountain, Be thou removed, and be thou cast into the sea; and they shall have whatsoever they said; because they shall not doubt in their heart but shall believe that those things which they said shall come to pass.

## Calvary and Eden Revisited

In the Bible, there was one guy who spoke to his mountain, and he believed; he was a thief who was crucified on a cross at Calvary, next to Jesus. Physical death for him was only moments away; and yet, in what can only be defined as a moment of divine intervention and revelation (reported in Luke 23:42), the thief spoke:

> 42 And²⁵³² he said³⁰⁰⁴ unto Jesus,²⁴²⁴ Lord,²⁹⁶² remember³⁴¹⁵ me³⁴⁵⁰ when³⁷⁵² thou comest²⁰⁶⁴ into¹⁷²² thy⁴⁶⁷⁵ kingdom.⁹³²

Jesus' response was revealing and very comforting. It tells me that before you take your last breath, if you go to Jesus with a contrite spirit and a broken heart (Psalms 51:17), He will forgive your sin and welcome you into the kingdom of God (1 John 1:9). To appreciate my interpretation of the thief's dialogue with Jesus, I need us to revisit briefly, the Creation Story and the Garden of Eden.

You know the story very well. God created man (Genesis 1:27). I say that that man was a spirit. God took dust and formed the man (Genesis 2:7a). In other words, God made a body for the spirit-man that He had just created. The man was now human. God then breathed into the nostrils of the human; and the combination of the created man, the dust, and the breath of God man became a living soul (Genesis 2:7b).

I define a living soul as a sinless human being in whose body the Spirit of God dwells. I am saying that the man that God created and made was a human being in whose body dwelt a spirit called man and a God-breathed Spirit called God. That God-breathed Spirit (Genesis 2:7b) would have been a spirit of power, a spirit of love, and a spirit of sound mind; it would not have been a spirit of fear (Genesis 3:10; 2 Timothy 1:7).

I am saying that God could not give to believers in the New Testament that Spirit of power, love, and a sound mind and not have given the same Spirit to Adam. The fact that God breathed His Spirit means that it is eternal and uncreated (Genesis 2:7b). The fact that the spirit called man was spoken into existence (Genesis 1:27) made that spirit-man a created being.

Now, it is my position that when Adam sinned, the Spirit of God left his body. Spiritual death results in spiritual separation from God. So, if we cannot prove how Adam became spiritually separated from God, we have a problem.

Relocation of the man from the Garden of Eden to a world of thorns and thistles was only one aspect of the penalty for sin (Genesis 3:18). A changed internal condition of the spirit-man was the other. Adam had sinned. The body that was once holy had become unholy, so God had to remove His presence from within the body of Adam.

The Bible teaches that to be saved an unbeliever must receive the Spirit of the risen Christ (John 1:12). Now if that is true, how could it have been any different for Adam? How else could Adam have named all the animals had it not been for the fact that Adam had to have had the Spirit of God living within his body? No man knows the things of God except the Spirit of God lives in him (1 Corinthians 2:10-11). That's Bible.

If it is true that in the beginning, Adam's body was a house for a spirit called man and a Spirit called God, what happened when Adam sinned, and the Spirit called God (Genesis 2:7b) upped and left? May I tell you?

That space that God occupied became filled with satanic spirits because when Adam disobeyed God, immediately, he became Satan's servant.

The Bible says in Romans 6:16,

> Know ye not, that to whom ye yield yourselves servants to obey, his servants ye are to whom ye obey; whether of sin unto death, or of obedience unto righteousness?

### Seven Devils Entered

Because of Adam's disobedience, Satan became the God of this world (2 Corinthians 4:4). And as God of this world, what do you think Satan did with Adam's body over which he now had control? Here's my take on the matter

When the Spirit of God left, the spirit of the god of this world entered Adam's body, and he brought with him seven devils. We read in Ephesians 5:6; 2 Timothy 3:13; Proverbs 6:16-19; 1 Timothy 4:2; 1 John 4:18; 2:16 that they were the devils of

1. Disobedience
2. Deception
3. Lying
4. Fear
5. Lust of the Flesh
6. Lust of the Eyes, and
7. the Pride of Life

So, whereas Adam's body was fashioned by God to be a house for two spirits (his spirit-man and the Spirit of God), once Adam sinned, God moved out, and the spirit of the god of this world moved in and he and his minion's established residence in Adam's body.

In the former case, as Creator and Maker, God was the self-appointed Master of the created spirit called man. In the latter case, the devil exercised his right to become the master of the fallen spirit-man named Adam.

## No Man Can Serve Two Masters

Fast-forward to the Cross and the Resurrection.

- The blood of Jesus had been shed on Calvary's hill.
- Jesus has regained the keys to death, hell, and the grave (Revelation 1:18).
- With the shedding of His blood, He paid in full the penalty God demanded for Adam's sin (Romans 3:23-24; Hebrews 9:22).

- And by His death, burial, resurrection and ascension into heaven, Jesus thus provided a new body for all who would choose to believe in Him, so that they can live again in the newness of life in His glorified body in heaven (Romans 6:4).
- The body that He provided is a body that was
  - sown in corruption and raised in incorruption.
  - sown in dishonor and raised in glory.
  - sown in weakness and raised in power.
  - sown as a physical body and raised as a spiritual body (1 Corinthians 15:42-44).

**From Dirt Body to Glorified Spirit Body**

Whereas Adam's body was made of dust and contained blood and water, the risen Christ had a glorified body that was made a quickening spirit and it had neither blood, nor water, nor flesh, nor bone (1 Corinthians 15:45)!

**From Closed Wound to Open Wound**

Whereas God closed up Adam's side after He took out the rib and made the woman (Genesis 2:21), and so established that every human being MUST come out of Adam, with Jesus' body, the wound in His side (John 19:34) was left open (John 20:27). This was so that whenever "whosoever" confesses Jesus as Lord (John 3:16), Jesus can take their procreated spirit-man (Genesis 4:1) and hide it in Himself (2 Corinthians 5:17; Romans 8:1; 2 Corinthians 12:2), even as He, who is the Spirit of the Risen Christ, is hidden in God (Ephesians 3:9).

**Let's Go Back to Calvary**

This brings me back to the thief on the cross. Luke 23:42 says that just before he took his final breath, after which his inner procreated spirit-man would have left his body which would have signified his physical death,

42 And²⁵³² he said³⁰⁰⁴ unto Jesus,²⁴²⁴ Lord,²⁹⁶² remember³⁴¹⁵ me³⁴⁵⁰ when³⁷⁵² thou comest²⁰⁶⁴ into¹⁷²² thy⁴⁶⁷⁵ kingdom.⁹³²

And the Bible records in Luke 23:43

43 And²⁵³² Jesus²⁴²⁴ said²⁰³⁶ unto him,⁸⁴⁶ Verily²⁸¹ I say³⁰⁰⁴ unto thee,⁴⁶⁷¹ Today⁴⁵⁹⁴ shalt thou be²⁰⁷¹ with³³²⁶ me¹⁷⁰⁰ in¹⁷²² paradise.³⁸⁵⁷

To understand fully how the thief could be in paradise "today," you need to interpret that verse side by side with the parable of the vine (John 15:5-6). In that parable, Jesus said,

5 I¹⁴⁷³ am¹⁵¹⁰ the³⁵⁸⁸ vine,²⁸⁸ ye⁵²¹⁰ are the³⁵⁸⁸ branches:²⁸¹⁴ He that abideth³³⁰⁶ in¹⁷²² me,¹⁶⁹⁸ and I²⁵⁰⁴ in¹⁷²² him,⁸⁴⁶ the same³⁷⁷⁸ bringeth forth⁵³⁴² much⁴¹⁸³ fruit:²⁵⁹⁰ for³⁷⁵⁴ without⁵⁵⁶⁵ me¹⁷⁰⁰ ye can¹⁴¹⁰ ³⁷⁵⁶ do⁴¹⁶⁰ nothing.³⁷⁶²

6 If a man abide not³³⁶² ⁵¹⁰⁰ ³³⁰⁶ in¹⁷²² me,¹⁶⁹⁸ he is cast⁹⁰⁶ forth¹⁸⁵⁴ as⁵⁶¹³ a branch,²⁸¹⁴ and²⁵³² is withered;³⁵⁸³ and²⁵³² men gather⁴⁸⁶³ them,⁸⁴⁶ and²⁵³² cast⁹⁰⁶ them into¹⁵¹⁹ the fire,⁴⁴⁴² and²⁵³² they are burned.²⁵⁴⁵

Now, if Jesus is the Vine, can you see Adam as the branch? When Adam sinned, the penalty for his sin was that he was cast forth as a branch (Genesis 3:23-24). Fact: God drove him out of Eden (Genesis 3:24).

When you separate a branch from the vine, you can say that the branch is "dis-membered." The same was true for Adam when God drove him out of Eden. He became spiritually dismembered or spiritually separated from God and with him so too did the entire human race who were but seeds in his loins.

The consequence of Adam's sin was twofold:

1. God removed His presence (or His breath) from within the body of Adam. The glory had departed (1 Samuel 4:21), and

2. God removed Adam from Eden, which was the very spot where His presence was (Genesis 3:23).

And so, I believe that when the thief said to Jesus, "Lord, remember me when thou comest into thy kingdom," He was not implying that God or the Lord Jesus had ever forgotten him, because He hadn't. When the Son of God—who was the eternal Spirit who took the form of a man (Philippians 2:6-7) and became the person we know as Jesus Christ (Matthew 1:21, 1:25)—came into this world, among other things,

1. He came "to seek and to save that which was lost" (Luke 19:10). And,
2. He came to "destroy the works of the devil" (1 John 3:8).

So clearly, Jesus' coming was never motivated by or predicated upon the fact that God had ever forgotten man.

The word "forget" is usually interpreted as being the opposite of the word "remember." But in this case, that is not so.

In this case, Jesus came with a purpose.

He came to shed His blood so the fallen, sinful, procreated spirit-man that occupies the body of each and every human being would be given the opportunity to choose to be restored into right relationship with God the Father who lives in heaven (Romans 5:1).

So, if I might paraphrase Luke 23:42 and tell you what I believe the thief meant when he said, "Lord, remember me when you come into your kingdom," it would go like this:

"Lord Jesus, there was a time when I was in the Garden of Eden with my great-great-great-granddaddy Adam. I was yet in seed form in his loins, but I knew that every day You used to come and have fellowship with him. And then he sinned. When he sinned, You drove him out of Your presence, and

You withdrew Your presence from within his body. He was but a branch on the vine that You were and are. And because of his sin, you cast him out. From that moment, he became a dismembered branch.

"And so, Lord Jesus, now that You have paid the penalty for his sin, seeing that as a spiritual descendant of sinful Adam I have confessed with my lips and believed in my heart that You are the Son of God and that God is going to raise You from the dead on the third day, Lord Jesus, I ask You to forgive me of my sin, wash me in Your blood, and restore me into a right relationship with You and with Your Father, Jehovah God, who lives in heaven."

And the Bible records in Luke 23:43 that after that conversation,

> 43 And[2532] Jesus[2424] said[2036] unto him,[846] Verily[281] I say[3004] unto thee,[4671] Today[4594] shalt thou be[2071] with[3326] me[1700] in[1722] paradise.[3857]

## The Re-Membered Man

If I know nothing else, I know that the inner spirit-man of the thief on the cross was one hundred percent re-membered to the Vine, and that vine is Jesus Christ! And, I know that, since then, that thief has been in heaven or in paradise with the Lord. There is no question in my mind that the thief on the cross is a re-membered man!

My definition of a re-membered man is inspired by John 1:12. A re-membered man is a procreated spirit-man who has received Jesus Chris as Lord and Savior, and to whom is given the power to become a son of God. A re-membered man is a man whose soul has been redeemed.

## The Redeemed Soul

If your soul has been redeemed, then you need to know that for the present time you may "see through a glass, darkly" (1 Corinthians 13:12). It may not yet appear what you shall be. But I know and you need to know, from 1 John 3:2,

> 2 Beloved,²⁷ now³⁵⁶⁸ are²⁰⁷⁰ we the sons⁵⁰⁴³ of God,²³¹⁶ and²⁵³² it doth not yet³⁷⁶⁸ appear⁵³¹⁹ what⁵¹⁰¹ we shall be:²⁰⁷¹ but¹¹⁶¹ we know¹⁴⁹² that,³⁷⁵⁴ when¹⁴³⁷ he shall appear,⁵³¹⁹ we shall be²⁰⁷¹ like³⁶⁶⁴ him;⁸⁴⁶ for³⁷⁵⁴ we shall see³⁷⁰⁰ him⁸⁴⁶ as²⁵³¹ he is.²⁰⁷⁶

The Prophet Job was not kidding. It is written in Job 19:25-27 that Job said,

> 25 For I⁵⁸⁹ know³⁰⁴⁵ that my redeemer¹³⁵⁰ liveth,²⁴¹⁶ and that he shall stand⁶⁹⁶⁵ at the latter³¹⁴ day upon⁵⁹²¹ the earth:⁶⁰⁸³
>
> 26 And though after³¹⁰ my skin⁵⁷⁸⁵ worms destroy⁵³⁶² this²⁰⁶³ body, yet in my flesh⁴⁴⁸⁰ ¹³²⁰ shall I see²³⁷² God:⁴³³
>
> 27 Whom⁸³⁴ I⁵⁸⁹ shall see²³⁷² for myself, and mine eyes⁵⁸⁶⁹ shall behold,⁷²⁰⁰ and not³⁸⁰⁸ another;²¹¹⁴ though my reins³⁶²⁹ be consumed³⁶¹⁵ within²⁴³⁶ me.

The one single act that seals the deal for all who believe is the fact that we would have confessed and made the Spirit of the risen Christ, Lord of our lives (Romans 10:9-10; John 1:12).

We who have accepted Christ know that even if there were no noticeable or immediate change in us, the fact that by faith, we choose to believe and not doubt that God's Holy Spirit has breathed on us guarantees us that our souls have been redeemed. We know also that there's coming a day when Jesus shall make all things new (Revelation 21:5). When that day comes, as it was in the beginning (Genesis 2:7b), so it is and shall be in the end (John 20:22).

And so, Beloved, as I close, I say: Thank you for the time we have spent together.

As I quote from 3 John 1:2, please know that

> 2 ... I wish²¹⁷² above⁴⁰¹² all things³⁹⁵⁶ that thou⁴⁵⁷¹ mayest prosper²¹³⁷ and²⁵³² be in health,⁵¹⁹⁸ even as²⁵³¹ thy⁴⁶⁷⁵ soul⁵⁵⁹⁰ prospereth.²¹³⁷

Know also (from John 3:16 and 3:18),

> 16 For[1063] God[2316] so[3779] loved[25] the[3588] world,[2889] that[5620] he gave[1325] his[848] only begotten[3439] Son,[5207] that[2443] whosoever[3956] believeth[4100] in[1519] him[846] should not[3361] perish,[622] but[235] have[2192] everlasting[166] life.[2222]
>
> 18 He that believeth[4100] on[1519] him[846] is not[3756] condemned:[2919] but[1161] he that believeth[4100] not[3361] is condemned[2919] already,[2235] because[3754] he hath not[3361] believed[4100] in[1519] the[3588] name[3686] of the[3588] only begotten[3439] Son[5207] of God.[2316]

"And so, shall we ever be with the Lord" (1 Thessalonians 4:17b). Thus, saith the Word of God: "To him be glory and dominion forever and ever. Amen" (1 Peter 5:11).

CHAPTER 13

# WHAT OTHERS BELIEVE ABOUT THE SOUL

## Bible Verses

**Mark 16:16**

He that believeth and is baptized shall be saved; but he that believeth not shall be damned.

**Romans 10:11-13**

For the scripture saith, Whosoever believeth on him shall not be ashamed.

**Acts 4:12**

Neither is there salvation in any other: for there is none other name under heaven given among men, whereby we must be saved.

**Ephesians 2:8-9**

For by grace are ye saved through faith; and that not of yourselves: [it is] the gift of God.

### Romans 5:8

But God commended his love toward us, in that, while we were yet sinners, Christ died for us.

### John 3:5

Jesus answered, Verily, verily, I say unto thee, Except a man be born of water and the Spirit, he cannot enter into the kingdom of God.

### Matthew 7:21

Not everyone that saith unto me, Lord, Lord, shall enter into the kingdom of heaven; but he that doeth the will of my Father which is in heaven.

### Hebrews 3:12

Take heed, brethren, lest there be in any of you an evil heart of unbelief, in departing from the living God.

### Ephesians 5:6

Let no man deceive you with vain words: for because of these things cometh the wrath of God upon the children of disobedience.

### Colossians 2:8

Beware lest any man spoil you through philosophy and vain deceit, after the tradition of men, after the rudiments of the world, and not after Christ.

### Ephesians 4:18

Having the understanding darkened, being alienated from the life of God through the ignorance that is in them, because of the blindness of their heart:

**Romans 1:20**

> For the invisible things of him from the creation of the world are clearly seen, being understood by the things that are made, even his eternal power and Godhead; so that they are without excuse.

## Differing Opinions about the Soul

In this chapter, I give a brief overview of the beliefs of various religions so that you can see how many differing opinions there are concerning the soul of man. If you wish to study these or other religions in more detail, there is a great deal of information available on the web.

Your mission would be to study the information, ask the Holy Spirit for revelation, and then decide for yourself whether the soul of man is really the mind, will, and emotions, as many propose; or if indeed your soul is a spirit of power, of love, and of a sound mind that God deposits in you when you accept His Son, Jesus Christ, as your Savior.

## What Do Protestants Believe?

Protestants, in general, believe in the soul's existence. Those who follow Calvin believe there is an existence after death that is conscious. Those who follow Luther believe the soul is unconscious or asleep until the dead are resurrected.[41]

Question: Whom should we believe? Should we believe Luther? Or should we believe Calvin? Is the soul mortal? Or is it immortal? Is it conscious after death or is it not? I believe that if you read the account of the certain rich man and the poor beggar named Lazarus in Luke 16, you would conclude, and rightfully so, that hell is real and that all who go there are conscious; they can feel pain; they have the ability to see and speak; and they have at least one finger and a tongue.

> 23 And[2532] in[1722] hell[86] he lifted up[1869] his[848] eyes,[3788] being[5225] in[1722] torments,[931] and seeth[3708] Abraham[11] afar off,[575] [3113] and[2532] Lazarus[2976] in[1722] his[846] bosom.[2859]

24 And²⁵³² he⁸⁴⁶ cried⁵⁴⁵⁵ and said,²⁰³⁶ Father³⁹⁶² Abraham,¹¹ have mercy¹⁶⁵³ on me,³¹⁶⁵ and²⁵³² send³⁹⁹² Lazarus,²⁹⁷⁶ that²⁴⁴³ he may dip⁹¹¹ the³⁵⁸⁸ tip²⁰⁶ of his⁸⁴⁸ finger¹¹⁴⁷ in water,⁵²⁰⁴ and²⁵³² cool²⁷¹¹ my³⁴⁵⁰ tongue;¹¹⁰⁰ for³⁷⁵⁴ I am tormented³⁶⁰⁰ in¹⁷²² this⁵⁰²⁶ flame.⁵³⁹⁵

## What Do Christians Believe

Many Christians understand that the body is the earthly house (2 Corinthians 5:1) for their soul and the spirit. Many believe that when their body dies, their soul will appear before God to be judged (2 Corinthians 5:10) and at that time God will determine, among other things, whether their soul get to sit at God's right hand and spend eternity in heaven (Matthew 25:34) or whether it will end up on the left hand of God and be cursed, into the everlasting fire (Matthew 25:41) that God prepared for the devil and his angels.

For what it's worth, I must tell you that I believe firmly that there's a day of judgment coming for everyone. None is exempt. The Bible does not mince words. Here's what it says in 2 Corinthians 5:10.

> We must all appear before the judgment seat of Christ; that everyone may receive the things done in his body, according to that he hath done, whether it be good or bad.

And Matthew 12, verse 36 tells us that

> every idle word that men shall speak; they shall give account thereof in the day of judgment.

When that day comes, that is when the eternal destination of your soul and spirit will be determined. What's your opinion?

If you agree that God will judge the souls of men and women when they die, do you know for certain that your soul will spend eternity in heaven?

Compare your answer with these verses: Romans 3:10, 3:23, 10:10, 10:13, 6:23; Ephesians 2:1; and John 1:12.

## What Do Christadelphians Believe?

Those of the Christadelphian belief teach that we are all created out of the dust of the earth and became living souls once we received the breath of life, based on the Genesis 2 account of humanity's creation.

Adam was said to have become a living soul. His body did not contain a soul; rather his body (made from dust) plus the breath of life together were called a soul, in other words, a living being."[42]

Now hold on.

- Doesn't the Bible teach that when God created, HE spoke (Genesis 1:1, 21, 27; Psalms 33:6-9; Nehemiah 9:6)?
- Doesn't the Bible teach in Genesis 1:1 that

    1 In the beginning[7225] God[430] created[1254] [853] the heaven[8064] and the earth.[776]

- And, in Genesis 1:2, wasn't the earth "without form, and void"?
- If yes, then on what basis are we expected to believe that when it came to man, God had to take dust that was once without form and void to create man?
- Did God change His method for creating things? Is it that instead of speaking things into existence, when it came to man, He had to use a substance that He had created previously to create man?
- Whatever happened to His creative word? Why did He not speak man into existence as He did everything else? Well, the fact is that He did. The Bible says in Genesis 1:27,

    27 So God[430] created[1254] [853] man[120] in his own image,[6754] in the image[6754] of God[430] created[1254] he him; male[2145] and female[5347] created[1254] he them.

Question: Could it be that the Christadelphians' interpretations are biblically inaccurate?

## What Do Seventh-Day Adventists Believe?

Seventh-day Adventists believe that the soul "is a combination of spirit (breath of life) and body, disagreeing with the view that the soul has a consciousness or sentient existence of its own." They believe when you die "the body returns to dust and life returns to the God who bestowed it."[43]

As it is with the Christadelphians' view of man and the soul of man, the Seventh Day Adventists interpretation completely ignores and makes no provision in their theology for the fact that the Bible states in Genesis 1:27,

> 27 So God[430] created[1254] [853] man[120] in his own image,[6754] in the image[6754] of God[430] created[1254] he him; male[2145] and female[5347] created[1254] he them.

So, could the Seventh Day Adventists' interpretation of how man and the soul of man came into being, be biblically inaccurate?

## What Do Jehovah's Witnesses Believe?

Jehovah's Witnesses believe the "Hebrew word *nephesh*, which is commonly translated as 'soul,' to be a person, an animal, or the life that a person or an animal enjoys." They also think "the Hebrew word *ruach* (Greek *pneuma*), which is commonly translated as 'spirit' but means 'wind,' refers to the life force or the power that animates living things."[44]

As it is with the Seventh Day Adventists, the Christadelphians, and the Lutherans, the Jehovah's Witnesses completely ignore the Genesis 1:27 "man." They do not believe that the man that God created is an invisible being contained in a body that can survive apart from the body after death.

By clinging to that belief system, they ignore the fact that:

1. When God created, He spoke (Genesis 1:1, 1:21, 1:27; Ezekiel 28:15; Psalms 33:6-9; Nehemiah 9:6).

2. When God spoke, the words that He spoke were invisible words, in which there was life (John 6:63).
3. After God spoke, God then formed or made His "spirit and life words" into visible forms. Romans 1:20, Hebrews 11:3, and 2 Corinthians 4:18 confirm this. The passages are below. Let's read them.

> 20 For[1063] the[3588] invisible things[517] of him[846] from[575] the creation[2937] of the world[2889] are clearly seen,[2529] being understood[3539] by the[3588] things that are[4161] made, even[5037] [3739] his[848] eternal[126] power[1411] and[2532] Godhead;[2305] so that they[846] are[1511] without excuse:[379]

> 3 Through faith[4102] we understand[3539] that the[3588] worlds[165] were framed[2675] by the word[4487] of God,[2316] so that things which are seen[991] were not[3361] made[1096] of[1537] things which do appear.[5316]

> 18 While we[2257] look not at[4648] [3361] the things which are seen,[991] but[235] at the things which are not seen:[991] [3361] for[1063] the things which are seen[991] are temporal;[4340] but[1161] the things which are not seen[991] [3361] are eternal.[166]

As I see it, the things which are NOT seen are the creative words of God. The things which are seen are the things that God made visible with the invisible creative words that HE spoke.

This is why the Bible states in Genesis 2:3:

> 3 And God[430] blessed[1288] [853] the seventh[7637] day,[3117] and sanctified[6942] it: because[3588] that in it he had rested[7673] from all[4480] [3605] his work[4399] which[834] God[430] created[1254] and made.[6213]

The Bible needed to establish for us that there were at least two phases, or two processes if you will, that God used to make visible the invisible creative words that He spoke (Romans 1:20).

Observation: The Jehovah's Witnesses make no provision to account for the Genesis 1:27 created man.

Question: Could it be that the Jehovah's Witnesses' interpretations are biblically inaccurate?

## What Do Members of the Church of Jesus Christ of the Latter-Day Saints Believe?

In an article titled "What Does the Book of Mormon Teach about the Afterlife?" among other things the following was stated:

1. "Nowhere is the plan of salvation more clearly and fully taught than [in] the Book of Mormon."[45] In other words, the Bible runs a distant second!

2. "The Book of Mormon expands or clarifies several important truths about life after death."[46] In other words, the Bible's record was inadequate or otherwise deficient.

3. "While the Bible teaches about the spirit world and the resurrection, in the Book of Mormon those principles are laid out with great clarity. Without it, many Christians are unaware of the state of the soul between death and the resurrection."[47] Does this mean that Mormons alone are the recipients of God's divine revelation? And,

4. "Thanks to the Book of Mormon and these other revelations, Latter-day Saints today are blessed with greater knowledge about the next life than any other known group of people in history."[48]

So, what must the Christian do with the words that were written by "John The Revelator" in the book of Revelation, chapter 22, verses 18 and 19?

> For I testify unto every man that heareth the words of the prophecy of this book, If any man shall add unto these things, God shall add unto him the plagues that are written in this book: And

if any man shall take away from the words of the book of this prophecy, God shall take away his part out of the book of life, and out of the holy city, and from the things which are written in this book.

Just asking.

## What Do Bahá'ís Believe?

Concerning "Death and the Afterlife,", "Baha'i teachings state that the soul does not die; it endures everlastingly. When the human body dies, the soul is freed from ties with the physical body and the surrounding physical world and begins its progress through the spiritual world."[49]

However, in the Bible, Ezekiel 18:20 states, "The soul that sinneth, it shall die." Ephesians 2:1 states we were born "dead in trespasses and sins"; And Revelation 21:8 speaks of a second death. It states,

> the fearful, and unbelieving, and the abominable, and murderers, and whoremongers, and sorcerers, and idolaters, and all liars, shall have their part in the lake which burneth with fire and brimstone: which is the second death.

Question: Whose report are you going to believe? Ask yourself the question that Jesus asked in Mark 8:36: "For what shall it profit a man, if he shall gain the whole world, and lose his own soul?"

## What Do Brahma Kumaris Believe?

Brahma Kumaris teach, "This reservoir of positive energy can be called the soul. It's tiny and invisible to the human eye. The soul sparkles with spiritual power. The soul is naturally sweet and loving. The soul is peaceful. The soul holds memories. The soul is unique."[50]

Conclusion and Question: Brahma Kumaris' view of how man and the soul of man came into being is biblically inaccurate or otherwise inconsistent with Scripture. Among other things, they make no provision for the Genesis 1:27 created man or the John 20:22 "Redeemed soul." What's your opinion?

## What Do Buddhists Believe?

On the website *BuddhaSasana, A Buddhist Page*, Venerable K. Sri Dhammananda Maha Thera answers the question, "Is there an Eternal Soul?"[51]

> According to Buddhism there is no reason to believe that there is an eternal soul that comes from heaven or that is created by itself and that will transmigrate or proceed straight away either to heaven or hell after death. Buddhists cannot accept that there is anything either in this world or any other world that is eternal or unchangeable.

Also, in Buddhism, they believe that "Those who believe in the existence of a soul are not in a position to explain what and where it is. The Buddha's advice is not to waste our time over this unnecessary speculation and devote our time to strive for our salvation."[52]

Conclusion and Question: My question, therefore, is this: How do you reconcile the Buddhist's view of the soul with Jesus' view when he asked the question in Mark 8:36, "What shall it profit a man, if he shall gain the whole world, and lose his own soul?"[53]

## What Do Hare Krishnas Believe?

Some of the basic beliefs of Hare Krishna are as follows: "We are not our bodies but eternal, spirit souls, parts and parcels of God (Krishna). As such, we are all brothers, and Krishna is ultimately our common father. We accept the process of transmigration of the soul (reincarnation)." They also believe that "Krishna is eternal, all- knowing, omnipresent, all-powerful, and all-attractive. He is the seed- giving father of all living beings, and He is the sustaining energy of the entire cosmic creation. He is the same God as The Father Allah, Buddha and Jehovah."[54]

The fact that Hare Krishnas' believe that the soul is eternal is good. But that they believe it is part and parcel of God is bad. Also, they believe that the Jehovah God of the Bible is one and the same with Allah, Buddha, and Krishna; and that is inconsistent with what the Bible teaches in Deuteronomy 6:4-5:

> 4 Hear,[8085] O Israel:[3478] The LORD[3068] our God[430] is one[259] LORD:[3068]
>
> 5 And thou shalt love[157] [853] the LORD[3068] thy God[430] with all[3605] thine heart,[3824] and with all[3605] thy soul,[5315] and with all[3605] thy might.[3966]

Also, though Hare Krishnas believe in the eternal nature of the soul, they do not believe in the "new birth" or the "born-again" experience of the soul, but rather, believe in the "rebirth" or "reincarnation" of the soul.

It is my opinion that their view of how man and the soul of man came into being is biblically inaccurate or otherwise inconsistent with Scripture. Among other things, they make no provision for the Genesis 1:27 created man. What's your opinion?

## Bible Verses Referring to the Soul's Value

### Romans 12:1-21

> I beseech you therefore, brethren, by the mercies of God, that ye present your bodies a living sacrifice, holy, acceptable unto God, [which is] your reasonable service.

### Matthew 10:28

> And fear not them which kill the body but are not able to kill the soul: but rather fear him which is able to destroy both soul and body in hell.

### Mark.8-36-37

> For what shall it profit a man, if he shall gain the whole world, and lose his own soul? Or what shall a man give in exchange for his soul?

### 3 John 1:2

> Beloved, I wish above all things that thou mayest prosper and be in health, even as thy soul prospers.

### Philippians 1:6

> Being confident of this very thing, that he which hath begun a good work in you will perform it until the day of Jesus Christ:

### 1 Thessalonians 5:23

> And the very God of peace sanctify you wholly; and I pray God your whole spirit and soul and body be preserved blameless unto the coming of our Lord Jesus Christ.

## Compare Each Interpretation with the Word of God

Based on the preceding interpretations, where not one of them is in total agreement with any other, how can anyone decide which is one hundred percent biblically accurate and which is not? The only way I know is to take each interpretation, one by one, and line them up, side by side with the Word of God and then go with the one that fits one hundred percent accurately.

Why is this necessary? Because only then would you know the truth and it is that truth that you know will set you free (John 8:32).

Think about this: As far as Jesus was concerned, the salvation of one soul was everything and was worth more to Him than all the wealth in the entire world (Mark 8:36).

This is why the Bible says that "joy shall be in heaven over one sinner that repents, more than over ninety and nine just persons, which need no repentance" (Luke 15:7).

Jesus' message is clear; or it should be. Heaven rejoices when one sinner repents.

## Why Aren't More Souls Being Saved?

Now as to why more souls aren't being saved and why isn't there more rejoicing in heaven, I would imagine that that is because most people aren't even aware that they have a soul. There are others who aren't aware of the eternal consequences for failing to take the initiative by grace through faith and ask Jesus to save their soul. And still, others aren't aware that their soul needs to be saved.

Why is this so?

Well, it could be because most Christians have just a superficial view of the Gospel message of Jesus Christ, whereas non-Christians have absolutely no clue that there is a Jesus message.

Did you say, "the Jesus message"?

What exactly is the Jesus message?

I will tell you it is not a message of prosperity nor is it a message of sowing and reaping that says if you sow a financial seed into a TV ministry, God will fill your financial needs.

- It is the message the Jesus preached concerning the Kingdom of God.
- It is the Gospel message that Jesus Christ gave to His disciples just before He ascended into heaven.
- It is the message that Christians call the Great Commission (Matthew 28:19-20).
- It is the message where Jesus told His disciples to "Go ye into all the world and preach the Gospel to every creature" (Mark 16:15).
- It is the Christ-crucified message (1 Corinthians 1:23), wherein Paul told the Corinthian church, and the Bible has been telling everyone throughout the centuries since who reads it 1 Corinthians 15:3-4 and everyone who hears the message

3 how that³⁷⁵⁴ Christ⁵⁵⁴⁷ died⁵⁹⁹ for⁵²²⁸ our²²⁵⁷ sins²⁶⁶ according²⁵⁹⁶ to the³⁵⁸⁸ Scriptures;¹¹²⁴

4 And²⁵³² that³⁷⁵⁴ he was buried,²²⁹⁰ and²⁵³² that³⁷⁵⁴ he rose again¹⁴⁵³ the³⁵⁸⁸ third⁵¹⁵⁴ day²²⁵⁰ according²⁵⁹⁶ to the³⁵⁸⁸ Scriptures:¹¹²⁴

- It is the message that Paul says, "is the power of God unto salvation to everyone that believeth; to the Jew first and also to the Greek" (Romans 1:16).
- It is the Gospel message that the Bible says has the power to "destroy the wisdom of the wise and will bring to nothing the understanding of the prudent" (1 Corinthians 1:19).
- It is the message that men receive through the "foolishness of preaching" that is able "to save them that believe" (1 Corinthians 1:21).
- It is the message that Paul received not from man "but by the revelation of Jesus Christ" (Galatians 1:12).

Now if this Jesus message is so important, why isn't it being preached more often? Could it be because the enemy has outfoxed us?

I mean, think about it. There are some television and radio stations where you do get non-stop Christian programming. This I think is a good thing. The Word of God needs to be preached. And thank God, we have TV and radio stations that are dedicated to spreading God's word.

But what percentage of those Gospel messages that are being aired around the world are actual messages that tell sinners that "today if ye will hear his voice, harden not your hearts" (Hebrews 4:7), because today "is the day of salvation" (2 Corinthians 6:2)?

Compare that number with the number of messages that keep giving people the biblical formulas for dealing with this, that, or the other condition. Count the number of messages that deal with money and the number of messages that say we can use a hanky as a point of contact to receive a blessing, and you'll see what I mean.

As well intentioned as they are or may be and as sincere as the preachers and teachers who deliver them are or may be, what is the truth?

Is it not true that the messages where we are being taught to seek the world and its "gold" first and seek this, that, or the other first far outweigh the messages where we are being taught to "seek ye first the kingdom of God, and his righteousness; and all these things shall be added unto you" (Matthew 6:33)?

If the ultimate goal of the Gospel message is to reach the lost—and the lost are everyone who has not as yet accepted Jesus Christ as Lord—then why not obey Christ and use his Christ-crucified message to the fullest to first save the lost, plug them into a church where the authentic Gospel message is preached, and then dedicate some time to mentor them so that their foundation in Christ can be strengthened?

I'll tell you why we don't.

We don't because the enemy has outfoxed us. The enemy doesn't care how many messages are preached. Go right ahead and preach them all. Just don't preach Christ crucified. Go right ahead and tell people or let people believe that while salvation is necessary, they don't have to take care of it today. Tell them they can do it tomorrow.

Here's what God said on that subject according to Luke 12:20:

> Thou fool,[878] this[5026] night[3571] thy[4675] soul[5590] shall be required[523] of[575] thee:[4675]

When Christ is lifted up from the earth, the Bible says that He will draw all men unto Himself (John 12:32).

When He is not, then the Gospel message remains hidden.

What's bad about that is that it is "hid to them that are lost" (2 Corinthians 4:3) because the "god of this world" (4:4) who is Satan who is also the "prince of the power of the air, the spirit who now works in the children of disobedience" (Ephesians 2:2) "hath blinded the minds of them which believe not, lest the light of the glorious gospel of Christ, who is the image of God, should shine unto them" (2 Corinthians 4:3-4).

Some time ago I heard a very popular televangelist say (and I'm paraphrasing) that since Satan is the prince and power of the air, Satan is the prince and power of nothing because (get this) air is nothing! Interesting!

Yet it has been my observation that it is through the airwaves that many of us (myself included) get access to our TV, internet, phone service, music, computer games, education, and information, not to mention the fact that the airwaves are also the gateways to a virtual cesspit of unwanted and undesirable pornography, pedophilia, and such like. Just one inadvertent click of the mouse and bam! It's there.

Now, when you add to that the fact that there are probably many who shall never see the inside of a church, either because of time, sickness, or whatever; and many who get their daily or weekly dose of Bible teaching and theology strictly from their favorite TV, radio, or internet-based preachers and programs; what have we got?

Do we not have a situation whereby our airwaves are being underutilized insofar as the spreading of the Gospel is concerned and maximized in the spreading of everything else? Of course, we do.

But do you want to know something?

Jesus knew that this day would come. Two thousand plus years ago, His words were recorded in the Book of Luke, chapter 17 verses 26 to 29. He said,

> 26 ... as$^{2531}$ it was$^{1096}$ in$^{1722}$ the$^{3588}$ days$^{2250}$ of Noah,$^{3575}$ so$^{3779}$ shall it be$^{2071}$ also$^{2532}$ in$^{1722}$ the$^{3588}$ days$^{2250}$ of the$^{3588}$ Son$^{5207}$ of man.[444]

> 27 They did eat,²⁰⁶⁸ they drank,⁴⁰⁹⁵ they married wives,¹⁰⁶⁰ they were given in marriage,¹⁵⁴⁷ until⁸⁹¹ the³⁷³⁹ day²²⁵⁰ that Noah³⁵⁷⁵ entered¹⁵²⁵ into¹⁵¹⁹ the³⁵⁸⁸ ark,²⁷⁸⁷ and²⁵³² the³⁵⁸⁸ flood²⁶²⁷ came,²⁰⁶⁴ and²⁵³² destroyed⁶²² them all.⁵³⁷
>
> 28 Likewise³⁶⁶⁸ also²⁵³² as⁵⁶¹³ it was¹⁰⁹⁶ in¹⁷²² the³⁵⁸⁸ days²²⁵⁰ of Lot;³⁰⁹¹ they did eat,²⁰⁶⁸ they drank,⁴⁰⁹⁵ they bought,⁵⁹ they sold,⁴⁴⁵³ they planted,⁵⁴⁵² they builded;³⁶¹⁸
>
> 29 But¹¹⁶¹ the same³⁷³⁹ day²²⁵⁰ that Lot³⁰⁹¹ went out¹⁸³¹ of⁵⁷⁵ Sodom⁴⁶⁷⁰ it rained¹⁰²⁶ fire⁴⁴⁴² and²⁵³² brimstone²³⁰³ from⁵⁷⁵ heaven,³⁷⁷² and²⁵³² destroyed⁶²² them all.⁵³⁷

There is a reason why Sodom was destroyed. We find the answer in Genesis 19:1-29 and repeated in Ezekiel 16:49. I invite you to read those verses and as you do, pay particular attention to Genesis 19, verses 8 and 19. Those two speak volumes because even as it was then, so is it now in the times in which we live. We live in a time when there are wars and rumors of wars, a time when nations are rising against nations, and a time when there are famines and pestilences and earthquakes in various places (Matthew 24:6-7).

And of these times Jesus said, "All these are the beginning of sorrows" (Matthew 24:8). But above and beyond all that, He warned us to "take heed that no man deceive you" (24:4). Remember, man is a spirit. And we are commanded in 1 John 4:1-3:

> 1 Beloved,²⁷ believe⁴¹⁰⁰ not³³⁶¹ every³⁹⁵⁶ spirit,⁴¹⁵¹ but²³⁵ try¹³⁸¹ the³⁵⁸⁸ spirits⁴¹⁵¹ whether¹⁴⁸⁷ they are²⁰⁷⁶ of¹⁵³⁷ God:²³¹⁶ because³⁷⁵⁴ many⁴¹⁸³ false prophets⁵⁵⁷⁸ are gone out¹⁸³¹ into¹⁵¹⁹ the³⁵⁸⁸ world.²⁸⁸⁹
>
> 2 Hereby¹⁷²² ⁵¹²⁹ know¹⁰⁹⁷ ye the³⁵⁸⁸ Spirit⁴¹⁵¹ of God:²³¹⁶ Every³⁹⁵⁶ spirit⁴¹⁵¹ that³⁷³⁹ confesseth³⁶⁷⁰ that Jesus²⁴²⁴ Christ⁵⁵⁴⁷ is come²⁰⁶⁴ in¹⁷²² the flesh⁴⁵⁶¹ is²⁰⁷⁶ of¹⁵³⁷ God:²³¹⁶

> 3 And²⁵³² every³⁹⁵⁶ spirit⁴¹⁵¹ that³⁷³⁹ confesseth³⁶⁷⁰ not³³⁶¹ that Jesus²⁴²⁴ Christ⁵⁵⁴⁷ is come²⁰⁶⁴ in¹⁷²² the flesh⁴⁵⁶¹ is²⁰⁷⁶ not³⁷⁵⁶ of¹⁵³⁷ God:²³¹⁶ and²⁵³² this⁵¹²⁴ is²⁰⁷⁶ that³⁵⁸⁸ spirit of antichrist,⁵⁰⁰ whereof³⁷³⁹ ye have heard¹⁹¹ that³⁷⁵⁴ it should come;²⁰⁶⁴ and²⁵³² even now³⁵⁶⁸ already²²³⁵ is²⁰⁷⁶ it in¹⁷²² the³⁵⁸⁸ world.²⁸⁸⁹

Being omniscient, Jesus knew this day was coming. Therefore, it is said in Acts 1:8, just before He ascended into heaven, He gave to His disciples the Great Commission to

> be witnesses unto me both in Jerusalem, and in all Judaea, and in Samaria, and unto the uttermost part of the earth.

He sent them to preach the Gospel throughout the world so that all men might be given the opportunity to hear it, believe in it, and then "call upon the name of the Lord" so that their soul "shall be saved" (Romans 10:13). But, as I said earlier, the enemy has outfoxed us.

Through deception, the enemy has managed to keep the essential message of Jesus Christ mostly off the airwaves; and when it is on, people aren't there to receive it because they are busy with the things of the world. Interesting, isn't it? Men seek after the things of the world, but Jesus told us to "love not the world, neither the things that are in the world" (1 John 2:15). He told us to seek His kingdom first (Matthew 6:33).

Why? Why did He say to seek the kingdom first?

He did because the kingdom was the first thing we lost (Genesis 3:24). And the way we regain the kingdom is by calling on His name and getting our souls saved. Once we do that, the Bible says in Romans 8:1-4,

> 1 There is therefore⁶⁸⁶ now³⁵⁶⁸ no³⁷⁶² condemnation²⁶³¹ to them³⁵⁸⁸ which are in¹⁷²² Christ⁵⁵⁴⁷ Jesus,²⁴²⁴ who walk⁴⁰⁴³ not³³⁶¹ after²⁵⁹⁶ the flesh,⁴⁵⁶¹ but²³⁵ after²⁵⁹⁶ the Spirit.⁴¹⁵¹

2 For¹⁰⁶³ the³⁵⁸⁸ law³⁵⁵¹ of the³⁵⁸⁸ Spirit⁴¹⁵¹ of life²²²² in¹⁷²² Christ⁵⁵⁴⁷ Jesus²⁴²⁴ hath made me free¹⁶⁵⁹ ³¹⁶⁵ from⁵⁷⁵ the³⁵⁸⁸ law³⁵⁵¹ of sin²⁶⁶ and²⁵³² death.²²⁸⁸

3 For¹⁰⁶³ what the³⁵⁸⁸ law³⁵⁵¹ could not do,¹⁰² in¹⁷²² that³⁷³⁹ it was weak⁷⁷⁰ through¹²²³ the³⁵⁸⁸ flesh,⁴⁵⁶¹ God²³¹⁶ sending³⁹⁹² his own¹⁴³⁸ Son⁵²⁰⁷ in¹⁷²² the likeness³⁶⁶⁷ of sinful²⁶⁶ flesh,⁴⁵⁶¹ and²⁵³² for⁴⁰¹² sin,²⁶⁶ condemned²⁶³² sin²⁶⁶ in¹⁷²² the³⁵⁸⁸ flesh:⁴⁵⁶¹

4 That²⁴⁴³ the³⁵⁸⁸ righteousness¹³⁴⁵ of the³⁵⁸⁸ law³⁵⁵¹ might be fulfilled⁴¹³⁷ in¹⁷²² us,²²⁵⁴ who walk⁴⁰⁴³ not³³⁶¹ after²⁵⁹⁶ the flesh,⁴⁵⁶¹ but²³⁵ after²⁵⁹⁶ the Spirit.⁴¹⁵¹

And the Apostle Paul said in Romans 8:38-39,

38 For¹⁰⁶³ I am persuaded,³⁹⁸² that³⁷⁵⁴ neither³⁷⁷⁷ death,²²⁸⁸ nor³⁷⁷⁷ life,²²²² nor³⁷⁷⁷ angels,³² nor³⁷⁷⁷ principalities,⁷⁴⁶ nor³⁷⁷⁷ powers,¹⁴¹¹ nor³⁷⁷⁷ things present,¹⁷⁶⁴ nor³⁷⁷⁷ things to come,³¹⁹⁵

39 Nor³⁷⁷⁷ height,⁵³¹³ nor³⁷⁷⁷ depth,⁸⁹⁹ nor³⁷⁷⁷ any⁵¹⁰⁰ other²⁰⁸⁷ creature,²⁹³⁷ shall be able¹⁴¹⁰ to separate⁵⁵⁶³ us²²⁴⁸ from⁵⁷⁵ the³⁵⁸⁸ love²⁶ of God,²³¹⁶ which³⁵⁸⁸ is in¹⁷²² Christ⁵⁵⁴⁷ Jesus²⁴²⁴ our²²⁵⁷ Lord.²⁹⁶²

## Paul Ought to Know

Of himself, he said that he was the chief sinner (1 Timothy 1:15). And yet Jesus saved him.

With Jesus, everything was, is, and ever shall be about saving the soul; and I dare say, many if not most people haven't got a clue as to what the soul is and why it is so important to Jesus.

And one of the key reasons why they haven't got a clue is because they have yet to understand that the soul is the Spirit of God

1. who comes and lives in the bodies of all,
2. who confesses with their lips and believe in their hearts,

3. that, Jesus Christ, is the Son of God,
4. who was crucified,
5. who died,
6. who was buried,
7. who rose from the dead on the third day,
8. who ascended into heaven,
9. and who is coming back for His church,
10. any minute now!

The Bible says it. I believe it. And that settles it for me.

## 1 John 4:1-3

[1] Beloved, believe not every spirit, but try the spirits whether they are of God: because many false prophets are gone out into the world.

[2] Hereby know ye the Spirit of God: Every spirit that confesses that Jesus Christ is come in the flesh is of God:

[3] And every spirit that confesses not that Jesus Christ is come in the flesh is not of God: and this is that spirit of antichrist, whereof ye have heard that it should come; and even now already is it in the world.

CHAPTER 14

# THE CONCLUSION OF IT ALL

## Bible Verses

### 1 Corinthians 15:36-38

[36] Thou fool, that which thou sowest is not quickened, except it die: [37] And that which thou sowest, thou sowest not that body that shall be, but bare grain, it may chance of wheat, or of some other grain: [38] But God giveth it a body as it hath pleased him, and to every seed his own body.

### Galatians 6:7-8

[7] Be not deceived; God is not mocked: for whatsoever a man soweth, that shall he also reap. [8] For he that soweth to his flesh shall of the flesh reap corruption; but he that soweth to the Spirit shall of the Spirit reap life everlasting.

### 1 Corinthians 3:7

[7] So then neither is he that plants anything, neither he that waters; but God that giveth the increase.

**Hebrews 10:5 and 10:7**

> [5] Wherefore when he cometh into the world, he saith, Sacrifice and offering thou wouldest not, but a body hast thou prepared me: [7] Then said I, Lo, I come (in the volume of the book it is written of me,) to do thy will, O God.

**Mark 4:13**

> [13] And he said unto them, Know ye not this parable? and how then will ye know all parables?

## What Is Next?

Well, we have had quite a journey, you and me. An appropriate question that you could or should be asking yourself at this time is, Where do I go from here? Or what should I do now?

Here are my thoughts on that subject.

**One:** Recognize that at birth, even though there was in you a procreated spirit-man, or a life force, if you will, that procreated spirit-man was born spiritually separated from God and because of Adam's sin (Genesis 3:6c) was connected to the god of this world. Before Adam sinned, his soul was the very presence of God—a spirit of power, of love, and of a sound mind (2 Timothy 1:7)—that was supposed to live in the body of every human being. Ephesians 2:1 confirms that every baby, no matter how cute, was born dead in trespasses and sins.

**Two:** Recognize that the fact that your spirit-man was procreated means that God DID NOT, repeat DID NOT, create you. Instead, God *made* you. Your daddy sowed a seed; your mom watered it, and God gave the increase (1 Corinthians 3:6; Galatians 6:7). The increase is the body in which your procreated inner spirit-man lives (1 Corinthians 15:38). God made a body for Adam (Genesis 2:7a); He made a body for Jesus (Hebrews 10:5); and today, He makes a body for every human being and every animal, bird, fish, insect, or plant (1 Corinthians 15:38).

**Three:** Understand that God does not want your procreated spirit-man that resides in your body to stay separated from Him. Instead, He wants you to ask His Son, Jesus, to save your soul so that you can be reconnected to and spend eternity with Him in heaven (Romans 10:9; John 1:12).

**Four:** Understand that between the time when you were hatched (your birth date) and the time when you are dispatched (your death), God would like very much to see you accept His offer of the free gift of salvation that He has made available to everyone, only through the shed blood of His Son Jesus Christ (Ephesians 2:8).

**Five:** Understand that the Man Christ Jesus (1 Timothy 2:5) is God's ONLY begotten Son; because unlike the inner spirit or earthly life force of every living thing which God spoke into existence at Creation (Genesis, chapters 1, 2, and 5), the inner life force that was within the body of the human Jesus was the verifiable Spirit of God (2 Corinthians 5:19), which God literally took out of His very bosom (John 1:18) and God did that even before He laid the foundation of the world.

That Spirit was called the Lamb that was slain (Revelation 13:8). The Spirit was the Word of God (John 1:1) minus His deity. That Spirit was the seed of God (Luke 8:11) that became the seed of the woman (Genesis 3:15) that publicly decimated Satan's kingdom of darkness (Colossians 2:13-15) and provided a way for everyone to have peace with God (Romans 5:1).

How do you accomplish all of this? The Bible gives us the formula

### Romans 10:9-11: Confess

> That if thou shalt confess with thy mouth the Lord Jesus, and shalt believe in thine heart that God hath raised him from the dead, thou shalt be saved. For with the heart man believeth unto righteousness; and with the mouth confession is made

unto salvation. For the scripture saith, Whosoever believeth on him shall not be ashamed.

### Acts 2:21: Call

And it shall come to pass, that whosoever shall call on the name of the Lord shall be saved.

### John 1:12-13: Receive

But as many as received him, to them gave he the power to become the sons of God, even to them that believe on his name: Which were born, not of blood, nor of the will of the flesh, nor of the will of man, but of God.

### John 3:3, 3:5-6: Know

Jesus answered and said unto him, Verily, verily, I say unto thee, Except a man be born again, he cannot see the kingdom of God....Jesus answered, Verily, verily, I say unto thee, Except a man be born of water and of the Spirit, he cannot enter into the kingdom of God. That which is born of the flesh is flesh; and that which is born of the Spirit is spirit.

### John 14:6: Understand

Jesus saith unto him, I am the way, the truth, and the life: no man cometh unto the Father, but by me.

This is so, and it is true because Jesus is no longer on the Cross. Instead, He now sits in heaven at the right hand of His father, forever making intercession for you and me.

Additionally, Jesus is the ONLY way because He has prepared a body for everyone who believes that was not made by human hands. It is an incorruptible and immortal body. It is a body that has no flesh and no blood for "flesh and blood cannot inherit the kingdom of God" (1 Corinthians 15:50).

## John 11:25-26: Believe

Jesus said unto her, I am the resurrection, and the life: he that believes in me, though he were dead, yet shall he live: And whosoever lives and believes in me shall never die. Do you believe this?

## Luke 13:3: Rest Assured

Except ye repent, ye shall all likewise perish.

# ABOUT THE AUTHOR

Desmond Langton is an ordained minister with the International Church of the Foursquare Gospel and a licensed home inspector. He attends Deeper Life Assembly in Orlando, Florida, where he serves as an assistant to the pastor and heads the bereavement ministry.

Originally from Trinidad, Desmond now lives in Apopka, Florida, with his wife, Pat. They have five grandchildren, two godchildren, and five children, one of whom is adopted.

## Special Request from the Author

If you enjoyed reading this book, would you consider writing a review? A review will help others learn about the benefits of this book, and your feedback will help improve the quality of my work. Just a sentence or two about what you enjoyed the most, what you liked the least or how I could make it better would be appreciated. Your review doesn't have to be glowing, only genuine and fair.

To leave your review, follow these instructions:

1. www.amazon.com/review/create-review/?asin= B07PRY95LB
2. Website: http://desmondlangton.com/

3. Facebook: www.facebook.com/desmond.langton
4. Email: desmond@desmondlangton.com
5. As an alternative, take a selfie with your copy of *What Is The Soul?* and post it on social media.

P.S.: If you were given a free copy of the book, state that at the end of your review. FTC regulations require it. It could be something as simple as: "I was given a free copy of this book for writing an honest review."

Subscribe to my blog www.desmondlangton/blog and be among the first to get updates on my next project.

Sign-up for my mailing list and receive a FREE Copy of "Rightly Dividing God's Word." Many books have been written on this subject. This is my contribution.

Thank you and God bless.

-Desmond-

# NOTES

[1] https://www.sacred-texts.com/bib/poly/mar008.htm

[2] "Nicolaus Copernicus," International Space Hall of Fame, New Mexico Museum of Space History, http://www.nmspacemuseum.org/halloffame/detail.php?id=123 (accessed September 9, 2015).

[3] http://www.sacred-texts.com/bib/poly/h5315.htm (accessed December 22, 2015).

[4] Ibid.

[5] J. H. Hertz, *The Pentateuch and Haftorahs*, 2nd ed (London: Soncino Press, 1971), p. 7.

[6] https://quod.lib.umich.edu/cgi/k/kjv/kjv-idx?type=simple&format=Long&q1=flesh+and+bone&restrict=All&size=First+100

[7] Genesis 1:27, Online commentaries, Bible Hub, http://Biblehub.com/commentaries/genesis/1-27.htm (accessed September 4, 2015).

[8] Genesis 1, Keil and Delitzsch OT Commentary, Bible Hub, http://Biblehub.com/commentaries/kad/genesis/1.htm (accessed September 4, 2015).

[9] Read these Scripture verses for confirmation of this statement: Hebrews 10:5; Luke 2:21; Matthew 1:16, 1:21, 1:25; John 1:14; 1:18; 3:16; 3:18; 1 Timothy 2:5; Acts 13:33; Isaiah 9:6; John 3:16; Hebrews 9:14; Revelation 13:8.

[10] https://www.sacred-texts.com/bib/poly/h3045.htm

[11] Lexi Krock, "Fertility Throughout Life," Nova Online, PBS, www.pbs.org/wgbh/nova/baby/fert_text.html (accessed December 10, 2015).

[12] https://www.sacred-texts.com/bib/poly/h1961.htm

[13] Myles Munroe, *The Purpose and Power of Praise and Worship* (Shippensburg, PA: Destiny Image, 2000). Dr. Munroe was the senior pastor of Bahamas Faith Ministries International Fellowship. He was also a best-selling author, an internationally renowned preacher, and a frequent guest on Christian television shows.

[14] Ibid.

[15] www.merriam-webster.com/dictionary/death (accessed September 5, 2015).

[16] www.brainyquote.com/quotes/quotes/a/alberteins148814.html (accessed September 5, 2015).

[17] "The Mystery of Death," The Truth About Death, Amazing Facts, http://www.truthaboutdeath.com/blog/id/1590/the-mystery-of-death (accessed September 5, 2015).

[18] Chris Higgins, "64 People and Their Famous Last Words," Mental Floss, Inc., http://mentalfloss.com/article/58534/64-people-and-their-famous-last-words (accessed September 5, 2015).

[19] Ibid.

[20] Ibid.

[21] Ibid.

[22] James 2: Barnes' Notes," Bible Hub, http://Biblehub.com/commentaries/barnes/james/2.htm (accessed September 5, 2015).

[23] *The Free Dictionary*, "graft," www.thefreedictionary.com/graft (accessed September 6, 2015).

[24] *New World Encyclopedia*, "surrogacy," www.newworldencyclopedia.org/entry/Surrogacy (accessed October 29, 2015).

[25] Ibid.

[26] "Using a Surrogate Mother: What You Need to Know," WebMD, www.webmd.com/infertility-and-reproduction/guide/using-surrogate-mother?page=1#2 (accessed October 29, 2015).

[27] Nick Vujicic, "About Nick: His Story," *Attitude Is Altitude* (blog), www.attitudeisaltitude.com/about-nick-his-story (accessed October 29, 2015).

[28] Julie Ganka, "Ask a Geneticist," *The Tech Museum of Innovation*, http://genetics.thetech.org/ask/ask420 (accessed October 29, 2015).

[29] Bert Thompson, "Biblical Accuracy and Circumcision on the 8th Day," *Apologetics Press*, www.apologeticspress.org/apcontent.aspx?category=13&article=1118 (accessed October 29, 2015).

[30] 1 Peter 2:2

[31] "History of Surrogacy: When and Where Did It All Begin," Surrogate Mothers, www.surrogatemothers.org/history-of-surrogacy-when-and-where-did-it-all-begin (accessed October 29, 2015).

[32] William C. Shiel, Jr., "Blood, How Much Do We Have?" MedicineNet.com, www.medicinenet.com/script/main/art.asp?articlekey=21474 (accessed October 28, 2015).

[33] James L. Lewis, III, "About Body Water," *Merck Manual: Consumer Version*, www.merckmanuals.com/home/hormonal-and-metabolic-disorders/water-balance/about-body-water (accessed October 28, 2015).

[34] https://www.sacred-texts.com/bib/poly/h5315.htm; Polyglot Bible, H5315, s.v. "nephesh," www.sacred-texts.com/bib/poly/h5315.htm (accessed October 28, 2015).

[35] See also Ephesians 2:1a; Titus 1:2.

[36] Used with permission.

[37] "United States v. George Wilson," Cornell University Law School, https://www.law.cornell.edu/supremecourt/text/32/150 (accessed December 30, 2015).

[38] See also Matthew 14:33; 26:63; 27:43; 27:54; Mark 1:1; 3:11; 15:39; Luke 1:35; 4:41; 8:28; 22:70; John 1:34; 1:49; 3:18; 10:36; 11:27; 20:31; Acts 8:37; 9:20; Romans 1:4; 2 Corinthians 1:19; Galatians 2:20; Ephesians 4:13; Hebrews 4:14; 6:6; 1 John 1:3; 3:8; Revelation 2:18.

[39] See also John 1:12; Romans 8:14, 19; 1 John 3:1-2; 4:15; 5:5, 5:10, 5:12-13, 5:20.

[40] "Mahatma Gandhi > Quotes > Quotable Quote," Goodreads, http://www.goodreads.com/quotes/22155-i-like-your-christ-i-do-not-like-your-christians (accessed December 30, 2015).

[41] "Soul," Wikipedia, last modified December 27, 2015, https://en.wikipedia.org/wiki/Soul (accessed December 29, 2015).

[42] "Soul Explained," A.B. Kryer, http://everything.explained.today/Soul/ (accessed December 29, 2015).

[43] Ibid.

[44] Ibid.

[45] https://knowhy.bookofmormoncentral.org/knowhy/what-does-the-book-of-mormon-teach-about-the-afterlife

[46] https://knowhy.bookofmormoncentral.org/knowhy/what-does-the-book-of-mormon-teach-about-the-afterlife

[47] Ibid.

[48] Ibid.

[49] https://bahai.org.mt/death-and-the-afterlife/

[50] https://www.brahmakumaris.org/8-iweb/196-en-gb-soul

[51] https://www.budsas.org/ebud/whatbudbeliev/115.htm

[52] Ibid.

[53] https://quod.lib.umich.edu/cgi/k/kjv/kjv-idx?type=simple&format=Long&q1=profit+a+man&restrict=New+Testament&size=First+100

[54] https://asitis.com/krishna/

www.ingramcontent.com/pod-product-compliance
Lightning Source LLC
Chambersburg PA
CBHW030432010526
44118CB00011B/607